One Master
one disciple
peeling of an onion

by

Jyoti Subramanian

GURU-SHISHYA PARAMPARA

When the student is ready the teacher appears
When the student is really ready the teacher disappears.

- Siddha Boganathar *aka* BoYang *aka* Lao-tse

One Master one disciple
Jyoti Subramanian

© Jyoti Subramanian
First Edition, 2007
Second Edition, 2019

All rights reserved. This book may not be reproduced in whole or part, or transmitted in any form, without written permission from the author, except by a reviewer who may quote brief passages in a review; nor may any part of this book be reproduced, stored in a retrieval system or transmitted in any form or by any means electronic, mechanical, photocopying, recording or other, without the written permission from the author.

Requests for permission should be addressed to jyotihamsa@gmail.com

ISBN - 978-1-7334970-0-8

ADESH

*Let not precious moments slip by
Seek now the ultimate Truth
Jeevahamsa spread your wings to fly
Immortal realms which death defy.*

– Yogiraj Siddhanath

Table of Contents

Author's Note 2019 xi
Acknowledgements xiii
Preface 2004 xv

1. The Opening of the Door 1
2. Daughter Wife Mother Seeker 15
3. On the Path of a Yoga Teacher 66
4. Expanding Awareness and Kundalini Experiences 111
5. The Disciple's Pilgrimage 155
6. The Flowing River of life 178
7. The Home of the Hamsas 199
8. Around the Campfire 232
9. Personal Sadhana and Inner Transformation 265
10. Kriya Yoga The Antidote 289

9 ancient yogic techniques 296
WINGS TO FREEDOM Illustration 300
Glossary 302

Author's Note 2019

Writing a book for me was like birthing a baby, there was conception, an inception, a period of gestation and finally the moment of birth. There were moments of exhilaration and desperation, pain and pleasure. Like a child a book comes with its own *Karma*, power to persevere and to resurrect. The first draft of this book was written in 2004, published in 2007 it has been through all the nuances of pleasure and pain, criticism and acclaim and near death. The publisher recently returned the book as an unprofitable venture for them. Knowing the book has helped many seekers, keeping much of the original manuscript intact, I decided to publish it again with fresh perspective backed by fifteen more years of sadhana and realisations.

Heraclitus says you cannot step into the same river twice, for it's not the same river and you are not the same person. I realised how deep this simple statement was while bringing out this revised edition. On the spiritual path there's a continuing transformation in the practitioner, the evolution of a sincere *sadhak* is not static but is fluid, the practice and the practitioner impacting one another dynamically. Add to that the presence of a living master aiding in the alchemy and augmenting the process and the blessings become manifold for the sadhak as it did for me with the presence of Gurunath.

About the title, I want to clarify that I use the word Master for lack of an English word for the Sanskrit Satguru. Like many other words in yogic terminology this word too does not have an equivalent in the English language. A true guru is more than a guide or a mentor or a master of the subject that is taught. True gurus bring to light the inner wisdom already present in the disciple often by merely being present; the prescribed practice given only to induce discipline. No definition adequately brings forth the contribution of a true master in a disciples journey.

Being inspired but not enamoured by the many mystical incidents that occurred regularly in my journey, helped me to keep balance on the path. It's human nature to feel superior about our experiences and overawed by those of others. History is witness that we place such people on pedestals of worship and form religious orders around their truth. Though it's great to be inspired I have constantly striven to build insight on the foundation of personal realisations. Every incident has to pass the lens of whether it's based on reality, hallucination, delusion, flight of fancy or mere whim and only the experiencer, in this case me, could interpret its validity and message. I have, without seeking endorsement from others incorporated these personal incidents into my spiritual growth to live life joyously.

Despite these wondrous incidents I understand and reiterate that all experiences are experienced through the lens of the mind, however purified that mind might be; absolving the mind to remerge into the spirit is the purpose of the *yog sadhana*. Empowered by Gurunath in 1998 in this life, I feel the connection of many lifetimes to the practice and to my master.

Acknowledgements

The first lotus I offer to my Satguru Yogiraj Siddhanath, lovingly addressed as Gurunath by disciples or simply Nath. Without his wake up call I might still be in deep slumber mired in the trammels of daily life. He is the spine of this book, the thread on which the words and experiences are strung.

When I look back it seems from the time of birth I was being prepared for what I am becoming now. I am grateful to my parents, my two strong grandmothers, my pious uncles from both sides and other friends of the family for cherishing and loving unconditionally a very unruly child and introducing me to a way of life that still stands the test of time.

My two daughters, a special thank you for making me realise I could do anything. For those moments of clarity, when you cried singly or in unison, "Ma cut the crap!"

To all my students a very warm benediction for their support, help with their inputs and suggestions and critiques. Every moment teaching in class is learning for me. Often I feel I should pay them for attending my class. It's a journey of love with them by my side. I have used their real name when recounting an experience or incidents related to them and thank them for allowing me to do so.

Warm regards to all those who have seen my life unfold and insisted on this revised version as an inspiration to others.

They are close friends with unconditional access to my home and hearth and heart.

Disclaimer

The book is my interpretation of events, spiritual, paranormal and personal as they unfolded in my life and the lessons learnt are subjective. I share them without prejudice with everyone, those who may be inspired, those who may disagree and those who may doubt and disbelieve. The book is not an attempt to convert, coerce or cajole people into a particular way of life or being.

Preface 2004

I wrote this book in spontaneity, as if pushed by some inner force; I had sat down in front of the PC, and with the soft blip of the screen, started writing. It was an exciting task, putting into words apparently bizarre experiences that could not be explained. Lifetimes of intellectual debate and discourse could not compare or compete with a millisecond of these factual experiences. The difference between knowing and realising... well, had to be realised. Faith then became the sum total of all my combined experiences, from this and many past lives. As in any other research field, this path too requires dedication and commitment while the master provides the spark for the 'inductive leap'.

I realise now that throughout my life, in all momentary happiness, I was really searching for this eternal joy, and in every adventure – the excitement of this search. The wellspring of which was always within, the master striking the spark to fire this lamp. *Hamsa Dvij* the twice born, *Sagura* the Initiated, *Khalsa* the Pure; all these were just terms of no significance to me. It was only gradually that the potency and magnanimity of the initiation seeped into me. All humanity has the capability to discard this body of flesh to emerge in a body of light.

In my case, it is the Himalayan master, Yogiraj Gurunath Siddhanath, who gave birth to this life, this light. He is the mother and the father who breathed new life into me. I see the divine umbilical cord connecting me to him and feel the nourishing, life-giving energy flowing through. This book is an offering to him who showed me the path and asked for nothing in return except steadfastness in practice.

CHAPTER 1

THE OPENING OF THE DOOR

I had a secret yearning as I lay in bed on the night before my journey to New Delhi to meet this yogi. I had never felt this way before, it was as if something within my body was stretching and pushing outwards. The closest that I can come to explain this yearning in human words, is that it was like the feeling experienced by a lover waiting impatiently to meet the beloved. The purity of this feeling is difficult to explain.

The reason I was taking this trip was a vision I had of *Yogiraj Gurunath Siddhanath*, as this Himalayan master was called. This vision occurred during a seminar in Chandigarh, North India, where twenty-five of us were sitting shoulder to shoulder in a stuffy room. In our avatar as new-age spiritual seekers, we were smiling and bearing up with the heat and claustrophobia. I remember wishing the ordeal was over and thinking to myself, "God, I have learnt enough to last me a lifetime." Then we were asked to get ready for a guided meditation. Our Reiki teacher had brought a cassette from Delhi, which he played, asking us to follow the technique. I tried to relax and loosen up but ended up doing just the opposite. From somewhere in the room a cassette player came on. The quality of the tape was poor, it dragged, and the directions for the meditation seemed to be in Hindi.

Trying to concentrate on the instructions all I could hear was a hissing sound and some reference to a lotus. So of course, at this cue, the lotuses in my chakra body started doing a jig; they were flying out on all sides. The lotus from my navel shot out like the lotus from Vishnu's navel and waved about in front of my face as I struggled to get it back in. Then, all of a sudden, my body felt light and weightless. The people beside me seemed to drift far away and the immense space around me filled with light. I saw myself walking up a path towards a bare-bodied person, who was standing a little distance away. He had a white beard and his silver hair framed his face like the mane of a lion; he was looking back as if beckoning me to follow him. I was to find out later that this path and location was in the forest ashram in Pune, Maharashtra, and the person was the Himalayan master Yogiraj Gurunath Siddhanath, whose guided meditation technique we were practicing at that moment.

All too soon, the picture faded and I was left feeling groggy and disoriented. I was most excited with this vision and could not wait to share it with others. Novitiates have a habit of collecting visions, experiences, miracles, healings, real or imagined, and a feeling of superiority when one has all these. Being a fresh entrant into new age philosophy I was no different.

The Opening of the Door

As I described the experience and the person I 'saw', my Reiki teacher and his assistant, who had met this yogi and recorded the technique that we had just followed, pointed out the similarity in appearance. There was general consensus that I must meet the master who had so definitely summoned me. The feeling of weightlessness stayed for a couple of days. I was literally 'floating' while going about doing my daily chores at home. This was amazing, because during my regular practice of various new-age techniques in the recent past, even what I had thought of as my most intense experiences were naught compared to the after-effects of this vision of a few seconds.

I had to wait for a few months, though, before the desired meeting with this master could take place. Finally, I got a call from Delhi informing me of the visit of Yogiraj Gurunath Siddhanath to the centre and the programme of initiation into a practice called Kriya Yoga. Yogiraj was a disciple of *Mahavatar Babaji*, who is said to be an ever-living immortal still inhabiting the Himalayan ranges. As to what *Kriya Yoga* was, I had no clue.

Although I had read the book Autobiography of a Yogi a few years back, I had completely forgotten all about the Kriya Yoga or the *Babaji* mentioned in it. I must be one of the rare students who did not seek Kriya Yoga after reading this book by Yoganananda!

The experience of the vision had faded somewhat by the time I got the message from the Delhi centre and along with it, my initial excitement. Therefore, I was in two minds about making the trip to Delhi, a city two hundred and fifty kilometres from where I lived. The fact was that I had learnt so many techniques in the past few months that I did not see how more time could be set aside for a new practice. I had done three levels of Reiki and was hoping to soon become a Sensei; I was a certified master of Kwan-Yin's Magnified Healing, I had taken part in Native American Shaman rites like sweat lodge and making prayer beads, fasting and dancing around the sacred fire, dabbling in crystal healing, and a course in reflexology from Australia concluded the list. Being a conscientious student I practiced them diligently and felt I had scant time for another commitment.

Therefore, I decided to give it a miss, and just stick to what I had learnt, and not add anything more to my already over-flowing repertoire of practices. Still, as the day of the visit came closer, I began to get restless, irritable and distracted. Compelled by an inner urge, I called the centre and registered for the course, little knowing how it was about to change me in such intense ways.

❃

The first meeting

I arrived in Delhi and reached the centre in the evening, filled with excitement and expectancy. As I read the information leaflet, I saw that Gurunath had received his education at Sherwood College in Nainital, Uttarakhand. Since my husband was from the same school, the first thought that came to my mind was, "Oh no, I don't need a guru from Sherwood, I have enough dealing with a husband and all his friends from there." But, even as I sat silently thinking these thoughts, waiting for a guru who was already an hour late for the seminar, I could not help feeling a warm glow of happiness.

When he walked in, he seemed so ordinary, dressed simply in a white *kurta pyjama* and *kolhapuri chappals*. He strode faster than the people accompanying him, who, though younger, had trouble keeping up. One look at him and I recognised the face from my vision, the same demeanour and the flowing hair. Before starting the programme, he moved around the audience, halting by each one and exchanging a few words.

I especially remember him stopping in front of an elderly man and asking him if he had recently undergone a heart surgery. When this person assented with surprise, Gurunath told him that the operation had not been performed properly and that there seemed to be complications. Though his manner was gentle and kind, I was shocked because I felt such insensitive behaviour was unbecoming on the part of a 'realised' master. Steeped as I was in recently learnt techniques that constantly promoted 'love' and 'compassion', I felt mortified to see a master behave like this, apparently without sympathy. After that, the elderly man attended the rest of the seminar lying on his back, as if unable to deal with this alarming revelation. Since we were all seated on the ground, as is customary during yoga seminars in India, the prostrate figure went unnoticed. Nevertheless, even though I was irritated at such conduct, deep within me, I wondered if this is how it felt to be exposed to the proverbial fire that burns all ignorance.

This incident rankled in my mind, and on a subsequent visit, I took the opportunity to check up on this person with whom, I felt, the Himalayan master had been unduly blunt. He surprised me by confessing that because of the timely warning by Gurunath, he had consulted with another specialist the next morning, and a tragedy was averted after a minor correction. With my limited perception, all the time that I had thought him to be lying down, disheartened, during the seminar, he had actually been receiving Shaktipat transmission from Gurunath. My attitude of indignation at Gurunaths behaviour had been dictated by a preconceived understanding of how masters are supposed to behave.

However, on that day, I was unsure and nervous as this Himalayan master walked towards me, wondering what sordid secret from my past would be aired in public.

He stopped in front of me and said, "You are connected with Sherwood College, aren't you?"

My mouth fell open in amazement, because I had shared this information with no one while reading the information.

"Yes, my husband studied there," I replied.

"What's his name?" he went on to ask.

"Jujhar," I said, concerned at the turn this conversation was taking. My husband, now ex, being totally non-committal about spirituality, I felt we should waste no time on him.

"Do you know what it means?" he asked and, without waiting for me to answer, continued, "It means, Jhunjhar, a warrior. Tell him the war to be fought is within and not without." The preciseness of the message stunned me, for my husband was always agitating against injustice in his surroundings, the family, as well as society. He is a visionary and is often thwarted by those who are short sighted. I was a little put out, though, that the subject of the conversation was not my spiritual ambitions.

This is how I met Gurunath, as Yogiraj Siddhanath is called affectionately – for the first time.

❦

The Opening of the Door

Experience of Shaktipat, Pranpat and Shivapat

Gurunath then went on to give the transmissions of *Shaktipat, Pranpat* and *Shivapat* as mentioned in the leaflet. His satsangs are more experiential than talks as I came to know later. I did not have any intellectual comprehension of these words, unschooled as I was in this terminology. So, there I was, sitting expectantly, not knowing what was about to happen.

During Shaktipat, Gurunath explained, a satguru is capable of transmitting the evolutionary Kundalini energy into the chakras of the disciples. In a manner, sharing the energy accumulated by the master through personal practice, with the disciples. The master, to the extent the disciple is ready to let go, gently pulls out debilitating qualities such as jealousy, lust, fear, doubts, or sorrow, so the disciple may flower spiritually and as an individual. The true guru does this out of love and compassion for the disciples, untainted by any other ulterior motive. With my association with Gurunath over the years I also realised that the audience received what they needed, healing or a boost to their evolution as per their preparedness.

My experience during this transmission was as if I had been released from the body – flying up and out. One minute I was sitting in the audience looking attentively at Gurunath and next I felt myself expand out of the physical body, flowing out through the top of the head. This experience is not mine alone. I later came to know that thousands of Gurunaths disciples, and many who are attending his satsang for the first time, experience variations of this liberating sensation like melting, spinning and elongating out of the body.

During the second transmission of *Pranpat* or the karma cleansing breath as it is called, Gurunath instructed us to sit relaxed, and without resistance, as he was going to breathe through our breath in our spinal channel. This, he said, to a certain degree, lightens the karmic load being carried by the aspirant, from this and past lives. Once again, I sat and tried to pay attention to my breath. First, it was difficult to feel any sensation in the spine but, gradually, I became aware of a sensation like a gentle breeze blowing up and down the vertebrae. Then, at a sign from Gurunath, there was a sense of lift as of a sudden gust and my breath kept increasing in length. The most amazing part in this transmission was when Gurunath asked us to wilfully stop our breath. I held my breath, squeezing my eyes shut as well for better control. But, imagine my surprise, when even though my breathing through the nostril had ceased, there was movement along the spine that performed the function of keeping me from suffocating!

It is said that one finds a guru after one's own heart. The quality that most endeared Gurunath to me that day was his directness. "Do not follow a guru blindly. Question and test them," he said, cautioning gullible seekers. "A guru cannot sit solemnly in a state of samadhi, smiling gently, without giving the disciples an experience of this state," he continued with a smile, imitating the popular depiction of serene yoga gurus in lotus posture. With a twinkle in his eyes, he said forcefully, "You have to demand it of them… you have to say to them… 'Hey guru, what is this state of no-mind, or unmani avastha, that you claim to have? Show me a glimpse of it'. And if that person is a satguru -a true Guru, they can and must do this for all their sincere disciples."

During *Shivapat*, Gurunath shared his state of thoughtfree awareness with those present in the audience. On that first occasion, it was very difficult for me to focus my eyes as they kept watering, and I had to blink constantly during the transmission. It was, I understood later, a psychic burning of the veil of ignorance. It took me many subsequent attendances, at such experiential satsangs, to see and feel the energy transmissions of Shivapat more clearly. The slowing down and then cessation of thought waves, as described by Gurunath, took a long time coming! In this later stage, I saw visions of saints and sages of ancient days. There were, especially, visions of two persons that would recur every time, and it was only afterwards that I understood that they were both from my past life connection with Gurunath, one from 30 B.C. and the second from my life as a Sufi devotee.

The transmission evoked different experiences in the audience; some saw a black hole at the spot where Gurunath was sitting, while a dozen or more perceived an expanded golden aura, while still others felt him convert to light and disperse. The vision of rapidly changing faces, reflected on Gurunaths countenance, was experienced by a very few. Of course, I was busy wiping my eyes constantly to keep them from watering to see anything clearly that day.

Every transmission was done so casually that my brain, at that time, did not seem to have the capacity to comprehend the meaning or understand the experiences wholly. It was only after attending many such transmissions that I started to realise what was happening – that he was giving his life energy to an audience, most of whom were new, and a few of them, of whom I was one, understood fully the magnitude of the event. In fact, everyone kept urging him to give the transmission repeatedly, little realising that every time he transmitted the energy he was infusing us with his life force and, in a sense, dying unto us. However, he obliged us each time, making sure everyone responded to the transmission. Of course now I know he is an unlimited source of this energy and for him this was mere child's play.

All present in that audience were healers and practitioners of various new-age techniques, but, I feel now that all of us were like babies playing with sea shells on the shore of mysticism, without any understanding of the ocean that was being revealed to us. The generosity of this person, in sharing the spiritual energy accrued by him after years of meditation, was beyond my comprehension then. In my journey until here, I had heard of many spiritual teachers and self-styled masters who made much ado of the little that they gave their disciples. Yet, here I was in the presence of a householder yogi who, very simply, had brought the mystical transmissions of the Himalayan masters to a farmhouse in Delhi and was happily sharing it with a mostly ignorant audience.

As I matured into my practice and in the past twenty-two years of attending innumerable such gatherings and being in close proximity to Gurunath, I have understood that Gurunath transmits these energies all the time. It's the disciples who absorb according to their capacity. Gurunath is forever giving, radiating twenty-four hours, everyday of the year like the sun without any bias or condition, it's the disciples who block or absorb according to the clarity they have developed. In fact, even without his physical presence the disciples can connect with him and be recipients of all three transmissions, this I have observed in all my classes where I lay out an *asan* –a seat for him and his presence is palpable and felt by all.

My understanding of the Shivapat also became clearer with time and experience. Seeing and hearing others see the many faces of past masters on Gurunaths face, some known some not, gave me a perspective of this unique phenomena. When Gurunath heightens the awareness of disciples by sharing the state of samadhi, the veil that covers the past, present and future is lifted for that moment and the master lifts the disciple to the same plane of revelation as his. The glimpse of persons revealed at this point could be the past life entities of the master and or the disciple's connections with those personas in the past. At this moment there is no barrier between the master and the disciple and their past and future lives, there is only Truth, a moment of clarity.

※

Wings to freedom

"Often, true masters contribute to the yogic treasury of knowledge by adding to the already existing knowledge, some nugget of information, or technique, that is unique and effective," explained Gurunath. "*Babaji Shiv Gorakshanath*, the originator of all yoga techniques, in his treatise on Hatha Yoga has revealed the connection of the mind to the breath and given us the precise, rational, and detailed science of *pranayam*. He has tabulated the exact measurement and patterns of breath to control various moods and mind fluctuations."

"On Babaji's authority, Sri Yukteshwar Giri could give the experience of complete God-realisation by a mere touch. Many masters are thus working for Babaji in the external as well as inner spheres of consciousness for the speedier evolution of the human race," Gurunath continued his assertion.

Similarly as directed by Babaji, Gurunath revealed he has contributed to this yog paddhati, or yogic treasury, by giving us the Shivapat, a unified field of consciousness that is the yogic still-mind state of soul awareness, which we had all experienced earlier. In simpler terms, as master, he communicates to the audience, wordlessly, the consciousness of natural enlightenment, transforming the ripples of thought in their mind into awareness devoid of thought. The second contribution of Gurunath, to the yogic treasury, is the legacy of the jivhamsa – the soul swan, a blueprint of where the jivatma resides in the body. Indian yogis have often referred to the Hamsa within in poetry and prose; but Gurunath has shown the exact location of this swan-like image in the physical body. The formation is clearly visible in a biological cross-section of the brain (see Illustration on page 300)

Initiation into Kriya Yoga

After the open satsang, those not interested in the initiation into Kriya Yoga were asked to leave, as the process of initiation is sacred and secret. Only those already initiated or those seeking initiation could attend. I was surprised to see many people get up and leave, even after confessing to powerful experiences during the transmissions.

A few of us were then given initiation for the practice of Kriya Yoga. Gurunath eased us into the technique, at the same time clearing our spinal channels with his breath, which he said would help us overcome numerous difficulties in our spiritual practice. Several students later reported how constraints of time and space for the practice disappeared; new avenues opened up at work and business, removing financial or job-related worries, giving them ample time for the practice. For me, in the following days, it translated into a sense of freshness and rejuvenation with an experience similar to the dawning of a new day. All feelings of guilt for sins committed, pleasures stolen, and self-perceived wrongdoings fell away gradually over the next few weeks. This is an on-going process; over the years, as practice has increased and strengthened, there is a constant sloughing off, of negative deposits in the physical, emotional and mental bodies, steadily improving clarity in my actions.

Gurunath explained the speedy result of the Kriya Yoga practice, as compared to others, graphically. "You can take a mala, and keep chanting *palak paneer, palak paneer, palak paneer* when hungry," he said. "The human cerebral system has the capacity to crystallise this dish after many lifetimes of constant chanting with complete devotion and one-pointed concentration. The practice of Kriya Yoga, on the other hand, empowers the practitioner to prepare the field, plant the seed, and harvest the crop. Then, lighting a fire, the practitioner can cook the meal and satisfy hunger. Sitting and gazing at the menu will not fill your stomach," he further clarified, stressing on the importance of active participation as against intellectual deliberation. I understood that Gurunath said this not to deride other practices but to allow the seeker to choose the path that most suited the seeker's temperament. It suited mine perfectly for personally being a person of action, it's not my nature to sit and wait for something to happen.

The initiates were to have brought an offering of five fruits for him, symbolising the offering of their five senses that are to be sublimated and introverted by the master. As I had not been informed, I was unable to complete this obligation and left carrying this burden with me. Next day I was back in Chandigarh, left to fend for myself. There was no local teacher to guide me in Kriya Yoga and no written literature, so I managed as best as I could. The thought of the five fruits kept nagging me until one day I mailed five different dried fruits – an almond, a raisin, a walnut, an apricot and a cashew all in their shell to Gurunath who was in Pune.

During the months that followed, I was surprised by the simplicity of the practice. The technique itself was so easy to practice, that it seemed too much to expect miracles from following it. Personally, I thought much more complicated exercise and hard work was required for any type of substantial spiritual advancement – but carried on with the practice regardless.

As if to show me the fallacy of my reasoning, during the following days, I had these experiences. The feeling of a hand placed on my head, not just a mental or psychological feeling or even symbolic, but a strong physical sensation, as though someone had placed the whole palm and five fingers on top of my head. Then, sometimes, as I clearly saw through my mind's eye, the fingers and the hand would turn into the hood of a five-headed snake. This was followed by a vision of the planets in our solar system, aligned along my spine. Both these experiences, though uncanny, were exhilarating.

I know now that I have been a practitioner of Kriya Yoga in the past, having been initiated by Gurunath in many other lives; enlivened after the resumption of my practice from where I had left it in a previous life. I believe that spiritual gains accrued in the past are the one commodity that a soul can transfer from prior lives to the present one.

CHAPTER 2

DAUGHTER WIFE MOTHER SEEKER

There was a time I would not have ever thought that I could be part of a group that 'followed' a guru. My view being gurus moralised and pontificated, interfered in their follower's personal lives, and attempted to tie them down with traditions. It was only after being with Gurunath, a Nath yogi and Himalayan master; I understood that it was not a follower that gurus want but a disciple who will be steadfast and alert in the practice given by them. I had the freedom to practice and experiment and learn my personal lessons within the boundary of the set discipline. A true guru sets the disciple free. Liberating the sadhak, step- by-step, from the bondage of narrow conditioning, the master finally enlightens the earnest pupil to move beyond the restricting cycle of mortal birth and death to enlightenment.

Looking back at my life today, I wonder if the years before I met Gurunath were simply a preparation for meeting him. The earlier thirty-six years now seem to have passed in a dream. Whatever the depth of darkness I imagined myself to have sunk into, I eventually emerged from the quagmire to move towards the light. The instant I had made the effort, pathways opened up, leading me to the moment of meeting the master.

※

Days of innocence

Emerging feet first from my mother's womb, I have been told that a grand Shanti puja was performed at my grandmother's house in Mumbai, erstwhile Bombay. As soon as my mother and I came back from the nursing home where I was born, Brahmin pandits were specially summoned to appease the gods, to avert any obstacles for the child and mother arising from this breech birth. Over the years, as I grew, blame for all my childish tomfoolery was squarely placed on this occurrence by Bombay Ma. I lovingly addressed my maternal grandmother as Bombay Ma. The oft-repeated remark over my pranks was, "How can she do anything right – she was born upside down!!!", she would say with exasperation at my antics.

Ours was a small Palakkad family from Kerala living in Calcutta, now renamed Kolkata. It included *Chitthi* my paternal grandmother, *Amma* my mother, *Appa* my father and *Chittappa* my father's brother. I was an only child to my parents for a very long time, my brother being born when I was thirteen. My parents, though loving and full of concern for their cherished child were, however, not physically demonstrative in their love. I hardly have any memory of being hugged or cuddled by them – a grudge for many years, until both of them finally had to make amends by hugging me when I was forty!

I was, however, surrounded by other adults who hugged me aplenty. Most of my father's friends were bachelors or newly married with no kids, and found plenty of time to play with me and fulfil every one of my childish demands. Moreover, our family lived in a portion of a huge mansion rented from a Bengali family of four brothers and their wives, who had let out a portion of their house. Their children had all either grown up or left home and I was a pet to all of them. The men would carry me away to the park for a ride on the bicycle or to the corner shop for a treat. Their wives would ply me with all kinds of goodies and I had the run of the place. I gave them all names in bengali in my childish way, *cycle mama, upor mami, kakima, borodada, bubudada*. My mother had no chance to discipline me, although she tried hard.

A lot of my initial emotional nurturing came from my Chittappa, who transferred his job and came to live with us after my birth. I remember him feeding me and putting me to sleep, singing and patting me on the back while rocking me in his arms. Nothing was too good for his beloved niece and, as I grew, I heard him arguing with everyone in the family, either to allow me to stay up late, or forego dinner, or play for a little while longer! Chittappa was more a mother to me than uncle. I always felt safe in his presence, as if no harm can come to me. His love was like a warm protective hug. When he passed away in 2017, he reached out to me and I miraculously saw the message of his demise through a shattered phone screen. It was as if he summoned me from another dimension and I was able to attend and be there at the cremation and subsequent immersion of his ashes. It was for me a completion of a circle of love.

Chitthi was, without any doubt, the head of this family. Every morning, she would roast and then grind fresh coffee to percolate. I remember waking up daily to this intoxicating smell and the signature tune of All India radio. My grandmother came from a distinguished, landed family. My grandfather, whose act of youthful defiance had been to run away to Singapore, a family trait of rebelliousness, that I believe was passed on to me and then by me to my daughters, we all have that streak of wanderlust in us. My grandfather had later returned to marry and manage the family property as the only son. He died at a young age and my grandmother, widowed with the heavy responsibility of bringing up five children, had lost all her property to greedy relatives. To pay for her children's tuitions, and boarding and lodging at her brother's house, she had to sell off all her possessions. Yet, she had not lost her graciousness. Guests were always invited to stay for meals; no leftover food was served to anyone, and there was always something given in charity on a regular basis. All customary festivals were celebrated with due pomp, continuing the traditional preparation of the long list of homemade sweets and savouries.

Amma was born into a family that had settled in Rangoon in Myanmar erstwhile Burma for several generations. Her family, however, came back to their village in Kerala in southern India, during World War II, leaving behind all their properties and possessions. The family later moved to Mumbai. My mother was an entrepreneur, and very fashion conscious for those times. She used to tailor garments for some posh shops before she married my father. Even then she had refused to marry when first approached with the proposal for my father, citing the reason that she needed to support her family at that moment. The astrologer predicted that if my parents marry it would be to each other or they would stay single. So after two more years of my father looking for a bride the proposal went back for my mom who was now ready for marriage as her brother was now settled into a job.

She carried on her style experiments in tailoring on me, and as a child I was always wearing clothes that were different from everyone else's. One can see that in my photographs, I am the kid with patchwork dungarees, peculiar shorts or skirt but looking very spiffy in them. I have heard her reminisce longingly that had she been born at a later time, she would have made a really successful fashion designer, which I did not doubt for a moment.

Much later, in the days of cable television, she loved to watch Fashion TV with my daughters. She would laugh delightedly at some of the fashion statements made by modern designers!

Amma's other passion was classical Carnatic music. She had been trained from an early age. She loved to sing, and would not hesitate for a minute when asked to sing at public gatherings or at friends' and relatives' homes, as is the custom in South Indian families. "Can't you at least wait till they ask you a second time?" I would say to her, thoroughly exasperated at her apparent lack of coyness. Her favourite, and mine too, was a Tamil devotional song begging lord *Krishna* to appear before the singer, while also beseeching him not to move, for when he moved he made the whole galaxy shake and roll. Whenever she sang this song, I could see baby Krishna before my eyes, adoringly addressed as '*Kanna*' in the song, dancing with abandon and making the universe slide and shift.

Appa had a weakness for sweets and savouries, and always came home from office bringing goodies like chocolates, wafers and cakes. At eighty-six, he still does this, and he spoilt my daughters in their childhood, just as he had spoilt me at that age. He introduced me to the world of books at the British Council library in Kolkata where I accompanied him to borrow books. I would spend hours browsing in the children's section there, which at that time seemed to me like an endless gallery of bookshelves filled with secret getaways. One of my greatest pleasures in life was when he would take me to a bookstore just before the long summer holidays and buy me as much as seven or eight books to read at one time. No possession has been so priceless since.

Appa was also an avid movie buff and a fan of yesteryear Bollywood icon Dev Anand. In his younger days, he would copy the inimitable hairstyle of this favourite actor. On festival days, I recall, he would be up early, washing and chopping vegetables and helping my mother in the kitchen. His chopping was mathematically precise, just as his accounting must have been in the office, and each piece of bean, carrot or pumpkin would be of the same length, breadth and thickness once he had finished with it!

He also introduced me to the practice of *asanas*, I remember going with him to a *yogashala*, where a teacher very gently would make the group of students practice yoga postures on rattan mats laid out on a mud floor. Appa continues to this day practicing his yoga every morning in a very set disciplined manner. And the hatha yoga I share today, the foundation of it was laid on that mud floor; more than the practice it is the essence of yoga that I remember from that age that I bring to my class, the simplicity and joyous austereness.

Throughout my childhood, whenever I tripped, fell or got hurt, my father would react by scolding me. This was very confusing to me, and I felt a great sense of injustice over the fact that through no fault of mine I was getting a dressing down from Appa. Much later when my brother, who also had to face this behaviour, and I confronted him, Appa told us that he had read in some psychology book that to take away the pain and attention of the child from the trauma of getting hurt the parent should immediately chastise the child. We could not believe that a major portion of our childhood agony had been based on some misguided theory of psychology that our father had adopted in good faith. What a laugh my brother and I had as this dawned on us. This also made me understand how we carry grudges about our parents actions which they probably enacted out of love for us.

Sunday morning, unfailingly, started with a march to the *Bal Vihar* classes, a Sunday school for kids organised by the Chinmaya Mission. The founder of this Mission, Swami Chinmayananda, was a great preacher of *Sanatana Dharma*. There was a set format for chanting mantras, which all of us remembered 'by heart'. Since I had a loud and clear voice and good command over Sanskrit pronunciation, trained as I was at home, I would show off by reciting ahead of the rest of the class or chant at a loud, different pitch. Then the teacher, who conducted the class, would promptly reprimand me and make me stand outside for the rest of the class. What a pain I must have been.

An older sister of a friend in this class, one day, conspiratorially told us that if we rubbed spit with a cloth between our eyebrows, it would open the Shiv-Netra! My knowledge of this extra appendage was only from photographs of lord Shiva, and the tales I had heard from my grandmother about the awesome incendiary effect of the opening of Shiva's third eye. So, I started in right earnest, rubbing the brow surreptitiously with a corner of my dress whenever I was alone. Till, sore and painful, it led to mild infection and fever, putting an end to the pious endeavour.

My mother was very possessive of me in those early years, and would not let me out of sight. I especially remember an incident when I had won a prize in reciting the Bhagavad Gita in the Bal Vihar class, yes despite being banished from class, and during the same period, ranked first in class at school. I was to receive the prize personally from Swami Chinmayananda. The prize distribution was to take place in front of a large gathering in a noisy hall, with children from all the collective Bal Vihars, their parents and teachers being present. I kept hearing my name being called on the mike and tried to free my arm, but my mother would not let go, and so I missed this opportunity to receive the prize from Chinmayaji. It is amazing how I managed to feel that grip on my arm for such a long time and have managed to let go of that sensation only some years after I began my Kriya practice. I never asked her why she held on to me so, but assume that in the noisy mass of people, she could not hear the announcement and was worried about losing me in the crowd.

I spent my childhood amidst discussions and deliberations of elders at home on the meaning of the Bhagavad Gita and Upanishads, interspersed with *brahminical* chanting of Vedic hymns and mantras, with special emphasis on the correct Sanskrit pronunciations. During my adolescent years, I would listen as my father and his study group chose verses from ancient texts and examined their meaning threadbare, in all perceived nuances. The whole exercise started to seem very futile, the incessant debate and tomes of deliberation, the only result of it to prove one's intellectual superiority. So one day, I just refused to sit in anymore on these discussions. To this day I have, what I consider a healthy aversion to lengthy discussions of treatise by past masters. Therefore, I found it infinitely refreshing when, during the first seminar at my first meeting, Gurunath said emphatically looking straight at me,

"Write your own Gita, spirituality is an individual effort by the soul searching for freedom. Every person has the capability to create a Gita or a Bible. Crystallise the Krishna within you." I had, at last, found a path that involved personal creative endeavour, as against the dry intellectual discussions that I was exposed to at home in my growing years. Though of course now I understand that those early years were a preparation for my later education with Gurunath.

There is deep nostalgia in my mind for those years in Kolkata, remembering lazy afternoons spent engrossed in stories about Chaitanya Mahaprabhu, a Bengali *vaishnav* saint, and Vivekananda, an atheist who, with a touch, was given the experience of God-realisation by his guru Ramakrishna Paramahamsa. The story telling was not complete without macabre tales of ghouls and black magic, which seemed to abound in West Bengal, of human sacrifice and victory of good over evil. I recall combing and braiding my mother's long hair and eating a peculiar but delicious mixture of mangoes, bananas, curds, beaten rice and puffed rice, generously sprinkled with jaggery made from date palms. I felt important when allowed to hold the kite strings for the older boys of the parah engaging in kite fights. This experience in kite flying has given me a similar analogy using the kite and its string that I use to help my students understand training the mind. There were picnics at the Victoria Memorial and in the botanical gardens. I remember my own expression of terror looking at the goats being led for sacrifice at the Kali temple.

Those were days of exciting times getting soaked trying to catch the fish swimming in the tank in our landlord's bathroom, where they were kept live and fresh in a large tank, until it was time to cook them. What I remember the most about the people of Kolkata was their generosity and capacity to share and welcome everyone. On certain days of the month, we would patiently wait for long lines of refugees from Bangladesh to come by, receiving alms of rice, sugar, saris, or dhotis from everyone in the lane. On Durga and Kali pujo days, I felt as though my heart beat louder than the drums or the fireworks, hiding behind people and flinching every time the loud firecrackers were set off.

Growing Pains

Major changes in my way of life occurred at about age eleven, when my father took a transfer, with promotion and enhanced perks, to Patna, in Bihar. Abruptly uprooted from a huge extended family, I found myself pretty much alone. Patna was a smaller town of mango orchards and *Amaltas* trees laden with flowers. On the way to school, I remember breaking fresh tamarind from trees and sucking on the sweet and sour pulp until my teeth felt raw. In the summer, bare bodied, I would sit and eat mangoes that were immersed in a bucket of water to keep them cool, refrigerators not being a common household item at that time. The taste was heavenly and there was no limit to the number I could consume. Sundays were spent splashing in the river Ganga, while the afternoons had to be spent shuttered and safe inside the house, listening to the *looh* – the exceedingly hot and dry summer wind blowing relentlessly outside.

This was the first time that I was formally introduced to yoga, at the Patna branch of the Bihar Yoga School, whose teachers came to train us in our school. I took to the practice of *asanas* very naturally, and did well in the yoga exhibitions. The rest of the time I spent alone, reading and daydreaming. At the same time, hormonal changes were taking place, bringing about confused, disturbing feelings, vague sensations, and fascination with the physical body undergoing maturation, leading to attractions to boys and men. Having no sibling to share my life at home and no close friends, there was no one to discuss all this with. Patna was fascinating because of the connection to ancient India, Pataliputra, the ruins of Nalanda University and the Buddhist Stupa at Rajgir that we visited often. The other attraction was the proximity of the river Ganga, where Appa would take a group of us some Sunday mornings for a dip and as he was a good swimmer he would swim out while I splashed around on the side, feeling the sand underneath, the tug of the river. I never learnt to swim then only to enjoy the immersion in the river.

※

Of periodic cycles

A radically unconventional incident took place at this time that I feel impacted my approach to life in general and patriarchy in particular. It is customary in south Indian families for women to sit isolated during the time of their periods usually for three days. They in those days do not enter the kitchen, do any puja and are generally left alone. I had seen my mother and other ladies of the house sit aside and really did not have any thoughts on this custom as it did not influence me then and I could see my mother really relax with this break from all household chores, reading her books and generally catching up with her hobbies while either Appa or Chitthi did all the housework on those days. I guess this 'tradition' may have started as a relief for women suffering from PMS but as with all traditions took on notes of a taboo.

When I got my periods at age eleven my grandmother suddenly decided enough was enough and pronounced the diktat that this day hence no one would be isolated to a cordoned area of the house and that there would be no discrimination against any woman during these days at our home. I was allowed to participate in all religious functions at home, enter the kitchen and in fact there was no change in my daily life. The onset of the menstrual cycle is celebrated in the south with some pomp as a coming of age of a girl to fertility. My mother was quite happy to comply with Chitthi's wish and my father unconcerned did not even blink. I wonder today what light of wisdom propelled Chitthi my grandmother to take this stand and how wonderful this liberation must have been for her. For me personally throughout my life I felt no different during these days, in school I could play tournaments during this time unlike a lot of girls traumatised by cramps, heavy flow etc. And yes I could hop on my cycle during the cycle and speed away!

Later in life too I don't remember putting my mind to this very natural biological phenomenon. It is, for me like any other bodily functions, respiration, excretion, assimilation and digestion; a necessary development for reproduction, just as the appearance of sperm in boys. I felt the same way in my spiritual practice and would practice my yog sadhana with ease, as I would play sports when young. Menopause came similarly at age fifty, just ceased without a glitch over two years with none of the accompanying trauma. My personal conduct does not mean I ridicule others who follow such customs or try to influence them, a healthy deliberation on this topic is of course stimulating, but as a rule I steer clear from fanatic discussions. "In spirituality, there are no fanatics," I have heard Gurunath say.

Hence when the Sabarimala incident broke on the collective psyche of *Ayyappa* followers, I was appalled at the apparent aggressiveness of some women bludgeoning their way into the temple in the name of reform, apparently during their periods. Even though I personally do not support keeping anyone out of temples for any reason whatsoever and do not think the god's care either. For those who are not aware, Sabarimala is a temple in Kerala dedicated to Swami Ayyappa a celibate divine being, highly venerated by his followers. Since ages women in the menstruating age have not been allowed entry into the temple, both my parents have been on this pilgrimage and one of my uncles has lead the group from Mumbai every year for the past fifty years. I remember having debates about this custom imposed upon women in certain temples, but never did the thought arise of insulting established customs and storm the bastion of religious belief. For some it may be difficult or distasteful to perform certain activities during the cycle, for others it may not matter at all but both according to me should ideally resist imposing their views on the other, as it's a matter of personal choice, often dictated by social conditioning.

My courtesy is simple in this regard, I will not overstep others comfort zones, I will respect norms laid by them while I am in their personal space and if their belief system bothers me to such an extent as to be disturbing I will stay away, this applies across the board to home, religious place, hotel, club or country. Being natural, doing what comes naturally works for me and keeps me straightforward. I truly believe one should do what's comfortable and on the spiritual path, it helps if one is in tune with ones own body and its circadian rhythm. What works for one person may not often work for another, this is true in all aspects of ones life. Sometimes students in their desire to gain wisdom ask the teacher to throw light upon a subject, my answer when asked this question is always, "Where is your effing torch?" *Swadhyaya* or self-study, being one of the tenets of *niyama* in the eight steps of yoga that I hold close and highlight while teaching, it's an important lesson learnt from Gurunath.

❈

The tumultuous teenage

Then, in three years, it was off to Bhubaneswar in Orissa, following yet another job transfer for my father. New school, new friends and a new set of teachers I was quick to adapt to. After-school lessons were done under the shade of a Banyan or Peepul tree, in the courtyard of the ruins of old temples that surrounded our house. It was here in the last two years of my school years that I suddenly one day started writing creatively. It was magical as if some switch in my brain had been activated. I still remember the essay our English teacher gave as homework, 'A walk in the moonlight', was the topic that triggered a creative flow that never stopped. I went on to score very high in all my English compositions. My English teacher, Ms. Nalini gave me very high scores but always retained one or half a mark and when I asked her why, she would say I have to keep something for Shakespeare and Thomas Hardy…very hilarious.

My brother, Jagannath, named after an aspect of Vishnu worshipped at the temple of Puri, Orissa, was born here when I was thirteen. I was pretty embarrassed that my parents had a child after all those years, and I kept it a secret from all my friends. I was at an age when it was disturbing to accept that parents too indulged in sexual activity. In my private moments at home though, I was secretly happy that I now had a sibling. Since he was much younger than I was, my feelings for my brother were more maternal than sisterly. It was only much later that I developed a more chummy relationship with him.

Unbelievably, my father gave me my first puff on a cigarette around this time! I had never before seen Appa smoke, nor had I imagined that he would have any liking for it, but I saw him standing with some friends one day, puffing away on a cigarette. The look of sheer incredulity on my face must have been provocation enough for him to offer me a puff, seemingly in jest.

Then, it was my mother's turn to be shocked for she appeared suddenly from inside the house and that made his friends depart in a hurry. She could not believe that any honourable father could do such a thing to his own daughter. I never saw my father smoke ever again. As for me, I never fancied smoking myself, nor was I enamoured by the glamour of it, even though many of my friends did smoke in school and college.

In school, keeping the company of rich classmates, I was always short on cash, so once when I had collected money for a school fête, I spent it on movies and in the school cafeteria! The guilt of this embezzlement lay on my conscience for a long time. Also, it was in Bhubaneshwar that I had my first romantic encounter, in my last year at school at age fourteen. Though I never directly met this boy, taking only guilty glances at him around town, we spent endless hours on the telephone talking about God alone knows what. The excitement of doing something forbidden was exquisite. Today in the time of social media, I am once again in touch with friends from this time after over forty years. Though at that time Appa discovered the romance, I think, by inadvertently listening in on the extension phone, and he promptly nipped it in the bud by asking for another transfer, which happened to be to Chandigarh in Northern India.

Some memories are indelible and I remember our frequent visits to the Lingaraj and the Puri Jagannath temples and the Sun Temple at Konarak. Recently I had visited Bhubaneshwar again and in Puri went to visit the Karar Ashram of *Sri Yukteswar Giri*. And as I walked in my memories of the time when I had visited this place before with visitors from Kolkata flooded back. Wistfully I wondered if my visits to this ashram in early 1970's ever coincided with that of Gurunath visiting to meet his guru Hariharananda here. Did my Guru leave his footprints in the sands of time for me to follow and did he casually see me then and know I would be recalled later to join the path of Kriya Yoga at his ashram in Pune?

But in 1973 there I was chug chugging on the train to join college in another city. It was a brand new city, for it had been planned only as late as 1950. College was fun. I was part of a group of girls and we took part in all events organised by the college – debates, drama competitions, quizzes, fashion shows et al. The remaining hours were spent in the library researching on Philosophy, my favourite subject. This was a great period of growth for me, and I read everything I could lay my hands on without prejudice. Little did I realise how all this philosophy would be peeled away later, in the course of spiritual unfolding, leading to utter confusion at times.

Being fairly intellectual in college, I used to take great pride in my work. Looking at a subject from many points of view, I could put forth arguments for and against any philosophical treatise. Once, as a special project, I had to submit a paper on 'What is the mind?' I recall winning accolades for it from my Philosophy teacher. The project had run into fifteen or twenty pages, and I had felt very superior about my intellectual prowess after completing it. Writing on theories about the mind according to Spinoza, Plato, and Descartes, I had attempted to understand the mind, and actually felt I had a grasp on it! So, later, whenever I battled with my thoughts as I sat to meditate, this amusing effort would come to 'mind', and never fail to evoke a smile or guffaw from me. Interestingly, Indian philosophical thoughts were not part of the curriculum then.

The paradox on the spiritual path, contrary to all I had learnt in logic, also had me stumped and yet enchanted, like going with the flow is actually when life is under control; and in diving deep into spiritual practice, you emerge out into light! How is one to understand the contrary qualities of a yogi – that is, of a fearless fighter combined with sweet surrender! This paradox has been expressed beautifully in a Sufi rendering. "Jo ubhra so doob gaya; jo dooba so paar" the dervish sings, which means that, "The one who surfaces has drowned and the one that drowns has crossed over."

At home, this period was marked by many arguments; my father, unconventional in many ways, was unreasonably against short skirts, sleeveless shirts, tight tops and dance parties. In me, he had a daughter who saw no harm in all of this, so life at home resembled a battleground at times! Yelling and shouting matches with parents became common, leading to much slamming of doors, stomping out and bouts of sulking. Therefore, I felt I had won a major battle when I got Appa to agree to let me wear sleeveless shirts. But, dance parties were another matter, for he had this fixed idea about boys and girls dancing together, as if they were in an orgy, and nothing I said would change his mind which was stubbornly prejudiced. That was one of the reasons I started listening to and reading books by Rajneesh, just to exasperate him further. Rajneesh later known as Osho, became infamous as a sex guru in India, especially amongst folks who had not cared to read or listen to him.

Since most of the girls at that time were facing similar circumstances at home, we resolved it by holding dance parties in the daytime during college hours, so we could return home like little angels back from studies. We danced with curtains drawn, pretending it was night, with apple juice substituting for beer and, often, it was only girls at these events. Very harmless it all was – no drugs, no alcohol and mostly no boys either. This came back to bite me when my elder daughter would apparently go for her tuitions but I would find her red scooter parked outside the only disco in the city; they were carrying on the tradition of daytime events for girls, I would of course stomp in ready to pull out my daughter and her best friend who were innocently dancing on the floor. But since I had already gone in I could not help but groove a bit and get into my dance moves, deciding to deal with the girls later. Her friend reminded me of this recently at my daughters wedding while we were dancing. Music and dance is part of my yoga training and my students and I often go to do some Bollywood style dancing at a local club. Dancing till one a.m. then sitting down for a meditation and then often its regular yoga class in the morning, a few shots of tequila may make their appearance during the night.

As a teenager I would insist on paying for myself on dates, now I suspect I got asked out only when the boys had no money to invite the more fancier girls. Even then, for all my rebellious nature, I realise I must have been quite a prude, not interested in indulging in casual physical intimacies that many others did, which, I suspect, was another reason for the dates petering out.

The claustrophobia of my own adolescent life, where I was restricted from carrying out perfectly harmless activities due to my parents' fears, led me to develop a more lenient attitude towards my own daughters during their teenage years. Whenever Jujhar, my husband, enacted the heavy-handed Papa routine, whether in their wearing strapless dresses, going out for movies with boys, or throwing parties, the girls had my support. I usually encouraged them to be more fearless and free of guilt in conducting themselves, while at the same time, playing peacemaker by trying to persuade Jujhar to see their point of view. Not an easy task this; believe me, mediating between two strong-willed and rebellious girls and their equally opinionated, sometimes hypocritical father. Of course, I had my share of sleepless nights waiting for either of my daughters, Rukmani or Sukhmani to come home from a party, worrying about the late hour. Fact is when you draw a boundary for your kids and you think you are being liberal and it's further from where your line was; they always want to step over that limit, that's the nature of the next generation.

※

Early marriage and life on the farm

I was eighteen when I met my husband, Jujhar. He and his friends were playing 'seven tiles' – an Indian game called *stapoo*. It consisted of chucking a ball at a pile of flat stones stacked one on top of another, and trying to get them back together without getting hit in turn by the ball. I was watching, and it seemed like they were having a lot of fun. So, when invited, I happily joined in. Instantly, I felt a part of the gang; they were all from the same school Sherwood College in Nainital, the girls were from the sister school All Saints and had they had all been friends for a long time. Flirtatious by nature, Jujhar did not waste much time before he started charming me, and I was immediately bowled over, unschooled as I was in understanding men.

We became friends, and despite everything that happened between us later on, this underlying thread of friendship is what saw us through all the difficult periods. Even today, after being formally divorced since 2010, we live and share space and income at the same farm we lived for thirty years as a married couple.

In 1980, being a rebel with fierce independence and no guidance in such matters, I had no qualms about premarital sex; being in what I thought was deeply in love. It was the first time for me and, retrospectively speaking, we were both pretty naïve and inexperienced. He taught me swimming and driving, skills that I used to always admire in others.

These were sunny, fun-filled days, and I had thought nothing would change after marriage. The quick courtship ended in a wedding six months later in December 1980, a week before I turned nineteen.

My father had many reservations about my marrying into a different community, but he was helpless in the face of my determination. Jujhar was a Sikh, with a public school education. He belonged to a landowning family with vast estates, deeply into farming and allied activities. The two of us were from as disparate backgrounds as two people could ever be! We had a Sikh wedding ritual at the Gurudwara, not for any religious reasons but because of convenience, as it seemed the easiest and quickest ceremony at that time. It was attended by a small gathering consisting of my parents and a few of my college friends. The parents of his friend accompanied Jujhar; they stood in as family for him, as no one from his immediate family attended the ceremony. The eldest brother was not in favour of the marriage (though no specific reason was given), and did not attend, Jujhars sister had recently been widowed and was grieving, and the other elder brother, a Captain in the Indian army, was out on a military exercise and sent us his best wishes.

Both my parents were solemn and, after the ceremony, my father had a few words to say to me. He called us both together and said, "Jyoti, you are marrying against our wishes, but I want you to know that in spite of our displeasure, our doors are always open to you. Don't think we will abandon you at any point in life."

Though at that time I was bemused at this unusual form of adieu, it was much later that I realised the strength that it gave me during later events in my life, and his wisdom in communicating this to me in front of Jujhar. I have tried to give the same kind of unconditional support to both my daughters, explaining that whatever course their lives may take, their parents' home is a place they can always come back to. Today himself a father of two daughters, Jujhar often remarks, "You know, I think it was rather brave on the part of your parents to consent, even under protest, to you marrying me. They knew nothing about me, had not met anyone from my family and I was taking you to a one room shack on the farm, with no comfort whatsoever."

We set up residence in an overhead farm loft with no kitchen or bath. It was a tiny twelve-foot by twelve-foot enclosure, with many windows all around; it gave a feeling of being out in the elements. In fact, there had been no door to the room until the morning of the wedding day, when Jujhar had paid a carpenter to fix a door. I still remember with amusement how we sat demurely and waited for the guy to finish the job that he seemed in no hurry to end, finally leaving at midnight with a sly grin!

A rickety ladder led up to the room, which had to be pulled up at night to safeguard against robbers and miscreants. Bath was a bucket in one corner, kitchen a stove at the other end, and toilet was the riverbed nearby. I used to cycle ten kilometres to college every day, for I still had to finish my graduation. I loved life at the farm, the sense of space, and as we added to the livestock – cows, poultry and three dogs. The serene pace of farm life was wonderful.

The little cottage we built after our marriage took two years to complete, with work coming to a standstill whenever funds dried up, which was often. With no help from anyone, we still managed to survive. In the course of the years that followed, we gradually developed the area surrounding the house. Though the house itself was a small, 800 square foot structure, consisting of a bed-sitter, a study, and kitchen, it had almost half an acre of land around that could be developed. The remaining two acres went towards building the poultry farm. Planting trees, shrubs, roses, other flowering plants and fruit-bearing trees gave the place real character. In due course of time, it evolved into a picturesque postcard setting – a scene straight out of a country novel. The small quaint cottage with honeysuckle on the front porch, the green hedge, the clinging ivy; the puppies, of which we had three, chasing their tails on the lush lawn, filled my heart with joy. The sound of the clucking chicken and the occasional mooing of cows completed the pastoral setting.

Jujhar was ever the farmer, relegating all conveniences of modern living to second priority, preferring to develop the farm first. I remember having a heated debate about whether to buy a refrigerator or a cow with the limited funds in our kitty. He thought the latter would be a more practical investment, since a cow would give milk and birth more calves that could be sold for a profit. So I carried our first calf home, straddling and hugging her to my chest on the scooter behind my husband; the refrigerator came a year later. Fresh milk, butter, cheese, eggs – "Wow!" everyone would exclaim with delight, and I even managed to plant a kitchen garden. Over the years, the house has aged and mellowed with a glow that is warm and welcoming in essence. Today, friends drop in casually for coffee or an informal lunch or supper. Students of course, never want to leave and have to be pushed out. My kitchen today is a hub for students to sip coffee and munch on spiritual discussions after class.

The poultry farm grew as well, from a few hundred chickens in the beginning, to thousands in the following years. Forgetting all about my own ambitions I was totally entrenched in farm work. Working alongside and supporting Jujhar in all his ventures, not that he would have paid any attention to my dissent as I learned painfully.

Both my daughters were born within the next four years and by age twenty-three I was already a mother of two. At this time, we took on the added responsibility of taking care of my husband's widowed sister and her two young children who came to live with us. Doing the daily household chores, taking care of two small kids, helping Jujhar with the farm… the days went by in a blur. My sister-in-law moved out to her own place after two years, though we continued the responsibility of looking after their needs. Despite being so busy in the day, I joined journalism classes at an evening school, driven by a desire for a more meaningful life. It had never even crossed my mind, in that initial phase, to question if I was cut out to be a farmer's wife.

❃

A few short breaks from work

Jujhar was not very fond of travelling and sightseeing and considered this a frivolous pastime. Another reason for him not wanting to go away on long vacations was the nature of his work. The poultry required constant monitoring of the livestock for disease, daily overseeing of feed intakes, managing fickle labour and especially the fluctuating egg prices demanded instant decision on sales. However, having spent his childhood in the hills of Nainital, in Sherwood College, he had a love for trekking in the mountains. Therefore, our tours took us to the hills of Nainital, Mussourie, Manali and Dalhousie, all in the lower Himalayan ranges, though most of our getaways were trips into the nearby Shivalik hills. One of my memorable treks was one that we took immediately after I stopped breast-feeding Rukmani, which meant I could take a day trip away from home. A school friend of Jujhar's came up with the idea of trekking up to the hill town of Kasauli. Perched high on a mountain, this town is visible from Chandigarh and, on clear nights, the lights from the hilltop houses would twinkle brightly. The trek was to take four to five hours by a trail that started at a village on the outskirts of the city.

I prepared some sandwiches and armed with high-energy food such as chocolates and dry fruits, and our bottles of water, we were ready to start. I had left Rukmani with my mother for the day. An hour into the trek, our friend realised that we had taken the wrong track and the trail had become more and more difficult, until finally we were walking along a dry riverbed full of massive boulders. Trying to scare us, Jujhar started talking about flash floods and about how people had been washed away in recent floods. After two more hours of this gruelling walk, tired and hungry, we somehow managed to climb out of the rocky riverbed, and found our way to a village. This being the onset of winter, fresh *jaggery* was being made from sugarcane and the whole area was alive with this wholesome fragrance. Nothing had ever tasted as good as the fresh sugarcane juice that the farmers freely gave us, extolling us to have more. The generosity of these poor farmers touched me and I could not help comparing it with the behaviour of city dwellers that loathe sharing anything without some hidden motive.

The villagers enquired about how we came to be walking in this hilly terrain. The incredulity on their faces was amusing when we told them we were walking from Chandigarh to Kasauli. "But," they said with surprise, "there is a bus service from the city." With their harsh lifestyle, where they had to farm, hunt and forage, they could not imagine anyone walking such distances voluntarily! Anyway, we managed to arrive at the hill town by evening after a total walk of about ten hours, and as we entered the main market square the last bus was leaving for Chandigarh, so we got on to it and returned home.

As the children grew, they joined us on these holidays. During all of these treks, Jujhar was undoubtedly in his element. His knowledge of the flora and fauna was vast, his ability to observe details – to point out hidden nests and find tracks of wild animals and birds, to guide us unerringly on jungle trails – made him undisputed leader of the pack. Though most of our vacation time was spent in the hills, we did manage to go for a longer trip to the South as part of giving Jujhar and the kids a taste of my part of the country. Because of having a good season in poultry, we could afford to travel by air. It was Jujhar who pointed out that it was the first time that each one of us had got on to an aircraft, Jujhar in his early thirties, me in mid-twenties and the girls four and two years old. The ten days spent travelling in Kerala was a new experience for all three of them, and for me it was homecoming to god's own country. We visited my Chittappa in Thrissur and went to my village in Palakkad to meet my cousins.

The last leg of this journey was spent in Kovalam, a beach resort in Kerala. It was the first experience of the sea for all of them and Jujhar was as overawed as the children with the vastness of the ocean. We spent all five days dressed in swimming costumes and shorts. The freedom to dress as I pleased without anyone staring at me was a forgotten memory since I had gone to live in Chandigarh. Jujhar was amazed to see women in the village working, or relaxing at their doorstep, top bare or with just a thin covering. More amazed was he by the fact that the men paid scant attention to them. I was of course not new to this as my childhood memories was of my grandmother barebreasted, fanning herself in the summer with one end of her sari with no inhibitions.

For me today that graphic image is quintessentially one of total liberation. It was only after we shifted to Chandigarh in the north that my father insisted she start to wear a blouse and I remember how mortified she was the first time and how uncomfortable. She kept complaining of how the stitches were giving her a rash and how she couldn't breath. Till finally Amma improvised a blouse for her that was loose and could be tied up instead of buttoned. I know there's much historical conjecture about the breast no-tax apparently imposed on low caste Kerala women who were excused tax if they kept their breasts bared, I'm not sure whose narrative it is, but throughout my childhood I have sat besides my grandmother and many of her friends in our very orthodox Brahmin *agraraham* -village in Palakkad, and never felt an iota of oppression in them. A dress code considered a symbol of oppression by historians became for me a symbol of liberation.

Terror and religious divide in Punjab

Soon after we came back from our holiday began the awful days of terror in Punjab. Truth was intangible, and all we heard were stories of encounters and mass murders. We witnessed a vicious circle of terror perpetrated by both the police and the insurgents upon the ordinary citizen. The simple folk in the villages of Punjab bore the brunt of this violence. They faced the brutality that was unleashed on the pretext of controlling the situation. Many young boys disappeared without a trace, their last known stop being the police station! With no recourse to any judicial process, the families were left to grieve and wait for children who would never return. There were first-hand reports of extortion of the landed farmers, first by the terrorists and immediately thereafter by the police, both of whom seemed to be acting hand-in-glove with each other, sharing priceless information about which party had coughed up how much of the 'blood money'! In a way, I feel the spirit of the brave people of this land was broken by all the atrocities heaped upon them during this period, and they are still struggling to recover.

Throughout all this, we continued to live on the farm keeping a low profile, not daring to draw attention to us. The girls, only seven and nine years old then, had to stop wearing skirts to school and donned the traditional dress of Punjab – the *salwar kameez*, with legs fully covered and the modest *dupatta* covering the upper torso – under the diktat of the fundamentalist forces.

There were undercurrents of the Hindu-Sikh divide wherever we went – at first subtle, but more audible with each passing day. Jujhar and I were invited to a party at my friends' place in the town of Jalandhar around this time, and after a while, we realised that Jujhar was the only Sikh there. Since he does not wear a turban, and is 'clean-shaven', he is not easily recognised as a Sikh. At the party, there was a tirade of criticism and *Sardarji* jokes, most people there being from staunch Punjabi Hindu families. On our return journey, we visited Jujhars cousins' family in the neighbouring town of Ludhiana, where we were treated to a plethora of jokes and denigration of Hindus and their customs, with barely a thought about how I would take it. We were in splits of laughter at this foolishness the moment we got into our car, while at the same time aghast at the behaviour of people. Operation Blue Star drove the last wedge into this divide, by splitting the hitherto homogenous community into Hindus and Sikhs. I felt divided and took up cudgels for both, feeling the pain of both communities, and anger at the State atrocities, which seemed unforgivable.

Personally, religious rituals never played any part in our daily life. I did not have to change the religion I was born into when I married, even choosing to continue my maiden surname. With Jujhar being quite unconcerned about such details, it was never an issue. When our first daughter was born, we named her Rukmani after my grandmother, and the second daughter was called Sukhmani – a traditional Sikh name. When a visiting guest once asked the girls whether they were Tamil or Punjabi, Rukmani, after a pensive pause, answered, "I am English." In her innocence, she thought the question pertained to which language she spoke, and English was the common medium of speech at home. She was only three at the time. The children visited all religious places without prejudice, visiting the temple with my mother, their grandmother. They used to sometimes help her with arranging the flowers and participate in her devotional sessions at home. Going into fits trying to hide their giggles at the Murugan chanting which in Tamizh, went muruga, muruga, muruga, muruga and murga in Punjabi meaning a chicken! In fact, it was rather convenient not to follow any custom at all. We never celebrated any religious functions at home. It did not mean deriding or disrespecting religion but just not being effected by any or inspired to be part of one.

I can truly say that today we have no allegiance to any organised religion. My daughters had non-religious wedding functions. Sukhmani choosing a court marriage in New York and Rukmani had their friend perform the wedding ceremony in LA. Diwali. Dussehra, Gurpurabs and other holy days come and go without a blip in my life, I might light a lamp on Diwali or not. My connection to the Sikh people of course went back to a past life, discussed later in this book but it didn't translate into devoutly celebrating Sikh religious functions in this one. So today when yoga aficionados, by their admission, escaping from the restrictions of their own religions start to follow 'hindu' customs, covering their heads, putting on bindis, acquiring other cultural habits replacing their own, I'm quite amused. For me attending a kirtan is not much different from attending a chapel choir, both equally enjoyable or not. Trading in one religion for another does not appeal to my sense of liberation.

Never a big fan of dress code, I chafe at being told what to wear, other irritables' being separation of genders and too much external show of devotion. I remember once a lady asked Gurunath if she should have a bath before her Kriya Yoga practice and Gurunath jestingly told her not only must she have a bath but also put flowers on her hair, light a lamp and incense and by that time he pointed out that there will be less time for the main puja, the practice. The straightforwardness of Kriya Yoga is very attractive to me.

Sometime after I met Gurunath, one day at a seminar he recited a poem he had written about the Joy of Festivals in Dhyan. For a yogi immersed in sadhana it's festival day everyday he explained. While Gurunath rendered the poem he transported me to the land he was talking about. That is the hallmark of a living master for me, to be able to bring alive the fragrance of that land for the disciples giving them a glimpse of that supernal space. In a voice filled with nostalgia, he sang in hindi, "*Hum pardesi ba des bhaye, jahan har din hori hoth*, a foreigner to this land, I belong to a country where the festival of holi is celebrated each day; There sprayed with the seven colours I am transformed, whirling in festive joy I become colourless, oblivious of my ego and body." In my mind I could picture this scene of spinning colours transforming into a purity beyond colours. Gurunath, his eyes misted with a longing for his true home carried on, "An outsider here, my country is where there is perpetual irradiant splendour, seven coloured wheels of mystic fire swirl within me and every day is the festival of Diwali." I am translating here for the reader but the poem was sung recited in hindi for us. "*Dasra naubat naad kare aur raag kare Omkar,*" Gurunath explained that at the festival of *Dussehra* the big drum sounds the *Naada Brahm* and the *raagas* reverberate the Omkar. In his simple style that seeped deep within he brought home to us the constant inner state of celebration that a yogi lives irrespective of outside show.

Recently while giving his blessings to disciples during *Gurupurnima*, a celebration to pay reverence to the master, he said something that in a flash took away the ritualism that priests invest into every sacred exchange. "Today is Gurupurnima," Gurunath expounded, "when the Guru is ready to offer his heart in order to serve humanity. But let me tell you, whenever a disciple is in total at-one-ment with the master, so many times it is Gurupurnima for the disciple." This fell like rain on my parched heart, more attuned to internal devotion rather than external show. "Every time a disciple connects with the master," he continued, "the master takes that soul into a nirvichar avastha a trance like state free of thoughts." This connected so deeply with me, the Satguru had put into words and brought out something I had always felt intensely within.

The true master frees the disciple gently from external trappings imposed by social norms and turns them to a higher devotion within connecting them directly with the guru, no intermediaries required. It's a timely warning to stay clear of the trappings of organised religion where priests, pundits and gatekeepers take over authority in the name of devotion, appointing themselves as the only spokespersons artfully inserting themselves between the divine and the devotee.

The dark era

Though compatible in matters such as religious beliefs, working together at the farm, and ideas about bringing up the girls, trouble had already reared its head in our marriage. The very flirtatious nature that had attracted me to my husband now began to rankle when it was so obviously directed at other women. I became overcome by jealousy and bitterness, emotions that were completely alien to my inherent nature. But somehow, I could not seem to help myself and every party, and many evenings, would end with me throwing a tantrum, sometimes accompanied by frenzied, mindless drinking.

My sense of shame doubled because the children were witness to such scenes of uncontrolled upheaval. Joy and sorrow had seesawed for the past few years, even through my pregnancies. I had known nothing about pre- or post-partum depression, which must have also influenced my mood swings. My sense of worth hitting an all time low, with Jujhar never happy with the way I looked or dressed or kept my hair or cooked.

During my second pregnancy, I had been very temperamental, strongly reacting to Jujhar and his on-going flirtations, especially with a visiting foreign national. Under the circumstances, I even had doubts about going ahead with bearing the baby. I took an overdose of sleeping pills while in the grip of a feeling of sheer desperation. All this had an effect on my younger daughter for, as an infant, she slept for long hours, and displayed difficult behavioural patterns in adolescence. When I became aware later of how a baby in the womb is so deeply affected by the mothers state of being, I was mortified to have put my baby through this.

There was a time during the period after the second daughter when, under subtle and overt pressure from Jujhar and some family members, I allowed myself to be persuaded into believing that it was my duty as a wife to produce a son and heir. I underwent two abortions after sex determination in this quest, and on the last occasion, I almost bled to death on the operation table. Doctors and nursing homes abetted the crime gladly. These experiments were kept a well-guarded secret from my parents, who would have felt deeply hurt, taking the blame upon themselves for this 'lack of culture and education' in their one and only daughter.

In retrospect, I consider this the darkest phase in my life. I was filled with self-pity, losing all sense of balance or perspective, ready to blame my husband for everything that I perceived as wrong in my life. The only redeeming feature was that the girls were never made to feel unwanted or inadequate and, as far as I am aware after frank conversations with them, they knew nothing about these traumatic events. Much later I discussed this subject with them, as examples of moral blindness that can afflict anybody. It also gave me perspective that if someone of my independent nature and attitude could succumb to pressure and go through such an experience willingly, how much more difficult it must be for those unfortunate women from less advantageous backgrounds. My personal experiences during this period of agony and self-defeat have helped me greatly now to understand without judgement people and their behaviour. I find it easy to empathise and look kindly on human transgressions knowing that everyone has the capability to transform.

A brief interlude

As mentioned earlier, in order to bolster up my depleting confidence, I joined an evening college for a course in Journalism. The couple of hours away from home in an environment of study and learning helped me stabilise in important ways. But there was no way I could take up a job, what with the farm work and managing the children. To be honest, there was no opposition openly from Jujhar but for me life seemed daunting enough without an added complication of a full-time job. So I consoled myself by honing my writing skills on a typewriter I had acquired. I submitted short articles, poems and letters to the editors of local English newspapers, many of which, to my surprise, were published.

By temperament carefree and joyous, I felt as if I was living a life completely contrary to my innate nature. I tried to compensate for this by finding solace partying with friends who were themselves in bad relationships with their spouses. Even the older couples around us had personal agendas and were not good advisors rather to the contrary they created more misunderstandings. Today as I help so many young and old students I wish I had myself as my advisor when I was young! But at that time it was a case of being surrounded by the blind leading the blind to the edge of a crevice. Though I wanted with all my heart to end the marriage, my love for my daughters and their love for their father held me back. I had no idea then how our strained relationship and constant talk of separating was affecting the children. And so it went on, our emotional tug of war. It was many years later, when I was sitting at the dining table with a friend discussing someone's divorce that Sukhmani, who was doing her homework, said, without looking up from her book, "When parents separate they should just kill their children." My heart had almost stopped then, suddenly experiencing the trauma that small children go through when forced to witness fights and choose between two people they love equally; not equipped as they are to understand human deviations at that age.

In the midst of all this I took my first vacation abroad. I boarded my flight for Australia in the summer of 1992, not realizing that nineteen years later I will be sent by Gurunath to pioneer his work in Australia one day. I was very excited as travelling widely around the world, visiting places I had read about in books, had been one of my dreams. I was visiting my friend in Sydney, with a break in Singapore on the way back. When I alighted at the Sydney airport I am sure I must have looked completely goggle-eyed, the true picture of a native exposed to a world conflicting to her own. The first few days, I would stop startled as automated doors opened magically; the escalators were a difficult task to be mastered and instructions on pay phones indecipherable. The variety of cars and the highways stumped me, I felt like a country bumpkin let loose in the streets of a city.

I was exposed to my first close interaction with people not of Indian origin. Though independent by nature I was coming from a comparatively conservative country and society and found the mind-set of the western people very refreshing. Especially at that moment of my life when I was feeling restrained and chained in an unwanted marriage, this pragmatic outlook on life and self-indulgence was very attractive and I enjoyed my holiday thoroughly by imitating them. It was three weeks of fun filled days, swimming, and sight seeing, watching films and meeting lots of interesting uncomplicated people. For the moment I forgot all my woes and indulged in myself unashamedly. The claustrophobic life in India seemed far away.

❀

A period of deep turmoil

I returned to life as a dutiful wife and homemaker, in a hopeless situation that seemed to be spinning out of control with every passing day. Though externally I was going through the motions of what appeared to be a full life – as wife, mother, homemaker, woman entrepreneur running a business, employing and managing a staff of forty, with an active social life, a house, a car, club memberships, loving parents, bright kids – there was still an inner sense of vacuum. After retuning from Australia my Amma and I started a small take away specialising in packed food for office people. The small business grew to managing the housekeeping of ten to fifteen offices and providing them with cafeteria services and employing a workforce of forty. But through it all I was as if in a daze, little realizing what I was suffering was a form of trauma.

At home explosive reactions to each other's behaviour started a continuous conflict between my husband and me that gradually drove us far apart. The atmosphere was now intolerable, with old issues brought alive again and again – our previous indiscreet affairs, the innumerable times we had hurt and been careless about each other's feelings, the combined mistakes that we kept trying to blame on one another, all became too much. Jujhars utter lack of respect towards me was disturbing and heart-rending. I tried to take refuge in memories of the past, reliving moments of joy that now appeared fleeting and which I seemed to have lost forever. At that time it felt as though I was losing my sanity, morale and everything I held precious. I carried on, nevertheless, like a shell-shocked person, feeling abused in body and mind. A moment did come when I offered to leave and go my separate way if we could come to some agreements but at that point Jujhar recanted and we were back together again.

It was about then that I signed up for a Reiki class, urged by my brother's girlfriend, as an escape from this empty life devoid of any spark. A full session of Reiki took almost one hour. It comprised of just lying down and connecting with the body and this gave me a sense of ease and comfort. Prior to this, I had not even spent ten minutes on myself in such a focused way.

※

Wake-up call

It just happened suddenly. One day, I was as usual hurrying somewhere, when I caught a glimpse of my own reflection in the mirror. I was living a very repressed emotional life by then, only I didn't know it. Though I was just in my thirties, I had stopped looking into the mirror a long time ago, grudging myself this act of narcissism. I now recognize this refusal to look into a mirror as an obvious ploy to avoid facing myself squarely. My attitude had become one of utter defeatism, self-deprecation and self-denial, believing I was worthy of all the unhappiness I was getting.

However, on that day, I stopped short in front of the mirror, utterly shocked by the image reflected in it. I looked like an empty shell, a walking, talking, working body devoid of all life. I was suddenly moved to tears at my own pathetic persona, vacant eyes and hollow smile. Whatever had I done to myself? Who was this person? This confrontation was like a sudden flash of illumination in the dark interiors of my very existence, a hard reverberating slap that is shocking in its revelation. The result was a clear thought that I had to fight whatever it was within me that had reduced me to this sorry state, so utterly devoid of personal meaning or purpose. It culminated in my decision to leave home and go away to some kind of a sanctuary. Though my brother was now working with a Silicon Valley software company in the USA, he was still struggling, and I knew he would not be able to help me. The only faraway place I could think of was Australia, where I had visited a friend a few years ago. Little realizing then that my connection with Australia was more than just a getaway.

The real reason for needing to go far away was to remove myself from the familiar surroundings that would lull me back into old routines. I had to be far enough to be able to step back and have clarity instead of slipping back into my old patterns of behaviour urged by family and friends. Sadly, some of my closest friends were instrumental in creating the maximum misunderstandings. I needed to get away from such friends who were aggravating the situation by giving contradictory advice to both of us, mischievously or otherwise, I didn't know. I really did not wish to claim a share in the farm, or ask for maintenance, or sue my husband or fight for custody as they suggested. I instinctively knew these were secondary subjects; I needed to make myself whole first.

So, after consultation with my parents, and secret visits to the embassy to obtain a visa, I was ready to depart. I wound up my business by simply handing it over to someone else without seeking due remuneration. All this was done surreptitiously and no one knew of my plans; that I was going to Australia was known only to my parents. There was no doubt that the girls would be safe and well looked after by my husband, for he was very responsible as a father and I did not fear for them from him. And the fact that they came daily to my parents from school gave solace to my heart, knowing the emotional support they would be to them both once I did not return from the short trip I told them I was going for. It was with a heavy heart that I left without revealing my plans to them but knew that was the only way.

I landed in Australia for the second time in September 1997, with hardly any money and no clue about what I was going to do. But doors seemed to open automatically; I worked and supported myself which helped in building my confidence. I received a warm welcome from my friend Happie, who I had made friends with at the club in Chandigarh, become very close to and visited a few years ago. It was in her company that I had rediscovered my original carefree and rebellious nature, to the discomfort of Jujhar, who mistrusted and derided her. In a way, the irreversible events leading to the process of leaving him and landing in Sydney now could be said to have triggered six years ago with this friendship. She introduced me to a friend who owned a crystals shop on Bondi Beach in Sydney. That started my romance with the stones, so to say. I held healing workshops there in the day, and in the evenings, I waited at tables in another friend's Indian restaurant. Going far from home brought perspective and introspection about my situation. Being away from outside pressures to either rebel or conform helped me to see my life in a detached way.

I was in Sydney for close to four months. My interaction with people was limited to my friend and her family, the people I worked with at the restaurant, and those who came in for healing. Most of my time was spent alone, as people were preoccupied with their own lives, and my need to be by myself to recover in isolation was very intense.

❈

Guidance from crystals and animal spirits

The months away were of great importance in terms of healing and rejuvenation. I discovered my affinity to crystals and was enchanted by the way they responded to me. I picked up those that spoke to me and intuitively started to interact with them. The time spent with crystals brought me in touch with my deepest roots. Holding each crystal in my hand, I understood I could connect with its spirit and move deep into the bowels of the earth. The mystic revelations that came to me via these crystals helped to heal the wounds of the heart. Crystals,

I understood, are a manifestation of the healing properties of the earth, as Mother to all the living creatures on this planet. She births them just as we are born of our mothers' bodies. Immersion in the aura emanated by the crystals was akin to the feeling of being securely held in my mother's womb. There was one particular piece that, though not the most perfect or beautiful in my collection, resonated deeply with me. I discovered that I could easily flow with it into the volcanic centre of the earth, connecting to the nourishing energy of the earth Mother, and return with a feeling of completion. A wholly physical sensation devoid of any thought, these journeys left me with an afterglow of supreme fulfilment and serenity.

In later years though, the crystals I met were hurting and bleeding. Because of the high demand for crystals they were being harvested and pulled out instead of waiting for them to birth naturally. I have now released all my crystals back into the earth in my garden where they now rest and radiate vibrations of love and peace. On my recent visit to Australia I visited a crystal mountain near Byron Bay and sat inside an amethyst crystal cave that has been transported from South America. I wonder what makes people acquire and relocate natural rock formations, a need to possess maybe. I, accompanied with a group of my students, sat inside the cave in silent meditation for close to forty minutes. The cave was still settling down, there was sense of longing for its old land but I felt that this will change and the original strength will slowly be restored. In fact there was a reverse energy flow and I ended up reassuring the energy of the cave.

During that time of finding myself in 1997, the spirits of a pair of Great American wolves became my constant companions. They were a silent presence in my room, and travelled with me on the train to work. I derived enormous strength from them, as the energy they radiated filled me with inner calm, stability and courage. A single swan completed my guest list. It was the wolves that led me to a portrait that was being sold in a garage sale on the way to my work.

I was drawn to this image of a strange old man, whose weather-beaten facial features tugged at my heartstrings; I had to bring it home, saying it reminded me of my grandfather, not knowing then how true this was. Sitting Bull it said on the portrait and later I learnt about his being a Sioux leader and medicine man whose love for his people and his land was legendary.

Though I was unaware then, this was also my first resonance with my Native American past life. The portrait adorned my house in Chandigarh for many years hung on a wall in the porch, facing north. It was exposed to the elements, as the porch is not fully enclosed, but I had an intuitive sense that the image wanted to be left outside, relatively in the open, facing the sun, the wind and the rain. And there he stayed until the elements faded and disintegrated the picture. In my subsequent visits to Australia I have had visitations from the indigenous elders from the astral realm and often accompanying them are the original natives of America. A connection between all these lands and their people goes back to Gondwanaland and that the spirits of the elders in both these countries are still connected and visit was interesting to know.

The lessons learnt from the swan were deeper; being single, she taught me to gather my energies in spite of the sense of bereavement because of being separated from my loved ones. I had to dive deep within to find the pearls of insight, the inner qualities that were hidden beneath layers of emotional hurt, anger and cynicism. The fact that it was a Hamsa, a swan that appeared was significant though I did not note it then. The vision I saw of Gurunath while following the recording of his meditation was also called the Way of the White Swan, now the Siddhanath Hamsa Yoga!

All three creatures disappeared as mysteriously as they had arrived, following my decision to go back to India eventually. I was now ready to move on in life, and it was as if they had seen me through the most difficult passage in the interim also lighting the course of my life once I came back.

※

The process of healing and recovery

Once back from Australia, I stayed at my parents place determined not to go back to a hurtful relationship. Yet the first moment of clarity was the moment when I decided to return to the relationship with my husband. This choice was uninfluenced by any other thought or desire, whether of compromising with an untenable situation, social or family obligations, concern about the children, or reasons of economic security. I now see that this firm resolution in my mind had, for the first time in my life, led to a clear action without any expectations or preconditions. Before that, everything I had done was a mindless reaction to something or the other in the environment. Even my most rebellious act of going away so far from home, had been a reaction to the events as they unfolded in painful sequence. So this was the first conscious turnaround, an action instead of a reaction that opened for me the future pathways to spiritual exploration and wisdom.

Throughout my sojourn in Sydney, I had no qualms about the girls, knowing fully well that Jujhar was conscientious as a father and would look after them well. In fact, sometimes, I felt that he might even be a better mother than I, being more meticulous about details like nutrition, physical wellbeing and appearance. Once the girls got to know where I was, which was a few weeks after I did not return, it became common for Rukmani and Sukhmani to call up every evening and update me about happenings at home. I was touched that Jujhar never interfered with these calls, and for a person who normally threw a fit at phone bills – he does so even now – he quietly shelled out the money at that time. In fact, he even wrote a couple of letters asking me to return, while indicating respect for whatever decision that I would finally reach but at the same time sent me papers to sign so he could sell my car while I was away so when I came back I was without a conveyance!

It was a difficult time for all of us and I can only feel relieved that it all worked out and with what seems to be minimal damage. Of course, for a long time, it became a habit with my younger daughter Sukhmani to blame her seemingly wayward behaviour on my 'abandoning' her at a young age. It took me a few years and many conversations to mend this particular fence! At first, I was overtaken by guilt and I genuinely apologized to her and Rukmani, for the seeming lapse on my part that had hurt them so much. I tried explaining how if I had not left at that point they would now have a defeated mother, who having lost all her spirit, would have been a pathetic figure, scarcely able to guide or educate them. Rukmani seemed to understand this much better than her younger sister, who I later realized, was just using this as an excuse for emotional blackmail. So I then had to sternly put a stop to it by explaining that what had happened then was a matter of survival for me and was now done with, and she was the one who had to take responsibility for her actions from now on.

❈

Lady Kwan Yin and Magnified Healing

Following my return to India, I entered fully into new age practices obtaining a Master's certificate in Magnified Healing, a healing technique the knowledge of which, we were told, came directly from Kwan Yin. Kwan Yin is considered the Goddess of mercy, compassion, and forgiveness; the female aspect of *Avalokiteshwara*. Lord Gautama Buddha was her master. She is also likened to Green Tara in Tibetan Buddhist terminology. Magnified Healing is a process by which the flames of love and compassion are awakened and steered to heal the earth and those inhabiting it. The third phase of Magnified Healing that I attended was the light Healing method given to two American women, Kathryn and Gisele, by Lord Archangel Melchizedek at the end of 1996. I learnt it from them soon afterwards, while they were visiting India. But the image that came to me of Kwan Yin was as the Devi riding a tiger, although at that time I did not know whether it was my imagination or fantasy, as my intuitive faculties were then in too nascent a stage, and there was no clarity in my vision. But I definitely enjoyed the whole process of channelling and directing the energy. I found myself slipping easily into the role of teacher and had a constant stream of students coming in. However, after initiation by Gurunath into Kriya Yoga and my empowerment to teach as Hamsacharya, this fell away as did all other techniques that I had learnt.

※

Native American Shamanism and the sweat lodge

A month after the Magnified Healing workshop, I took part in a Native American ritual workshop held in New Delhi by a visiting Shaman, Sally Perry. Sally was a middle-aged Native American woman of Cherokee lineage, practicing Spirit Medicine. This appeared to be a natural outcome of my experiences with the animal spirits. It also served to affirm my past life connection with Sitting Bull. It was during Sally's annual six-month tour of India in 1998 that I came to know of her and enrolled for the workshop.

I felt very comfortable with the Native American rituals that Sally made us go through. We fasted to purify the spirit, and made prayer beads for forgiveness from small pieces of cloth of varied colours wrapped around tobacco and sage. Though the fasting began to make me a little dizzy, there was a feeling of purity and tensile strength as the day progressed.

As dusk drew near, we watched with fascination as a small minuscule tent made of bamboo, tartan cloth, and mud was put up. A fire pit outside heated round boulders on wood fire and these were carried to a depression inside the tent that cradled the hot rocks. Sally entered the tent first and took her place in the centre, placing sprigs of sage and other herbs on the hot stones. Then the rest of us filed in to sit in a circle around the hot rocks. Sally started to chant and pour water on the rocks to produce steam. The tent began to heat up and fill with earthy smells. The atmosphere was eerie with all of us in shadow. Somebody started to scream wanting to be let out, while someone else sobbed silently. I was strangely exhilarated and when I looked up, instead of the roof of the tent, I saw a clear night sky with alien star formations.

Then, as instructed, I spun and danced around in the specially prepared circle outside, in a trance. The night passed in a dreamlike state and I did not know whether I was asleep or awake. Strange sounds and shadows kept flitting through my subconscious mind. When dawn broke, I got up surprisingly revitalised and alive.

A month after this, I attended the Reiki seminar, where I saw the vision that led me to Gurunath. This was followed by the initiation into Kriya Yoga, and a subsequent visit to the ashram in Pune, Maharashtra. Most of my clear and conscious visions and intuitions happened after the initiation. Before that, everything was an enjoyment of sensations without clarity.

✻

Clearing past torments

The period that followed was of healing the torments that came up again and again, as Jujhar and I tried to work on our relationship. It was impossible not to bring up old issues as we tried to comprehend the problems that had driven us apart. But the first change I noticed in myself was that the hurt and anger did not go as deep anymore, and there was a rising to the surface of these feelings, preliminary to disappearing forever. It reminded me of my childhood days when I would stand beside Amma, as she prepared sweets for some function or the other. Most entailed preparing syrup from sugar crystals. As the sugar began to boil, impurities within it would rise to the surface. Amma would patiently keep removing them by skimming the surface of the liquid with a cloth strainer, until the syrup was left clear and colourless. I felt like that during this phase of renewal of the old relationship with my husband. I could step aside with detachment most of the time, to watch as the hurtful words and anger boiled over and, gently, ever so gently, the process of mending started.

※

The Final Separation

In 2003 my younger daughter left for undergrad studies in economics and finance to Bristol, UK. My elder daughter was already away in distant Goa where she had got an internship after school. Unconventional and following her own heart she chose not to go to regular college. It was then that I started writing my book and intuitively the name *One Master one disciple* came forth. In 2007 my elder daughter too left for the United States for furthering her skills at film production getting admission and later a scholarship at a reputed college in Los Angeles. Both of them were doing very well in their chosen fields and that left Jujhar and me at the farm. As our responsibility towards children started reducing our relationship started to unravel at a rapid pace, though I was blissfully ignorant of it, thinking all was as usual in our marriage.

I was quite busy with my activities at Gurunaths ashram in Pune where I had started helping with retreats and camps since 2000. I had already written and published the first edition of this book in 2007. I had to face a lot of challenges regarding this book and almost came to the point when I was ready to trash it; then Gurunath suggested some changes that I applied and the book was resurrected. Here I want to reiterate that the bond between a master and disciple is uniquely personal and the master guides each disciple individually. An advice the master gives to one disciple in a given situation maybe diametrically opposite to an advice given to another disciple in the same situation. The satguru gives the disciple what is needed for speedier evolution not what the disciple wants as temporary placebo. My publisher felt the difficulties came because it was very rare for a disciple to write about the Guru while the Guru was still present. Most books by disciples about their gurus are written after the master has passed so don't come under so much scrutiny.

At home though my bond with Jujhar seemed to be loosening, I still had no inkling of the extent to which it had gone thinking it was not as worse as it had once been. But late in the year in 2010 one day at breakfast he blurted out that he wanted a divorce. He had already moved out of the main house by then to the children's room upstairs. Truth to say my first feeling was one of relief like a burden dropped. Knowing fully well that I would not have got this divorce if I had asked for it, I readily acquiesced.

Even then there was a sense of melancholy as I acceded to this demand and asked him to get the papers ready. My only request was that I would keep staying in the home we had built thirty years ago until it was sold to which he agreed. No alimony was set nor asked for; it was going to be a clean break. We signed the papers and the court gave us the mandatory six months to change our mind.

Throughout my discipleship and until today I have never taken my personal problems to Gurunath, never discussing or asking for a remedy on such matters that seemed mundane in the larger spiritual context. So when I was at the ashram at a camp I simply informed Gurunath about our divorce thinking that if he told me to go back and try once again, I will do it even if it kills me. But all Gurunath said was, "Jyoti, you are being freed for more spiritual work." Sure enough in 2011 few months after the divorce he sent me to reconnoitre and start work in Australia to teach and establish a community there. So there I was back to my romance with that beautiful country after a gap of fourteen years. Eight years hence, today in 2019 Gurunath accompanied with Ayi will be setting foot in Australia for the first time being welcomed by a thriving well set-in community of his disciples, some of whom have not even met him yet. I feel quite elated to be instrumental in this venture supported by some very strong local disciples whose sustained efforts has made it possible for this to happen.

After the divorce though, I was not sure what changes I would have to face. I had no idea about money or how I was going to manage. All I knew was in all my years from childhood to today I had never wondered where my next meal was coming from or about security or bank balance and I was not about to start now at forty-nine years. After the six months we went to court to sign the papers, I think we were both a bit sad but it was like the wheels had been set into motion and there was no turning back. The judge, looked at the papers, saw we had been married for almost exactly thirty years, he just asked where the two children were and we told him they were both working abroad. He noticed there was no financial settlement or alimony so wanted to know if I was okay with that and had no objection to a mutual decree, when I assented, I felt a flash of envy spark in the judge, wondering why his wife couldn't leave him like that and this thought brought a chuckle up in me and that set the mood for my divorce. I strongly feel that a divorce was not on the cards for me in this life but intense practice of Kriya Yoga speeded up the momentum and burned the seeds of attachment in this life itself. The beauty of it was because of the grace of the master the dissolution happened for me without the accompanying trauma, a fluid disengagement.

As it happens nothing much changed after the separation, we continued staying in the same space and settled into a different relationship of sort of space mates. The income is still shared as before and we managed to work out a way of being. When I am home I still cook and we discuss whatever family matters need to be discussed. It's been nine years of that now. If I don't mention it people visiting will not make out that we are divorced. But I like to live my life openly not restricted by norms imposed on me hence share my status without any reservations.

Today with the new cottage he is building for himself on the same property I guess we will move into another state of separation. And slowly the last vestige of partnership will dissolve. When I look at my journey from a troubled young woman to the self-contained person I have become at present I feel only gratitude to the person who made this possible, my satguru.

❈

Settling into the Path of the Sadhana

I remember in college during heated debates while we were passionately defending our positions, I would always reiterate that for me beyond a point nothing mattered – love, hate, pain, joy or grief. In the innermost centre of my body, I had this empty space into which all emotions would cease leaving me unruffled. At that point, my friends reacted by saying that I was unfeeling, shutting myself to life, and should not allow what they called, this dead portion in me to interfere with my passions to live life. I started to think that maybe there was something truly lacking in me. So, I withdrew from this core and deliberately let every joy and sorrow shake me up, believing that, at last, I was becoming more human. But today, I enter more and more easily into this core of silence, which had never disappeared but only retreated deep within. Now I have rediscovered this serene sanctuary, to which I return for healing and nourishment, only to emerge later ready to face all challenges. Gradually, the circumference of this centre is increasing to occupy more space, soothing all disturbances – physical, emotional and mental – leaving a tangible sense of inner calm and peace. A still core in the centre of my being that is expanding daily.

I realised that this stillness is what Gurunath reintroduces us to in his transmission of Shivapat. "The secret lies within," he says, "the witness is the God within." In that moment of the transmission, gently removing the veil that separates us from our own inner wellspring of divine bliss he brings us to face the divinity which is our core nature, the witness. In a flash he introduces us to the vaster consciousness that permeates the universe. This is an invaluable gift that he shares with thousands in the audience, calling it his service to humanity so they may realize that at the level of divine consciousness they are one. As our personal practice becomes steadfast we are then able to access this centre more and more easily to emerge rejuvenated and resuscitated.

As I spontaneously worked without expectation or attachment, doors kept opening to lead me to a preordained goal. From looking outwards for happiness and joy, I had turned inwards seeking another truth. I am still not sure what makes this turnabout possible but Gurunath says past karmas play a major role in this. When one takes care of residual past karmic debts, the seeker is ready to move on. Apparently, it is the nature of the individual soul to evolve. The lotus must pass through three stages: the mud of ignorance, to water symbolising resistance from inner passions and outer circumstances, to sunlight and air that symbolises realisation. My journey seems to be passing through a similar chartered path. According to Gurunath, windows of opportunity to take this leap comes to everybody from time to time, the person either takes it or if too enmeshed in the present circumstances lets it go by. Not all is lost though as their own karmas will again and again bring this opening of light till finally rid of the restricting past actions they will take the leap, Gurunath explains.

Now, in the presence of Gurunath, I only feel a deep sense of gratitude that it has happened to me. Thirty-six years of slumber had passed in a flash and I feel alive now. Touched in every aspect of my life by the initiation, I am constantly striving for perfection in my being.

Was my attachment to Gurunath instantaneous, or did it evolve gradually? A bit of both, as the mystical vision of his beckoning to me on the ashram pathway set the groundwork and the subsequent interaction pulled me closer and closer, guided by my steadfast adherence to the yogic practice he assigned to me. "The guru is like a magnet and the disciple the iron filing; through constant practice, the disciple comes into the magnetic field of the guru, and then sticking to the magnet, becomes a part of it," Gurunath often repeated this statement to emphasise the importance of personal sadhana. Then, laughingly, he would add, "So, dear disciples, move your butts and practice, and don't be a dead weight on the guru, obstructing his own take-off." Sincere and committed disciples are often taken on the higher flight path along with the master.

In the present day, I feel no separation from Gurunath, how much ever the geographical distance that separates me the disciple from him the master. The master's essence is always within and the sincere disciple is constantly in contact with that Presence.

CHAPTER 3

ON THE PATH OF A YOGA TEACHER

A few months after being initiated by Gurunath, I heard he was to be in Delhi again to give higher initiations. Though keen to go, I had a house full of guests and was unable to make the trip. Many others from Chandigarh attended the workshop and I was envious of them all. When they got back, they could not stop talking about their experiences, about Gurunaths transmissions and the changing faces they saw during the Shivapat transmissions.

When Gurunath gives this transmission of the state of thoughtfree awareness, all boundaries between the master and the receptive disciple dissolve, and one of the experiences is the vision of different images of the master from past life associations, which are revealed as quickly fleeting impressions superimposing on Gurunaths face. Many of the students had been initiated into higher practices. I hid my jealousy as well as possible, and consoled myself by thinking that maybe, for me, it was not yet time for higher initiation.

A few weeks later, I was in Delhi and, perchance, called up the centre to enquire about any on-going programmes. I was thrilled to hear that Gurunath would be stopping by again as he had been to Gwalior with some foreign disciples and was on his way back to Pune via Delhi. I waited the whole day at the centre in vain. Gurunath did not show up, so when I heard that he was invited to tea at another disciple's place, I shamelessly showed up at her house, uninvited. Such was my determination.

❈

Bestowed with the title of Hamsacharya

As I walked in and stood by Gurunaths side, he looked at me with pensive eyes and said, "I want someone to teach in Chandigarh." Then he asked for another disciple from Chandigarh with the same first name as me Jyoti, who had attended the entire earlier workshop, but she had already left. Then, Gurunath decided to invest in me the rank of *Hamsacharya*, giving me the authority to teach the practices of the Hamsa Yoga Sangh as the organization was then called. He initiated me into further higher practices also that same evening.

It is very difficult to describe this process of investiture, as this function authorising one to teach, was called. I was told that Gurunath would now, by this tradition of the *guru-shishya parampara*, authorise us to teach the practices of the Hamsa Yoga and Mahavatar Babaji Kriya Yoga. Though it sounds formal, the ceremony itself was simple.

During the ceremony, Gurunath puts his mantle, which is the cotton shawl that he uses, around the teachers to be invested with the authority to teach invoking Mahavatar Shiv Gorakshanath Babaji as he pulls the shawl tightly around telling them to hold steady. He then proclaims that from this day onwards the teachers would help in sharing his task of carrying out the work of Babaji by propagating the practice of Kriya Yoga, thus lightening his load. He also declares that they would consider themselves a servant of humanity, serving all humankind as part of their larger self. Enveloped in the shawl, which was warm from the heat of his body, I felt the sanctity of this ceremony that has kept alive the sacred contract between master and disciple. The full understanding of these words was impressed upon me much later as I sincerely began to teach. At that time though, I was too overwhelmed by so many initiations at once, to realise completely the responsibility I was being entrusted with.

As he completed this invocation, I felt swayed by powerful waves of energy that coursed through me. The feeling was as if he was preparing me to carry the weight of the whole world on my shoulders. Then a saturating sensation seeped in, making me feel protected, wrapped in a cocoon and safe from all life's turmoil. I remember I could not get up after the ceremony, feeling unable to make the effort to make my legs move. It was as if the load of all that I had absorbed was too heavy, but I did stand up after a while, as renewed strength surged into my legs. I understood that Gurunath had judged, with precision, the extent to which he could empower me into responsibilities without straining me beyond capability. Like a good physical trainer at the gym, he monitors the weight to make each disciple gradually stronger. The weight or responsibilities are then steadily increased to toughen the disciple more. This realisation became clearer to me, as I took on the errands of the organisation. Multi-tasking various activities, like organising satsangs, distributing invitations, posting flyers, community meals, Himalayan trips and initiation ceremonies, singlehandedly at first. I realised that though the task seemed too tough to be attempted, I would manage to deliver. Remember this was the year 2000; we were still far away from social media and electronic advertising. There were no tools available then, Gurunaths book Wings to Freedom was still in the process of being written, the film was yet to be made, no YouTube. So every effort was literally hands on.

Sometimes, I wonder how preordained everything was – my missing the main seminar, the other people leaving, my late arrival and, by default, being empowered and initiated. Was it really by default or was it always meant to be? I felt like a pawn in a chess move, being placed there for this specific purpose. How ready was I to teach? What could I teach? Did Gurunath see something I was unaware of? I was totally clueless, but at the same time very proud to be the chosen one, as the donkey must have felt when he was chosen to carry Mary and the unborn Christ to Bethlehem!

※

First visit to the ashram

A few months later, I had the opportunity to go to Mumbai and decided to visit Gurunaths forest ashram at Sinhagad, that was a few hours drive away from the city of Pune. I had only a city address for Gurunath in Kasba Peth. I didn't know where the ashram was except that it was in a forest near Pune. The idea was to reach Gurunaths house and go with him from there; I had already called and told them I would be coming. I arrived at the house after much bouncing around in an auto rickshaw through narrow lanes and found myself standing in the middle of the afternoon, outside a huge wooden door that we called *hathi darwaza* meaning a door made for elephants to pass. The door was solid wood with metal studs, written above it was Narsingh Bhavan, I couldn't see any bell to ring so I caught hold of the knob and knocked and waited patiently not knowing if anyone had even heard me. I knew Gurunath belonged to a royal family and the facade of his house amply proved it. The external walls of the fort like structure were made of heavy stone, though crumbling in parts it was imposing in its majesty.

Then I saw someone appearing on the parapet on top. He was an elderly gentleman and I knew instinctively that he was Gurunaths father; he looked crossly at me asking me what I want. I wished him good afternoon and told him I was a disciple of Gurunath and had come to see him. He replied gruffly that no one was home and he didn't know when they would be back. At that I blurted out how I was connected to Sherwood College Nainital, Gurunath having told us in Delhi how his father was in the old school building that had burnt down. At the mention of his school something happened, he asked me to wait, invited me in, and then sent his driver to take me to the ashram. I was very touched and enchanted to see how deep ones love and connection is to the alma mater, not knowing what made me mention the fact to him.

It was a magical moment when I walked in through the simple ashram gate. I went up the path and in front of me, looking back to see who was coming, stood Gurunath, exactly as in my vision during the seminar in Chandigarh. I recognised the path and the scene. I detected the bamboo hut to one side and the temple columns on the other as in my vision. It felt like a homecoming. The forest ashram was landscaped in such a manner that, even after entering the gate, no building was visible. The living quarters merged into the mango grove while a small Shiva temple at the top of the hill stood guard over the terrain. Gurunath and his wife Shivangini have built the ashram lovingly, over many years, while facing great difficulties. They had lived with their two sons in this panther-infested forest and Gurunath has performed intense spiritual practice here. Disciples address Shivangini as "Ayi," meaning "Mother." Ayi however was not at the ashram that day as she had gone to Mumbai with some of the disciples who had left and was expected back in two days.

There were only three other people at the ashram, since the camp had already ended. Mainly attended by foreign disciples, most of who had left by now. My reason for coming was a desire to learn the practices of Hamsa Yoga in detail, since I was now quite serious about my role as teacher. From day one, I started quizzing Gurunath about the various techniques, but, maddeningly, he would not allow himself to be pinned down. I stayed at the ashram for a few days. The few of us who were there enjoyed long walks with him in the adjoining hills, listened to music, and talked on myriad topics from politics and mythology to Bollywood films and songs. We shared jokes and gazed at stars, but Gurunath revealed not a word about what a teacher was to teach.

I gave up hope, thinking that maybe Gurunath was now doubtful about my capability as a teacher. However, on the last evening before I was to leave the next day, Gurunath asked us to gather in the temple room. This room is a simple structure with beautifully carved pillars, cool marble floors with ancient glass lamps hanging from the ceiling. A white and pink bougainvillea plant showered us with its blossoms as we entered its portal. Gurunath's seat was on a dais in the centre, with the copper kamandal, the chimta, and the wooden staff that supports the yogi when deep in meditation, laid out alongside.

On the exquisitely carved marble altar was the picture of the Siddha Yogi Guru Gorakshanath, a lamplight flickering before him. By his side, an image of Krishna and Christ smiled gently at us. There was also a small marble figure of a saint, whom I later came to know as Dattatreya. In a corner, almost as if he did not want to be disturbed, was a photograph of a mystic yogi deep in meditation, his body and locks dusted with snow. Above the altar a large picture of a yogi with flowing beard and his consort dominated, identified as Adinath and Parvati by a disciple.

Three of us laid out our mats and sat in a circle around Gurunaths asan. I was told that Gurunath had an underground meditation room below the dais where we were sitting. I was the lone new student, while the other two had been with Gurunath for a few years. Gurunath came in and took his seat, dressed in pale saffron-coloured robes, a black cloth belt tied on his waist; the rudraksh string around his neck glowed like embers.

He smiled at me with twinkling eyes and said, "Ok, now, let's get down to it."

Then in a span of forty minutes, he taught me the practices that I needed to know as a teacher. I do not know how I managed to learn what he taught me for I took no notes; the closest I can come to explain this is, it was like telepathic data transference. Gurunath spoke, and I absorbed the words. Without even trying, my attention was total and concentration complete. I know now that during the days preceding that I thought were wasted, he had been working on my subtler, inner self, preparing me to receive this initiation perfectly.

I had not known that Gurunath was also a solar master and taught powerful solar meditations along with Kriya Yoga. The lesson, therefore, included a series of exercises and mantras to invoke the sun and absorb pranic solar energy to heal and rejuvenate the body and mind. The next day, I took leave of Gurunath and Ayi, who was now back, in the traditional manner by prostrating before them. A feeling of tenderness, warmth and melancholy enveloped me as I journeyed back to Chandigarh, as if I had been separated from much loved and caring parents.

I returned to Chandigarh with a sense of lightness, having shed all my excess baggage. All the techniques that I had picked up over the years seemed to pale in front of this yogic sadhana, given by a master. Though simple, these intense practices made everything else I was practicing seem very tame. I felt all impurities in my body, mind and emotions torched, leaving me with a sense of being naked, pure and free.

Later to duplicate this cleansing feeling, whenever I felt disturbing thoughts and emotions churning inside, I started to employ the following tactic intuitively. I would imagine sitting on a burning pyre and the fire cleansing my body and spirit until I felt totally rejuvenated and reborn. I discovered afterwards that this is actually an ancient technique, part of *samshan* sadhana, practiced by yogis, to rid the practitioner of the fear of death. As time went by, I realised that apart from the obvious lessons, many unspoken techniques had also been communicated and stored in my memory during the initiation at the ashram temple by Gurunath. These started manifesting as my practice and my connection to the guru became stronger and aided me in my role as Hamsacharya, teaching Hamsa Yoga and Babaji Kriya Yoga.

※

Introducing Hamsa Yoga in Chandigarh

As soon as I was at home, I began to chronicle all that I had learnt in a systematic manner. This included the practices of *Surya Yoga, Hamsasanas, Gurunath Samadhi Yoga*, a special meditation of transformation, and the Mahavatar Babaji Kriya Yoga. As we had received no written matter, having to depend on our memory to remember the techniques when initiated, as teacher I felt this was necessary for students to have. The result was four booklets, including an introduction to Gurunath and the organisation Hamsa Yoga Sangh. It must have been through grace that the booklets were produced, for I had no inkling about where it all came from. Where I sat typing, on the wall behind me, were pictures of Gurunath, Mahavatar

Shiv Gorakshanath Babaji and lord Shiva, and while my fingers were on the keyboard the typing seemed to happen automatically. I could palpably feel the energy flowing from them into me. Subsequently all other pictures fell away from my altar leaving only that of Gurunath.

Those were the days of snail mail and I sent the booklets by post to Gurunath in Pune and waited patiently to hear when he received it. I was rewarded with Gurunaths elation when he opened the package and saw the booklets. Ayi told me on the phone how excited he was to get something tangible in his hands. Of course, many amendments and additions have been made in due course, but this was a beginning, and I was pleased to be a part of it.

Ayi suggested an auspicious date from the calendar, the Buddha Purnima, to start my classes and I made the announcements in Chandigarh, accordingly. It was the year 1999 and I was excited to have five students in my first class. I did not have my own place in the city, so the principal of the college I had graduated from arranged for my classes to be held in a school on weekends. The outcome of the class was often unpredictable. There would be days when I would sit alone waiting for someone to come. My emotions seesawed between dejection and elation, depending on whether anyone attended the class or not. Some would be unable to come in the morning, and others in the evening; some had problems during the weekend and yet others in the course of the week! In trying to please everybody, I started taking lessons three to four times a week at different venues and at different times. Many had a problem with the fee structure, and thought it too steep. I tried to break up the practice into smaller capsules thinking it would become more affordable. I was going crazy trying to please everyone. All this changed as I matured and went deeper into my own practice. I understood that for yogic sadhana a person has to have an inner hunger, a yearning, and the discipline for sustained regular practice. Many times, when my students complain of lack of time or finances, I feel it is more often on account of a lack of inclination. The bottom line is that seekers always find the time and money for what they really want – whether it is travel, wining and dining, shopping, beauty treatments, the gym, or other necessities. However, I think, when it comes to long term spiritual gains, most people find an excuse to put it off for another day since the results are not immediately tangible. Expecting quick returns, practitioners often do not realise that instant gratification is not a prerequisite on the path of spiritual pursuit.

Gurunath, in a lighter vein, calls the sadhana, "the manicure and pedicure of the soul." It is not enough to remove dead skin, dirt and ugliness from the body; the same polish has to be given to the soul. "Make a long-term investment in the soul," he often says, "this body of flesh and bones you leave behind at the time of death. It is the soul that lives forever."

In due course of time, I noticed that the group that came together seemed to be connected by an inner cord of familiarity. Intuitively, I felt many to have been practicing Kriya Yoga since earlier lives. It was as if we were coming together again under this living master, guided by diverse factors. Some would be attracted by Gurunaths photograph in the newspaper or promotional literature and come for the satsang, and then decide to be initiated; I was drawn to him by the vision. It turns out that many of those I have taught have later found pictures of Babaji, or Lahiri Mahasaya or Yukteshwar Giri, Pramahamsa Yogananda (all Kriya masters), tucked away, often unknowingly, in some corner of their homes. Some would find an old copy of the book Autobiography of a Yogi on their bookshelf. Many are attracted due to their fascination for the Nath Sampradaya and Gurunaths connection with

Gorakshanath. The feeling was as if some force was pushing us all together to make a network. This feeling kept increasing, strengthened further with experiences with my own students, and as I met more of Gurunaths disciples from around the globe and heard how they had been drawn to him. There seemed to be a system at work in the way the disciples were being guided that could not be explained away by mere coincidence.

※

The Panchvati garden

At about this time, Jujhar and I had the good fortune to lease an additional plot of land in Chandigarh that we developed as a garden to be used for weddings and social functions. Situated at the entry point of the city, it was a beautiful location, far from the city centre yet close enough for people to access it easily. The forest area flanking the rear gave it privacy, protecting it from any encroachment of the city, and a mango grove in front shielded it from the busy highway.

Jujhar brought alive this whole garden, which we named Panchvati. A book of names that I was scrutinising on the site for this very purpose, fell open on a particular page, and the name Panchvati leapt out of it to catch my attention. Taking it as an omen for good luck, we decided to call the garden Panchvati.

Special plants and ground cover were sourced from different places to be planted here. Jujhar, a champion of local varieties of plants and trees as against imported ones, made sure the garden was home to many Indian species of trees and plants. A cobblestone fountain and a lotus pond completed the garden. The lotus pond was filled with waters brought from many holy sources – the Ganga, the sarovar at Amritsar, from Gorakh Tibba at Jwalaji, the Beas, Hemkund and Indus to name a few.

My students too habitually transported sacred water for this pond. The lotuses, in hues of yellow, purple, pink and white, seemed to thrive in this and so did the ornamental fish. Then, one day I was surprised to see tractors ferrying huge boulders in their trolleys. Jujhar had arranged for these massive rocks to be carted from a nearby riverbed. He had them placed around the garden in patterns that seemed to aid us in meditation with their strong vibration.

The garden developed into this beautiful haven for birds and animals. Often, while meditating in the morning, I would see Nilgais, a species of a large antelope, grazing in the lawn. When the caretaker chased them, they would effortlessly jump the fence. Peacocks abounded in the forest area and a variety of birds chirped in the early morning hours. Fragrances from aroma bearing flowers wafted through the plot to regale the senses and the colours of the different varieties of flowers were a treat to the eyes. Fleets of egrets would carpet the lawn as they fed on the earthworm of which there were plenty, as no chemical pesticides were used in the garden. Once while meditating in the summer, sitting on the lawn, I felt my mat move with what I thought was the breeze. When I tried to tuck in the mat, I was startled to see this huge field rat cosy up to me. I screamed and jumped up, disturbing the other students. From the next day, I sat on one of the boulders, but the rat, a student pointed out, came to sit by the boulder every day. The grey rat would come after I sat to meditate, sitting still all the while as though absorbing the energy, and leave when I finished!

Every day at the garden was special, but I remember one day in particular. The early morning dew was still damp on the grass when I opened my eyes after a Kriya meditation. The sun had yet to come up over the faraway trees. With my eyes half open, I detected some movement over by the small hillock. It was a peacock accompanied by two peahens. I was surprised, as

I had never seen such beautiful peahens before; normally dowdy, these two were graceful, moving delicately as they foraged in the overgrowth at the edge of the garden. To my further surprise, the peacock suddenly decided to open his plumage and break into dance even though there was not a cloud in sight. It brought to my mind Karthikeya and his two wives. I sat and watched in fascination as the peacock continued his strutting dance for close to forty minutes, while the hens paid scant attention to him. It almost felt as if he was giving me the privilege of a personal audience. Even whilst writing about this incident the scene flashes upon my inner eye and gives me joy.

Gurunath comes to Chandigarh

Having this space where a large number of people could gather and with accommodation for some to stay allowed me to invite Gurunath to visit Chandigarh for the first time in the spring of the year 2000. However, during his first visit, the garden was not yet completely ready with the cottage still under renovation, the trees and plants still developing, and no enclosed boundary to give privacy. Yet, just sitting under the existing mango trees with the backdrop of cooing peacocks, there was an aura of serenity and an other worldly texture to the place.

Gurunaths programme got a mixed response. Hundreds attended his 'experiential' discourses and many of them found the experience overwhelming. His satsangs are called 'experiential' because here the audience is not subjected to long sermons but is introduced to the direct experience of Shaktipat – the Kundalini energy transmissions, Pranpat – the karma-cleansing breath and Shivapat – the state of thoughtfree clear mind awareness. Since this kind of discourse was a first in the city, many had trouble in relating to the experience while others were amazed and incredulous about it. To be able to assimilate the visions superimposing on Gurunaths face, to be aware of his breath moving in their body and, in some cases, instant relief from physical pain and discomfort seemed to be beyond the comprehension of many a rational mind. People flocked to the gathering and by the last day, the hall was packed to capacity as word spread about the mystical quality of the satsang. Of course, many who did not experience anything were left unimpressed, and went away with a sense of being let down.

The extent of the visions depends on factors such as the receptivity of the viewer, on whether the viewer is on any form of medication, antibiotics, tranquilisers and mood elevators, or steroids, which may dull the perception. A judgemental personality too would act as deterrent to any psychic revelation that is available. But from my personal experience even those who feel, see or sense nothing get the benefit of all three transmissions often seeping in later when they relax.

During the interactive satsang, Gurunath always asks for feedback from the audience about their experiences. During one such satsang, one woman kept saying she could not feel anything. Gurunath looked gently at her and said, "But the palace doors were shut and I have no authority to force them open." I smiled at Gurunaths insight for, as it happened, the woman actually belonged to an erstwhile royal family, and Gurunath had no means of knowing this.

In fact, the individual has to be willing and prepared for the experience to occur. Sometimes, even if our conscious mind feels ready, there may be subconscious obstructions such as a fear of the unknown or emotional and mental disturbances that prevent an experience. The master will not overstep boundaries of propriety to force the inflow of this higher spiritual energy into the reluctant human brain, as that would mean injuring the delicate organism of the cerebrospinal system. However, frequent attendance slowly does break down these inhibitions until one day the person is suddenly aware of the experience. Why are some people attracted to this fast track evolutionary path more than others? How come some experience all the nuances of the transmissions and yet others are left cold? Some are happy sitting by the side while others are compelled to dive deep in. Is this path so hard that only the toughest walk on it? Is it toughness or escapism as some call it? Even among the hundreds who experience something significant, only a handful take the first step to learn the practice. Is it because each person has to progress along the path at an individual pace, until the necessary karmic conditions are completed, enabling a paradigm shift on their path?

These were the thoughts that kept entering my mind in those early days. Until I understood how, while walking this path, the traveller is forced to realise that most of the things learnt about right and wrong, good and evil, are relative. Suddenly, there is no opinion about anything and every illusion is wiped clean as the seeker faces reality. All social conditioning and artificiality, personality traits, pretensions and acquired mannerisms eventually have to peel away. Maybe the mind, used to making us dance to its tunes, instinctively understands that it will gradually lose control over its idiosyncrasies once the first step is taken on this trail, and so resists the desire to join. Most sincere practitioners go through this stage of drowning in confusion. At this time, the satguru is the only anchor in the stormy seas of this unknown territory. Connecting to the master and practicing the sadhana given is the only way to tide over this treacherous period; otherwise, the traveller could and does fall by the wayside.

Gurunath visited Chandigarh yearly for the next ten years until 2009. It was a great honour to have been part of this initial organisation of his public events and making a success of it. Our community had grown over the years with strong practitioners and there were many volunteers who helped with their time and offerings for the practical management of the visit. In 2009 Gurunath expressed the desire to now pay more attention to the bigger cities and turned his attention to other major cities in India. His foreign travels had also increased to include more countries.

Many of my earlier students remembered how I used to urge them to spend more time with the master when he was in town as I could see a future when access would become comparatively reduced as number of disciples grew. But there's always something that comes up, your creature comforts, your will to take the necessary steps or just plain lethargy and then you realize the master has moved on. After ten years he once again expressed his desire to visit the city and we organised an event for him this year in 2019 and the city took off with more power from where it had left off in 2009. We had a packed hall and record number of students for empowerment. Disciples came from Taiwan, South Africa, The Philippines, Russia and Australia and many cities and towns of India.

※

Introduction to Babaji

The most captivating moments with Gurunath were those spent sitting by a campfire late at night, listening to stories of Babaji. Gurunath addressed him by various names – Mahavatar Shiv Gorakshanath, the Nameless One, the Lightning Standing Still, and Mahabinishkaran, the great sacrifice. "His name is 'Toba'," he would say, touching his ears in the popular Islamic style, moving effortlessly back to his life as a Sufi saint. Gurunath also called him *Aja Purush*, the one who is never born and never dies. The setting was enchanting and magical as we sat in the garden of Panchvati, singing praises of Babaji and listening to tales about his mystical phenomenon. We were like young yogis by the campfire and, as Gurunath pointed out, we could be anywhere in time as well as space. For, since time immemorial yogis have sat thus by campfires throughout the length and breadth of our country, exchanging fables of the immortal Babaji and other Himalayan masters.

My knowledge of this being called Babaji was minimal and when questioned by students in those early days about him, I was often confused. All the stories were known but the essence eluded me. As a result, I was filled with a longing to know more about this enigmatic figure about whom Gurunath said, "Naught may be said." Who is Babaji? Whom did Gurunath meet? Was he the same as Yoganandas Babaji in Autobiography of a Yogi? On the other hand, was he Nagaraj, the south Indian incarnation of Babaji as some claim? Who was the Gorakshanath who was Matsyendranaths disciple, who was resurrected from the dung heap? Who chanted "Jago Macchinder, Gorakh ayaa?" – a clarion call by the disciple Gorakh to his guru Macchinder as Matsyendranath was addressed in the local dialect, which meant, "Wake up Macchinder, Gorakh has come." My ignorance irritated me and I decided to ask Gurunath at the next opportunity. I had an intuitive feeling that the Gorakshanath that Gurunath spoke of was all this and more. Therefore, I mustered the courage to reveal my ignorance and to question Gurunath about the Babaji he had met. "There are so many Babajis. Whom did you meet?" I enquired. "Everyone seems to have met him. Is Babaji so easily accessible to everyone?" Gurunath then disclosed that the Babaji he had met was the infinite Gorakshanath, called the 'Consciousness of the Universe', born eighteen million years ago! Babaji had burst forth from the heart of lord Shiva, at the beginning of our world cycle, the date shrouded in mystery.

"In fact, he is Adinath Shiva himself," Gurunath clarified. In 1967 at age 23, Gurunath had darshan or experience of Babaji in the Jhilmili gufa in Badrinath, in the Himalayas, where Babaji first blessed him by revealing his formless light body, which then crystallised into his deathless body of flesh.

Gurunath also divulged that Mahavatar Shiv Gorakshanath is the Babaji in the book Autobiography of a Yogi by Paramahamsa Yogananda and guru to Lahiri Mahasaya. In his book Babaji, the Lightning Standing Still written later, Gurunath has proved this connection with ample proof. He is the first one to make this connection, though now I hear many others referring to the Mahavatar as Gorakhshanath. He further explained that many others are partial reincarnations of this Mahavatar, such as Baba Balaknath and Yogi Sri Chand, both of whom carried the ray of Babaji within them.

Born eighteen million years ago! My rational mind shut down at this and, devoid of speech, I could only bow my head with reverence. I felt that with my limited intelligence I could never understand the magnitude of Gurunaths experience.

❀

Connecting to the source

After Gurunath left, my classes gathered momentum. It was as if the place was blessed for the quality of meditation refined and improved here. Surprisingly, queries asked received spontaneous answers from me. Even I did not know where the response was coming from. All that I was aware of was being connected to a source from where the reply to all questions flowed. Some student would ask about the benefits of the practice, its effect on the body or emotion, ask a deeper question about life or death, or voice other doubts about yoga. Each time, the response would come effortlessly. It was like magic. Gurunath had given me no formal training in the theory of yoga, but he had established a bond that made acquiring knowledge easier than reading volumes of books and trying to remember them. It was then that I realised the potency of an initiation and how the disciple is drawn closer to the source by simply being in the presence of a master.

I gradually became so attuned to Gurunath that I would know when he wanted me to call him, and the moment the phone rang, he would pick it up and say my name without my uttering a word. Gurunath once initiated me into the method of Vivar, a whirling meditation technique he had recently formalised, over the phone. I was mentioning to him the Sufi tradition of whirling when he revealed where this practice had emanated from the time of Krishna and before and is kept alive such as in the dance of garba in Gujarat, in kolattam in the south and many other local forms. The meditation of the vivar as described by Gurunath facilitated the practitioner to spin and synchronise with the motion of the universal rhythms, pushing the disciple into an ever upwardly evolving vortex of energy. He pointed out that as the connection between us crystallised there would be no need of even the physical instrument of the phone and I would be able receive messages directly. I have ample experience of this now, as do many others of his disciples. The physical presence of the guru is not essential for a strong sadhak who could be capable of receiving messages and solutions to enquiry, by another medium, which, like an umbilical cord, connects the disciple to the satguru. Though often childishly we crave to hear their voice or feel the touch of the blessing on our head.

As the teacher connects intuitively to the guidance of a guru, the students who come to such a teacher's class are advised to listen carefully to instructions during class and follow them diligently, since the teacher is then working from a higher realm of understanding. Once, while teaching, I saw a shadow and a black spot in the aura of a student. There appeared to be some problem in the area of the uterus and I advised her to take adequate precautions. She had relationship problems with her grown children and, in her younger days, sexual ones with her spouse, and hence, the problem in this particular area. I was intuitively guided to give her some specific practices to combat this. I heard no more from her but, after three years, I came to know that a cyst had developed in her uterus, possibly requiring surgery. She admitted that she had not been practicing any of the given exercises, but was now ready to start again. I felt saddened. If only she had paid attention to my suggestion at that time, there had been a chance for healing to have taken place, since the directions had come from a higher source. With practice, I have also learnt to be more attentive to the instructions of the master that come telepathically. One of Gurunaths common maxim is, "The only sin of the mind is not to have paid enough attention." With sustained practice this detail to attention while in the presence of the master becomes more natural. Of course, the students must exercise discretion in what instructions to adhere, and not open themselves to any uncomfortable suggestions that goes against their deeply held truths, even if urged by others to. These are very difficult nuances for the beginner to grasp and only steadfastness to the teaching of the master brings the required clarity to understand them.

Being open to this source, the essence of the guru has enabled me to assist many students by a timely warning and prescribing practices to cure the impending ailment before it manifests in the physical body. Whatever the problem, even without analysis, just the practice itself helps to release pain and transform the disease. The problem is often related to the present way of being. By generating inner change through the practice of yoga, the outer symptoms can correspondingly be altered for the better. This is true for everyone though why some people connect more easily even though they may not practice regularly while others who are constantly sitting miss the mark, I don't know. I have seen healing happen to relatively new entrants while the older sadhaks struggle with issues. I guess karma has a play in this. All I know is continuing despite difficulties is key to a deeper attainment.

Once a journalist whom I knew called me and expressed she wanted to share something personal with me. She came over and said that she had read my book and had been practicing the exercises given in it at the end. The nine simple to follow yogic techniques were specially blessed by Gurunath before inclusion in the book. She revealed that some days ago she had gone for a drive uphill with her fiancée whom she had recently been engaged to. While returning they had got late and it was getting dark, when a few boys started chasing them on motorcycles on the deserted hill road. They managed to block and stop her fiancées vehicle; she was horrified and shocked when her fiancée at this time left her in the car, jumped out and ran away into the failing light. She said at that moment she felt she was surely going to be raped and killed that evening. But suddenly one of the boys looked back and shouted that someone was coming, at this all of them started their bikes and took off. As she regained her composure she saw that she was still alone and no one was around as the boys thought. She said she knew that it was Gurunath who protected her that day. Of course the first act of hers when she returned home was to break off her engagement. But I also wondered that maybe the whole drama of the boys was played out to expose her fiancée and protect her from a worse fate of marriage that there was actually no threat to her. Whatever the reason the outcome of the practice saved her life in many ways that day. But I have to share here that though she kept calling to take her initiation into Kriya Yoga after this incident, she never took it, though I am still in communication with her, the time for Kriya seems to be yet not near.

This incident made me wonder at the power of the practice that protects all who are even remotely connected to the source that flows from my master, even without knowing or having met him. In my time at the ashram I came across many such incidents when people would share how Gurunath appeared in the dreams of people who didn't know him and effected cures. Gurunath himself says he is not consciously aware that he effects such healings and is glad as it shields him from his ego. When he makes such statements about his own ego I feel humbled as I feel so proud sometimes of the really small things I do.

From 2003 to 2007 I along with a group of local farmers were involved with an intense agitation against the administration who were arbitrarily acquiring farmers land at pitiable prices and in the name of development passing it on to big corporates at huge profits for them. Of course corrupt officials were involved and big bucks. At that time my land was not under threat and I was warned by many not to take on this confrontation but it was as if an inner force drove me. At this time the CID and IB would often contact me, sometimes to intimidate and at other times to just get information. I was quite friendly to them all knowing that I was not doing anything wrong or disruptive, it was a fight for justice not for me but for others. I was very regular with the practice of the solar exercises that Gurunath had formulated and taught us. Spending time to absorb the energy of the sun for protection and healing. On one such day as I stood on my terrace facing the sun to form the solar protection with the powerful *Gorakhsha Kavach* mantra, I felt the sun expand and become more radiant and saw what looked like astral *shastra* -weapons descend and enter my aura to be absorbed by it. In that moment it was like a scene out of an epic, I instantly understood how power is conferred upon humans by the gods. There was a very matter of fact feel in the whole exchange and though no weapons were used in the agitation the pen being mightier than the sword showed its power as I got support from newspapers, my writing to various agencies and departments brought result and acquisition was blocked in our city by a procedure and till date no new acquisitions are taking place.

In 2004 when Gurunath visited us he came to our farm and casually asked us to do some puja around the boundary of the land. He asked Jujhar to do some of the sacred rituals that were quite simple though esoteric. A few months after that we learnt that the government was planning to acquire some portion of our land for expansion of the road in front which would have resulted in us losing our home and the temple centre for Gurunath on the terrace. This was followed some months later with notices to all of us. The government goofed up on the sections of the notice and we went to court to challenge this. Many other anomalies came to light and though our neighbours relinquished their land our case is still pending and in all probabilities it will be in our favour. Through this all I was quite calm about my personal difficulties, even leading the agitation was neither disturbing nor ambitious. I was working with a matter of fact attitude of an act that had to be done. The point I'm trying to make is that I was realizing what it means to act without reacting, a very important lesson for a practicing yogi.

※

Lessons learnt as yoga teacher

Teaching became a learning experience. While teaching, I had to understand the needs of every student, often intuitively; I had to answer questions from different levels of understanding – from complete novices to yoga experts, I had to be able to guide all of them to recover from physical and emotional trauma through the practice, and all this involved a great learning on my part.

On the part of the students, the reasons for coming to learn yoga were many. Health reasons were topmost, closely followed by mental stress and depression. Many who were already practicing Hatha Yoga were attracted to the practice of Kriya Yoga and intrigued by the transformative and healing qualities of the Surya Yoga and Hamsa Yoga. Of late, yoga has become a fashion statement and hence the attraction for many. Whatever the motive, every student who came was different and had a separate set of vibrations. Gradually, with guidance from Gurunath, I became adept at picking up on resonance frequencies emitted by the pupils who came to learn yoga. The frequencies would communicate to me the inner motivations of the student, often different from the apparent reason for finding a teacher. As understanding deepened about the connection of the physical to the emotional and mental state of the pupil, it helped me become more sensitive in my teaching.

"There are two ways to do genuine charity; one is to show people the path to God and the other to realise one's own divinity," Gurunath instructed. "The greatest good one can do is to show people the way to their own divine nature. Secondly, when a seeker attains samadhi through rigorous practice, an impetus is given to the evolution of this earth, this galaxy, and the stone evolves to lichen, the lichen to fish and so on up the evolutionary chain to ape, to man, then finally propelling man to God. This happens whenever anyone anywhere attains Buddhahood or the final nirvana." Here I have to chronicle an experience I had, though seemingly simple it left a great impact on me. It happened while I was driving to pick up the girls from school. It was afternoon and there was barely any traffic on the road. As I drove all of a sudden I felt as if the road had elongated and my car went into slow motion and suddenly in that moment I felt Buddha go into his enlightenment state and within less than a fraction of a second, almost at the same instant, I was in the car driving. It was as if there was no distance in time between these two events, the gap of 2500 years covered in an instant. The experience filled me with an exquisite exhilaration difficult to explain.

Although I would have loved to just indulge in intense private practice, I was instructed by Gurunath to teach, and personally began to enjoy this task. Sharing with others all that I had gained in my association with the guru gave me intense pleasure. While teaching, I felt myself connected to Gurunath and every session would entail some new learning for me too. There was no effort involved; it was a sense of filling up and overflowing. It did not require extensive hours of reading books or scriptures; the fount of knowledge was elsewhere. If any question arose to which I had no answer at that moment, the answer would follow after a period of time. Sometimes, the answer would arise out of an unrelated situation or incident, even to the point of a sentence jumping out while browsing through a book or an article, leading to a clear understanding. "Eureka!" I would cry joyfully at such times!

"Yoga is the evolution of human consciousness, the most comprehensive enterprise ever undertaken by humanity, besides which the greatest of human achievements pale into insignificance," said Gurunath, speaking at one of his many spontaneous satsangs under the mango trees at Panchvati. "It is an inner ascent through evermore refined and evermore expanded spheres of consciousness." As in any other refining process, depending on the individual practitioner, impurities are bound to release. These, I realized, surfaced as allergy, excess mucous, sweat, headache, constant yawning, and sneezing fits or sleep disorders. Equally, since yoga heals holistically, other emotional and mental symptoms would also rise such as anger, grief, frustration, doubts or fears. Many practitioners give up the training at this stage, not realising that it is the body ridding itself of toxins. Of course, all these symptoms need to be examined and proper care taken to cure them wholly.

Once, after being taught an advanced practice by Gurunath, I was warned that there might be reactions as the detoxification of the body intensified. Though instructed to take care while practicing, in my inimitable manner, I got fully into the practice, eagerly putting in two or three stints a day. One day I noticed a lump behind my ear that pained slightly when I pressed it. Without paying attention, I continued with my practice until the pain became unbearable and the lump larger. It was an inflammation of the lymph nodes choking as they tried to deal with the poison coming out of my body. Complete cure took a year-and-a-half and the symptoms included foul-smelling nasal emissions, which seemed to have accumulated inside since many years. With Gurunaths guidance, I learnt to lessen the intensity of my practice and gradually strengthen it again. Though doctors advised minor surgery, I preferred consulting an *ayurvedic* physician who prescribed some mild herbal medicines. After this, there was a great sense of physical purity as if cleaned from inside with a disinfectant! This incident also taught me to pay extra attention while instructing my students and making sure they intensified their practice gradually with the minimum discomfort.

※

Interpreting the importance of chakras

As I took my classes, various combinations of the main practice would be communicated to me, dictated by the need of the student. It was as if every practice taught by Gurunath could blossom into manifold permutations, each equally effective and powerfully personalised; such was the potency of the exercises. I attributed all this knowledge, without doubt, to the blessings of Gurunath and my connection to him. There was one particular exercise of cleansing the chakras that I taught to my regular students that was remarkably effective. Later, I described the technique to Gurunath and was pleasantly surprised to know that he taught this technique twenty years ago. He had discarded it when a foreign disciple, who had learnt it from him, started his own school of yoga based on this technique without giving any credit to the guru.

This often happens to the Himalayan masters who share everything they have learnt after years of rigorous meditation with seekers, who then go on to publish books or start their own yoga institutes. They pay no spiritual royalty to their masters and sometimes do not even mention the source from where they have received this insight, blatantly asserting their non-existent copyright or trademark. This is where the eastern belief that knowledge is meant to be free like the air and water clashes head-on with the popular western concept of trademark and copyright.

However, the masters pay scant attention to this, and since the fount of knowledge is within them, they can and do abandon the techniques that have been pilfered, and formulate other equally powerful techniques. The stolen techniques generally lose power without the backing of a master whose personal spiritual practice and connection to the source is what makes the technique flower to its true potency for the practitioner.

Through practice, my knowledge of the chakra system in the body kept increasing steadily without any acquired information from books. As all adept practitioners of yoga are aware, chakras refer to psychic vortexes of energy aligned along the spine. By and by, I could pinpoint the exact location of these centres in my body and dispassionately study their presence and activity. Through this understanding, I could better comprehend my own development through the years. Now I am able to help my students to holistic health through this awareness. Together, my students and I determine problem areas and work to clear malfunctioning in that particular chakra with the combination of yoga precepts that I have learnt from Gurunath and now teach. Gurunath, a solar master, meditates for long hours with the sun blazing overhead. His powerful yoga techniques to harness the energy of the sun are now used liberally by me for the healthy functioning of the chakras, and healing of physical and emotional ailments.

The chakras themselves reveal inner truths first about ourselves then about the universe we live in. The yogic belief that the body holds the blueprint of the universe is termed the *pind-brahmand* philosophy. The chakras were, for me, the gateway to this realization. At first as dedicated practice increased and purification of the chakras took hold, I could hear emanating from them musical notes of the sitar, sometimes the beat of the *tabla*, once the distinct sound of an axe on the muladhar. The chakras lost their rainbow colours; they expanded out of the body and took the form of galaxies and then in every chakra were the golden rim and the scintillating star. An experience of the macrocosm in the microcosmic body, a samadhi is possible in every chakra, I realized.

For me though, the small *mokshas* is a form of instant nirvana, as the chakras purify old stubborn habits, desires and patterns of behaviour dissolve leaving one with a freedom unimaginable, the final moksha can come when it does but I enjoy these small liberations for now. The journey through the chakras is individual and no two experience maybe the same, so learn the lesson from your own realisation, the satguru is always there for you to tune into for guidance and the teacher for support.

Throughout all this practice and realisation, Gurunath constantly guided me inspiring my understanding. "Your body is a medicine chest," Gurunath said. "It produces insulin and cortisone, adrenaline and all other chemicals required by the body. The yogi, through practice and by controlling the life force that is *prana*, learns to release these as and when required, and often the body of the practicing yogi makes the necessary adjustments by itself." The body has an innate intelligence to heal itself by paying attention to it and allowing it to function we can lead a life without modern medication. In 2019 it's been over twenty-four years since I have taken any chemical allopathic medication, not even an aspirin. Not that I don't exhibit symptoms of common ailments, but choose to heal myself with just giving the body time or only herbs. But of course this is something each individual has to decide after understanding their bodies intelligence and capacity to heal and so it's not an advice to anybody to stop taking their prescribed medications.

The yogis of old invested in the body only as a vehicle to realise divinity. In the realisation of divinity, all physical maladies are cured routinely. "Healing the apparent self... that is the body, of the ignorance of the true Self... which is the soul, is the ultimate essence of all healing," instructed Gurunath. "We are not practicing these techniques to get relief from constipation or joint pains but each of us is slowly transforming ourselves into Shiva, to Christ Consciousness, into Buddhahood. So don't cheapen the practice by confining it to the body, it is like using a paintbrush to sweep the floor," he cautioned. "The physical healing is a by-product of the yogic sadhana that transforms your body of flesh into a body of light." Characteristically, Gurunaths words were very inspiring and spurred me on to persevere in my personal practice and in teaching others.

As the number of students increased, it would bother me that many were not serious about their practice. Having become very regular with my own practice, and seeing the benefits thereof, I would expect the same from pupils who probably had many other interests and priorities that may restrict regular practice. It was a hard lesson to learn to let go of those who wanted to leave, and concentrate on such who were steadfast. I firmly believe that we have a hundred per cent free will and exercise it to make our choices. The teacher is there to give support when the students need it, but the decision to learn and persevere is theirs.

Whenever a new student joins, I always wish to know how many other courses the pupil has attended, whether regularity has been observed in the daily practice, and the reasons for the change. Sincere seekers, who learn out of genuine interest, give their best to any technique they learn. It is only when they find the path, or the guru, unsuitable to their temperament that they seek other practices. Others are like insatiable bees drinking honey from many sources; they casually go from one practice to another, one master to another, scarcely giving time for the exercise or the grace of the master to have the desired effect. When this leads to spiritual hiccups, they blame the path and the master instead of their own lack of discipline. "It is like planting a seed in a pot," says Gurunath, giving an example, "and then after every few days, digging it out to replant it in a new pot. Is it any wonder that it does not take root?" Similarly, time and effort has to be given to any learnt technique before it can show results.

Now it's a habit with me to meet with the student before they come to learn the practice, a sort of tête-à-tête. It is important for the student to form a rapport with the teacher and their interaction to be based on a foundation of trust in the teacher. Since I conduct teachers' trainings now, it's my fundamental instruction to teachers to form this bond of trust with their students. To students my advice always is if they do not form this connection with a teacher they must look for another, as this is a very sacred relationship based on mutual respect. In my book the students have the liberty to leave the teacher but this is not reciprocated for the teacher who has a responsibility towards every student and has to help them best strengthen the practice and connection with the Master. A living master is a rarity and the teacher who keeps away their students from them is doing a disservice with far reaching karmic consequences, according to me.

❈

Gurudakshina – an offering to the master and the teacher

Often, I meet people who cannot understand why a spiritual teacher should charge a fee at all. In India, there is a strong feeling of resentment when a guru is perceived to be indulging in material pursuits. The rishis and yogis in ancient India were regarded with a great deal of respect and received patronage from the rulers. The king and community looked after all their material needs of food, shelter, ashram and travel requirements. The stature of the sages was measured by the power and duration of their practice, the austerity with which they conducted their lives, and even their ability to influence natural phenomenon. These personages in return, or rather by their very nature, maintained the spiritual and moral integrity of the generation. This exchange was also a manner in which the satguru cleared karmic debts of the disciple and, in a larger context, the kingdom, by receiving munificence from the ruler. Today it is simplified, and the *gurudakshina* is normally a fixed amount as payment for their time, expenses incurred for travel or hiring a place. But still it's good to have balanced remuneration structure where the intention of the teacher is to share the sacred practice and not amass wealth from the teaching.

Here a distinction must be made between a teacher and the master, a teacher we can pay a fee to but a master we can never repay for what they do for us so whatever we give them is only a token of our gratitude.

According to Gurunath, with the new-age philosophy of 'what's in it for me?' the whole fabric of the *guru-shishya parampara* – the relationship between master and disciple, seems to be eroding fast, with most people not exercising the intuition to look beyond the obvious. Often, behaviour of both gurus and disciples are controlled by the apparent benefits they can give each other. It is here that the difference between the satguru and others becomes obvious. Since the true guru is responsible for the spiritual evolution of the *shishya*, every action of the master will be dictated by this fundamental motive. If the master allows greed or any other factor to interfere with this acceptance of gurudakshina, or if the pupil's intention in offering dakshina is corrupted, the fruits of this action will surely be extracted from them. Those giving as well as those receiving both need to work from the realm of a pure motive without agenda.

Many disciples, when invested with rank, erroneously imagine themselves to be of the same stature as the master. Often, in the course of my teaching, I secretly feel important when some intuition has been proved right, or suffer from this inordinate feeling of superiority when praised by those around me. At these times, I have a little exercise that I do to keep my humility intact. I imagine myself offering my head to *Durga* -the *Mahishasuramardini*. I visualise her glorious form, resplendent in all her finery, riding the tiger and wielding all her weapons. I place my head in front of her and watch as she chops my head off with her shining sword and then kicks it away over the horizon. At that moment, the extent of my ego I can measure according to the discomfort and pain at the time of the decapitation. Then, headless, I feel freed of an extremely heavy load until the next time this many-headed monster rises and the exercise is repeated all over again.

The teacher disciples, according to me, must not forget that they are chosen by the satguru for the purpose of spreading the word or practice formulated by the master. They are teachers with a title conferred upon them by the master, who is the only one who can judge their capability and has lent authority to them accordingly. For me personally there is only one hierarchy, there's Gurunath then there's all of us the disciples, old, recent and very old, teachers, senior teachers and very senior teachers alike.

Gurunath, I felt was reluctant to make me a Kriyacharya at a particular period of time when in fact many who had just come and who in my limited opinion were contributing much less, were bestowed this title. I'm sure he had spiritual reasons for the holdback probably to strengthen me. That apart, in my humorous way, I have a personal joke that to be senior in our organisation you should have the capacity to grow facial hair. Being quite competent in getting all my work for Gurunath done with the title I already was bestowed with, I did not really covet this trophy. So the incident of how I was made Kriyacharya was also typical for me. One day during Mahashivaratri of 2009, Ayi had gone out for some errands leaving the dinner preparations to me. We were to make cutlets and the kitchen staff had made the potatoes too mushy. So there I was with my hand in the gooey potatoes trying to salvage it before Ayi came back worried because she had asked me to layout the dinner on time. My reputation in the kitchen was anyways not popular with Gurunath, who thinks I always mess up. Suddenly a disciple, Amandeep who is also one of my first students, came stomping into the kitchen and said impatiently that Gurunath had been calling me asking me to come immediately to the satsang. I was not even given time to wash my hands but dragged with messy potato hands to the gathering on the terrace above Gurunaths house at the ashram.

Some senior teachers had been asked to sit in front of the rest of the group and Gurunath made a sign for me to sit with them and I did with sticky hands hid under my shawl. Then Gurunath started the investiture ceremony, one by one he put his shawl around the teachers and repeated the invocation making some of us *Kriyacharyas*, some others senior *Hamsacharyas*. As soon as the ceremony was over I was impatient to leave and get back to the kitchen before Gururmata Ayi came back, but was waiting for permission as is customary, then Gurunath looked at me with twinkling eyes and a smile and said, "Now you can go," and I scooted off to the kitchen. The potency of the initiation flowered slowly in later months and years as increased spiritual responsibility. This year Gurunath reinforced the investiture for a few of us in Rishikesh as if to strengthen once again our collective shoulders to push the wheel of the Guru's work with more ease.

※

The master-disciple relationship

One day, as I sat in meditation, I became aware of a figure sitting back-to-back with me. Facing the sun, the figure was swallowing the fiery rays that were being emitted by the sun. Startled, I realised the form to be that of Gurunath sitting with his spine seemingly superimposing and supporting mine, though the spines were not touching, I could feel the support like a wall behind me, I was facing the other way with my back to the master, yet could see what was happening. I observed with awe as he ingested the blazing waves of solar emission. Then this same energy, now toned down and gentler, was transferred to enter and flow in my spine. In that instant, I comprehended the service done to the disciple by the master. Taking care that the disciple does not harm the delicate cerebral and nervous system with the direct inflow of the

Kundalini energy, the master transmits the requisite amount, according to the need and dictated by the level of preparation of every sadhak. In this manner, the master is attached to each of the initiated disciples individually. The true master, I then understood, helps the disciple to move towards completion not only through the teaching of certain practices, but also by subtly working and guiding the development of the pupil at an astral plane.

The satguru for the disciple is like the sun and they the planets that circle the sun, each disciple receiving according to their connection. As Gurunath says, "You are god to the extent you know god." Picture the *raas leela* – a Krishna with each *gopi*, engaged in the everlasting dance of celebration. This image, for me, symbolises the master with the disciples. The eternal dance of the satguru and disciple is as sacred and mystical as the spinning of the galaxy. In the macrocosm, it is duplicated in the orbiting of the moon around the earth, the planets around the sun, the whole galaxy in this incessant dance of evolution. In the microcosm within the atom, the same endless movement as the proton and electron revolve and dance, creating and evolving life.

It is the slush of the untutored mind that sees eroticism in this play. The uninitiated can often misunderstand this close relationship between the master and disciple. A woman once came up to me and asked crudely, "Do you sleep with your guru?" Though taken aback, I answered her, "No", I replied with some inner wisdom that kept me unruffled at this shocking question, "but my intimacy is deeper than that. For the guru's breath flows through mine and the guru's essence permeates me." How could I explain a relationship between master and disciple that transcends the physical to a person steeped in the corporeal, I wondered. How could I explain the process of the transmissions that break down all barriers between them?

There is no sense of gender between the master and disciple and those who see it are in my evaluation, at a very base level of spiritual evolution. For me Gurunath is not a 'male' guru, his physical body may be male but the guru's essence that radiates and that I connect to is without gender. Similarly when I teach I don't connect to my students as male or female. Gurunath instructs acharyas during teacher's trainings that when they teach, they are a soul teaching a soul.

In the bond between the master and disciple, teacher and student it's the latter who are more vulnerable in the relationship. The master knows how to take care of this but I have realised that as a teacher it's always helped me to remember this dependency on the part of the students and take extreme care not to take advantage of it.

When I first began the practice of yoga, I paid scant attention to the primary limbs of *yama* and *niyam*, considering them to be a lot of moral bullshit. However, as I move deeper into the practice, they are revealed to me as a guideline for the conduct of both master and disciple. Following them without awareness, I feel, would move the practitioner towards an insufferable 'holier than thou' moral attitude, but when used with intuitive understanding they guide the one on this path to perfect behaviour.

Sometimes the disciple may find the behaviour of the master arbitrary towards the followers. Receiving gifts from some, while seemingly spurning others. I have seen Gurunath accept, refuse, and give away gifts that he receives from pupils apparently randomly. Once, when a pupil spent a paltry sum on Gurunath for some purchase, he asked me to return the sum to the disciple. I, either unintentionally or because it was such a small amount, did not pay heed and was admonished by Gurunath later and told to go and pay the sum immediately. Seeing my woebegone face, he explained that as a yogi moved on the spiritual path every action has to be weighed on a different scale of karmic repercussion. It serves well to remember at such times that the satguru works from a more sensitive plane, seeing more than is apparent to others. Similarly at another time, a foreign disciple had just offered him an expensive pashmina shawl, when another disciple walked in and exclaimed in admiration at the beautiful gift. Gurunath, without a moment's hesitation, offered the shawl to this disciple. "Once you have given away a gift it's the receiver's to do as he pleases, don't be attached to it like this," he said, seeing the dejected face of the disciple who had originally brought it. Gurunath frequently refuses offerings under the tenet of the *niyama- aparigraha*, which means 'non-hoarding' or 'non-collecting'.

The exotic chocolates that he receives find their way into other disciples' stomach. I am quite fond of raiding his stock along with his grandchildren, I like to think quietly like a mouse but of course the master hears!

❈

Finding the right guru

"How do we know this guru is right for us?" asked a student. This is an oft-repeated question. It expresses a fear of being cheated by a guru. It is not surprising as in today's age charlatans abound in this field as in any other, and exploitation of the spiritually gullible is common and new events surface everyday. Students seeking a guru or teacher need only have a clear heart and even words spoken in vain can lead them to the light.

It reminds me of a story I heard as a child from my grandmother. A fisherwoman would go to sell her catch every day in a nearby town. She had to cross the river to get there.

Under a Banyan tree in the town square sat a saint, surrounded by his disciples, giving daily discourses. As she passed him one day, she heard him say that just chanting the lords' name could enable one to walk barefoot across rivers. This impressed her greatly, for she realised that by following his advice she could save the few annas that she paid the ferryman every day to cross the river. Therefore, from the next day she decided to chant God's name and walk across. This went on for a month and, as crossing the river had saved her some money, she decided to invite the saint and his followers for lunch to her house. The saint readily agreed, and on the appointed day she came to take him to her house across the river. When the party reached the riverbank, the fisherwoman got ready to walk across it in the habitual manner of walking across, but the saint waited and asked her to bring the boat!

What must her reaction have been at the time? Did she lose faith despite the fact that, based on overheard advice; she had been performing the miracle of walking on water? This is not to make light of genuine concerns but the example shows that if the disciple is sincere, even words spoken by gurus who only preach and bestow no experience can act as an impetus. In my experience the true master surely arrives when the disciple is ready for discipleship. Until then just as we learn from our other relationships in life we learn from this too.

One of my students was in a dilemma once. By his own admission, as he sat for meditation one day, he wondered what he had got himself into. As a challenge, he mentally asked Gurunath to give him some sign of his powers and prove that he was a genuine guru. The student almost jumped out of his skin when he felt a sharp knock on his head, which was repeated three times to put to rest all his doubts for good. Many disciples get such signs during doubtful phases, but may be too distracted to pay attention. There are many such examples and incidents repeated by disciples from over the world. Gurunath would often say that if the disciple considered him a friend, he will be a friend; if the disciple followed him as satguru, he will be a satguru, and if the disciple considered him a piece of rag, that is what he will be for the disciple. Many disciples consider their master as God and the master becomes that for them. The seeker has to use perception in establishing the calibre of the guru. I see my connection with Gurunath always as that of master and disciple, for life after life and for me I have no concept of God as a separate entity. Merging into the Guru *tattwa* or essence is merging into God for me.

The true guru will always be there to guide sincere disciples when they are disturbed. In the course of writing this book, a time came when I was assailed with doubts. I was anxious and had qualms about my ability to produce anything worthwhile, and since Gurunath was away I felt even more abandoned. Nothing was going right. Worried and full of misgivings about any talent I might have, I was ready to give up. That night I sat to meditate and, as is my habit, connected to Gurunath to receive grace. Immediately, the room filled with a beautiful soft, blue light. Gurunaths face emerged in the midst of this light, and this reassuring message was communicated to me. "Jyoti," Gurunath said with a smile, "as you have written so far you will complete the rest. The people who are coming forth are being sent to aid you to bring your book to conclusion. So trust in nature that is ever nourishing and works in your best interest." I felt calmed and comforted by this transmission as my seemingly unwarranted fears were put to rest. The disciple needs to be open to such messages that are communicated by the master.

A good direction to know if the Guru is right for you is to follow the inner guide. At the start, observe the result of the practice, how much enjoyment the practice gives; the apparent benefits to the physical, emotional and mental bodies. Most of all make a fair assessment of the time contributed to the discipline, the noticeable potency of the practice, and the sincerity of the master. A satguru transforms the followers by infusing them with qualities of fearlessness, compassion, truthfulness, joy and bliss. Notice subtle changes in behaviour, how reactions to similar situations alter, how the master's words guide you in times of stress. Using these pointers, the seeker can go out in search for the guru with an open heart and mind. Do not let reports of charlatans, or experience of them, deter or dampen the search. Ever noticed a child learning to walk? Every fall is followed by the struggle to get up.

Like all true masters, Gurunath always draws from real life examples to teach us deep spiritual lessons. Our beautiful place at Panchvati became illegal under an order by the Chandigarh Administration disallowing farmers from using their land for any other commercial activity besides farming. Call it fate, call it the evil eye, but three years into our new business and our place came under demolition orders. A year after the demolition of Panchvati, Gurunath was to visit Chandigarh again. I was very worried, apprehensive about organising the event for there were no structures left standing at the site, no bathrooms, or toilets. There were no funds to hire a place, so I arranged the programme on the same site by putting up temporary tents and requisitioning a very ugly and impractical, temporary toilet from the municipal council. The debris from the demolition was all around us.

One evening during our usual talks around the fire, when a disciple asked how one should pray to God, Gurunath spread his arms and replied, "Like this! The external world may be in shambles, your life may be crumbling but look, here we are in the midst of these ruins, celebrating life and loving God." We spent the entire week in makeshift tents sleeping under the stars. It is one of the more memorable times in my life. The weather stood by us, even though it was the end of winter with chances of rain and thunderstorm. It also brought home to many of us how little we need to be truly happy.

Till date Gurunath mentions fondly that year at Panchvati as one of his memorable livingness camp, as we called the retreats in those days. "Apply the necessary means to achieve the necessary ends," says Gurunath, and practical application of this adage has made me more and more pro-active at times when nothing seems to move in life, whether sadhana or work, or just mundane household chores. To get desired results the seeker has to make the required attempt. So, just continue in your endeavour to look for the right master and the right practice until both are found, if that is what you long for.

When Gurunath is visiting, I invite people to come and meet him, extolling his virtues as a rare siddha who is also easily accessible. Many would come to stay while others would leave, unimpressed by his simple demeanour and directness. A very high-ranking government official once came to meet Gurunath. He was a learned man, a teetotaller and a strict vegetarian. If impressed, he could help our organisation greatly. I was aghast when in his presence, Gurunath accepted a glass of beer from another disciple, and casually began talking about the pros and cons of diet in a yogi's life. He said he would rather go out in the jungle, to hunt and eat the meat of a deer, than kill a poor defenceless vegetable that cannot save itself by running away from him. He even related the story of two meditating Nath yogis. Apparently, they were so famished after their continuous sadhana of more than a decade that when they found a body burning in the cremation ground, they immediately took a few bites to assuage their hunger! Needless to say, that government official never came back. I knew Gurunath preferred a vegetarian diet for practicing sadhaks, often likened intoxicants to gutter water, and was very harsh on those pupils who were regular addicts, constantly helping them to give up their habits through the practice.

Later, I argued that this was an important person who could have helped our cause and maybe Gurunath should have impressed him with some astounding insights. I did not realise that I was trying to use the master like a performing artiste to attract a crowd. Many a time, the people who came to meet him would be more interested in airing their own knowledge about scriptures and holy books rather than be open to learning from this meeting. I would be amused by how some would even keep interrupting to put forth their own views, rather than hear from the master. Gurunath would then keep quiet and allow them to carry on, his eyes filled with kindness and compassion. "Jyoti," he would say later with insight, "they came for high tea and polite conversation, they didn't come here to die." I understood what he meant but still felt frustrated that what was so obvious to me was not so for many.

I felt saddened by the thought that when there is a living master before us, we are suspicious of his motives and critical of his teachings and views, but when they are gone, we lament that we missed the opportunity to learn and rue that there are no more such exalted beings today! As for me, a living Gurunath has more significance than innumerable Krishna's or dead saints and sages.

As I understand, the guru is like a person atop a high mountain, who has an overview of the lay of the land, while the disciples are making their way up. From that position, the master can see the dangers lurking on the path, such as a ferocious animal behind a bush or a boulder on the course, and guides the disciples accordingly. Sometimes what seems like a needless detour is actually a tactical manoeuvre to make things easier for the disciple, a rough patch necessary to make them strong.

One Master one disciple

The disciples are given what they need, to speed them on the path of spiritual evolution, and not what they want. There is a unique relationship with disciples, and the master deals with them individually, building some disciples ego while subjugating the others, gently smoothing rough edges. There is no cause for passions like jealousy or envy amongst the students as the guru is there, in totality, for each disciple. It is the disciples who, with their limited understanding, know not how to accept or comprehend fully this abundance. "Drop competition," Gurunath advises us constantly.

True gurus often descend down to human levels in order to connect with the disciples, I have seen this very often with Gurunath when he joins us in our snow fights in the Himalayas, lobbing snow balls at his disciples and encouraging them to hit too without restraint. Complaining about his aches and pains or normal difficulties he reaches out to the disciples in their pain and frustrations. His interaction is unique with each one of the disciples and they all remember tender moments that happened seemingly only between the two of them.

That, for me, is the beauty of the one master one disciple relationship, that each disciple can chart a course with experiences with the master that is unique only to them. And even though these experiences may differ and even contradict with those of others they are exclusively personalised for them by the master for the evolution of their individual soul.

CHAPTER 4

EXPANDING AWARENESS AND KUNDALINI EXPERIENCES

The experiences mentioned here is a spin-off of the yogic sadhana given by Gurunath. Though enjoyable, Gurunath cautions pupils not to be excessively influenced by phenomenon such as seeing auras, intuitions about the past or the future, or experiences with spirits. According to him he does not consciously dabble in the Bardo Thodol. He often reiterated that the aim of yoga practice is to realise the truth about the journey of the soul, and for that the sadhana must be practiced with dedication. However, I had no control over these following incidents that happened unbidden. So while enjoying them with awe, I took them in my stride, with the understanding that they were a result of my practice and not a sign of any spiritual prowess.

One cold winter day just few months after my first meeting with Gurunath, indulging in the favourite pastime of most Indians, I was having a cup of hot chai. I had my hands around the cup for warmth and sat huddled in my shawl when I fell into the cup…I kept falling in like Alice into the rabbit hole.

There was a sense of falling and rising at the same time. I could see myself sitting still with the cup in my hands and at the same time I was in the cup... then, with a feeling of dissolving, I was in the tea garden; I was the tea leaf and I was the woman plucking me; I was drinking myself.

A few days later, I was reading a book on a warm, sunny afternoon when, suddenly, my body seemed to melt and flow into the wooden frame of my bed on which I was resting. Once again, there was the sense of falling and rising at the same time and I found myself in the forest – a thick dark jungle in the Northeast – I was the tall teak tree and the woodcutter cutting it. Everything blended the bed, the tree, the forest, the woodcutter and I. During both incidents, my awareness was enhanced manifold, so that I could smell, feel, hear and see with great clarity, the tea garden as well as the forest environs.

Things came to such a pass that if I were sitting in the garden I would soon be flowing into the trees, the grass and the flowers, feeling personally denuded when they were pruned or violated. A painful experience with Jujhar always ready with shears to cut, chop and prune plants and trees in the garden. While walking by the lake I started 'hearing' the thoughts of people passing me... mostly an electronic buzzing but sometimes a clear sentence. It was as if a floodgate had opened and I was helpless in controlling the flow.

These incidents kept multiplying and I became increasingly aware of energy fields, sometimes feeling exhilarated and at other times utterly discomfited. This happened when I had gone to pick up my daughter, Sukhmani, from her friend's place. I spent a mere ten minutes there but by the time I left I was feeling sick, and as I drove back I felt a slimy residue coating my car, my skin and my hair, sending a shiver of revulsion through me. The whole atmosphere in that area seemed to have been dense with some dark energy. Back home I had to scrub and bathe, standing for a long time under the shower, before I felt clean again. The neighbourhood I had visited was a housing colony for a particular segment of government officials. Their deeds seemed to have influenced the whole environment in that locality. Even if a few among them happened to be without blemish, they were too weak to make a difference in the aura of the area. I suppose in the same manner, good deeds and thoughts create a congenial aura, and that is why certain places give solace and others a feeling of discomfort. After this, I increased the intensity of a series of exercises taught by Gurunath that forms a light and sound shield around the body, protecting the pupil from harmful energy of places and people.

One day, a friend and her son dropped in and, while talking of auras and energy fields, I inadvertently made known to them my ability to sense them. Immediately, she started badgering me to read her son's aura. This was early on, at the beginning, and I had not yet learnt to be firm in my resolve not to do all this to satisfy idle curiosity. I believe, today, that unless the information is utilised in a positive manner, it is no use just knowing about the state of the aura. Therefore, I try not to use this ability frivolously. However, that day, excited with my newfound talent, I told them that the patterns in his aura showed him to be a secretive and non-verbal person who did not express his emotions. I asked him to practice some exercises to balance the relevant chakra. I came to know later that every day this boy would dress and leave for school but had never attended a class, spending his time hanging around the marketplace. His parents discovered this when they received a letter from the school. He had been playing truant like this for the past six to eight months. Whether he ever practiced the exercises that I taught him and if they helped him in any way, I never got to know as his parents stopped visiting me soon thereafter. However, with incidents like this, I realised that I could, to a great extent, gauge a person's state of mind by what their aura revealed.

These experiences, though, left me disoriented and vague in my waking hours. It was as if I was in my body and out of it at the same time! There was no desire to discuss them with anyone. Externally, I was apparently normal but inside me, there was a floating sensation. I was also plagued by terrible headaches at this time, but refused medication, intuitively knowing it was not a physical symptom but had its source elsewhere. I noticed that after every bout of headache the faculty to 'see' auras would improve substantially.

Sometimes, as I drove or walked, a cyclist or pedestrian would go past in a trail of multi-coloured hues. A splash of orange with some green, or predominantly bright blue with a tinge of red, and the colour would communicate something about the physical, emotional or mental state of the person. I learnt to enjoy the sight of the aura without being judgemental.

I started realising how easy it was to be struck by the glamour of the new-age phenomenon of reading auras, regressing people into a past life, divination into the future, and communicating with spirits through mediums – everything in fact that Gurunath had warned me not to be impressed by. This, rather than the actual spiritual practice which is the source of such talent, could take on more significance if I did not guard against it.

Soon, I was able to ignore and even turn off this faculty at will. For me, it is like peeking into someone's private life, and to do this for the sake of simple curiosity did not feel right. Now I barely pay attention to it, only when guided by a higher influence that I presume to bring attention to the problem area.

The magic of the Peepul tree and others

There is an enormous Peepul tree at the entrance to the Sukhna Lake in Chandigarh, where I have been walking regularly for over two decades. In all these years, I had noticed this tree only for its aesthetic beauty, without paying any special attention to it. But on this particular day, a warm summer evening of the year 2000, as soon as I got out of my car half a kilometre away, I was embraced by a golden energy. As I continued walking, the pull of energy kept increasing, until I realised the source of this to be the Peepul tree. There was a sweet, humming sound emanating from it, with the golden radiance covering the entire lake. The energy radiating outwards bathed all the walkers who were awash in this light.

As I passed under the tree my body felt saturated with the caress of this loving energy and my sense of hearing underwent a subtle alteration, enabling me to recognise the humming as the melodious repetitive chanting of '*Buddham sharanam gacchami…*' Gautama the Buddha had achieved self-realisation under a tree addressed ever since as the Bodhi tree. Had the surcharge of energy from that event elevated all trees in the world? Is it proof of what Gurunath had said of how when someone achieves enlightenment all nature gets a boost? I marvelled at this wonderful event. As I looked around, I realised that every tree and bush present was radiating energy in different hues, some more, some less, but all of them giving freely.

It seemed as if my ego and ignorance had, so far, kept me from consciously receiving this unconditional gift. The people walking here only needed to heighten their awareness to be able to perceive and partake of this largesse more freely. They probably do so without awareness for I have seen many people pause, apparently without reason, under the tree in a pensive mood. I felt my eyes brimming over as the selfless bounty of nature in contrast to my own selfish one was brought home to me. I have spent the days of my life chalking up credit and debit balance sheet, always wanting more than what I give in love, in relationships, in business, and in all aspects of life.

After this, my experiences with trees increased manifold. Once, I stood under the wishing tree of a temple that I visited. It happened to be a Peepul tree, and there were red threads strung all over, signifying wishes; people tie these while praying for the fulfilment of wishes such as passing an exam, a good job opportunity, a suitable match for their children in marriage, or success in business, among others. When these are fulfilled, they come back to untie a thread, and most of them end up tying another one for a new wish, as human needs are seldom completely satisfied. As I stood under this tree, there was again an alteration in my hearing and the whisper of a million wishes became clearly audible. The cacophony was horrible, with the desperate yearning of millions of hearts merging to create this inhuman buzz. It made me want to pull my hair and, shutting my ears, run far away. I felt the burden of all these wants weighing upon the tree and yet, the tree was carrying on in its service to humanity, and the inner expression was of joy at being able to do so.

During the following months, my consciousness opened up more and more and every day new messages would be communicated. When I started the search for publishers for this book, I got acceptance from two publishers in India. I was in a dilemma as to whom to go with, since one was closer home and would be very convenient, whereas the other was in a faraway city. As I walked at the lake one evening, I was trying to decide whom to reply to with final affirmation, wondering if I should just base it on what was being offered in the contract. Silently contemplating, I was gazing at the tree when a bright spark flew out of it and illumined what looked like the sea. A tree was growing and going all the way up a few floors to a window and, peeking in, I saw my book lying on the table. One minute I was walking by the lake and then in the next, a sort of illumination simultaneously outside and in the brain exposed the vision. With this insight, I decided to go with my present publishers from a seaside city. I was very thrilled when meting the publisher I shared this vision and I got confirmation about such a tree actually growing outside the publisher's sea facing office window. I am quite grateful to this publisher for taking on my book at that time when it would have been impossible for me to self-publish and also for returning it now so I can reprint with new inputs and revelations. All these experiences with trees reminded me of an incident at the farm that had happened quite a while ago. When newly married, we had planted a mango sapling in our garden, which, for many years, did not bear fruit. Then, I read somewhere about a ritual that was carried out by some tribal people in Central India. If a tree were not producing fruit, the gardener would take an axe and make some light cuts on the tree trunk, exclaiming aloud that the tree would be chopped for firewood if it did not produce a crop. On a lark, I enacted this one evening with my barren mango tree, accompanied by my two very young girls and an axe, laughing all the time at my foolishness. Imagine my surprise when the next season I saw the tree pollinating, and a lovely yield of mangoes followed and to this day we enjoy fruits from that tree. At the time, I put it down to some fluke chance, but I wonder now if my threat really did work and yes trees do have consciousness.

The relationship between trees and humans was further brought home to me when Ms. Chand, one of my friends, related the following incident. Living alone in a large house, she was exasperated with a Eucalyptus tree that littered her backyard and caused a lot of irritation to her workers who had to clean the area several times each day. So, one day, she called a local woodcutter and sold the tree for a few thousand rupees, as it was quite old and mature. The woodcutter even paid her an advance promising to come back for it the next day. That night, the spirit of the tree, in the form of a yogi, appeared to her in a dream and remonstrated about her decision to axe it. According to her, the spirit asked her to allow it to continue to meditate peacefully as it had done for so many years. The next day, she returned the advance to the disgruntled woodcutter and the tree still stands today, joyously littering that corner and providing mulch for the garden. I have been blessed with visions of many yogis meditating under trees in Chands garden, seemingly on a transit path. Her house is very close to the Sukhna Lake and, on other days, I have seen some of the same beings sitting serenely under the Peepul at the lake.

However, one of my most awe-inspiring experiences happened recently with another younger tree at the opposite end of the Sukhna Lake. One late winter evening, I was walking towards this side when I saw a beautiful blue light radiating from this tree. It was already dusk and the radiance spread in a circle, around the tree now, with flashes of gold and red mixed with the blue. I was taking pleasure watching it but could not decide whether to trespass and go closer or to step lightly and pass it by. As I watched thoughtfully, the entire tree transformed into the figure of Shiva with the Ganges flowing from his locks; I instantly felt bathed in the cool waters, which soaked me, seeming to flow into me through the Crown chakra – the Sahasrahar. Words are not adequate to explain this sensation; it was a complete drenching of the soul. The red and the gold transformed to Parvati and Ganesh and I was invited, through some unexplainable communication, to sit under the tree for a few moments, which I did. As I sat, swaying slightly with the power of the love coursing through me, I felt the tree offering me a gift that I was supposed to pick up. I waited for the feeling to become stronger, which then compelled me to move and search around the tree.

At the base of the tree, I found a bulge that I thought at first to be a part of the root but which, on closer inspection, was a stone that appeared to be growing out from the tree. When I loosened the stone, it jumped into my hands as if meant for me It adorned the room where I hold regular yoga classes for many years giving me glimpses of the Shivparivar – the family of Shiva. What is not very well known is that Shiva had a daughter called Jyoti, so childishly I felt as if I had sneaked myself into their family. The presence of this magical gift brought great joy and richness into my life in terms of advancement in all fields – physical, material and spiritual.

After many years while going into deeper sadhana I let go of this rock into the ground in my garden where all my crystals rest too.

   A very old Australian gum tree, popularly known as the eucalyptus, grows behind my house. It's not a native Indian tree but at some point the Indian government imported them in millions from Australia, I'm sure lining some deep pockets with the deal. This tree is as old as the years I have spent here, being one of the earliest trees we planted. I have always felt a tender affinity towards it dictated by the knowing that somehow it is connecting my songline with ancient Australia since my first travel in 1992 and from my past life association with that land. In my recent visits to Australia for establishing Gurunaths community, I met a lady who had learnt Kriya Yoga from our local teacher was herself a yoga teacher and was organising my event in Ballarat, Victoria. During my course I would stay at her farm in the outskirts in a cosy room facing the farmland.

   One day sitting for sadhana late at night I could feel the absolute stillness around me. As I went deeper I started to hear what seemed like poignant singing in some old language. It was beautiful and pulled at my heartstrings with tenderness. I realised it was a song emanating from some ancient tree telling the tale of the land; she wanted someone to hear it before she passed on. I shared this with my friend Susan the next day. We then made our way to a very old tree on her property, which had been there for many decades. Guided internally we did a simple ceremony to acknowledge the contribution of this ancient matriarch who was keeping the story of the land from being lost. It's interesting how this tree was so purely matriarchal, while the tree in my backyard I call the matripatriarchal tree, a term coined by me imbued as it is with both qualities of the mother and the father, the essence of balance, fortitude, nurture, strength, wisdom and courage whose vibrations of stillness permeate the whole area. The roots of the tree are firmly entrenched into the foundation of my house and in the floors inside.

※

Paranormal experiences from other realms

One day in early 2001, I walked out into my garden and was startled to see a spectre sitting on top of the greenhouse. The image of this spectre shimmered as if it were made of no substance but was a play of air and light. At first, I thought my eyes were playing tricks, but when I looked again, it was still there. The first emotion was of pity for the pathetic wispy thing just watching me. I must clarify here that, though sexless, there was something definitely male about it. This charade went on for a few days with me pretending to ignore and wishing it away, and the spectre keeping watch attentively. Then, one day when I went out to pluck some vegetables from my garden, the apparition, with a fluid movement, floated down and prostrated at my feet to abjectly offer its services. Though the conversation was mental and no words were spoken, there was still perfect understanding. It offered to do anything for me, from arranging foreign trips and money in the bank, to the ability to attract more students and great recognition in my chosen field. However, somehow, warning signals came on before I could accept this attractive offer. By this time, I was already well into the practice and had the intuition to realise that if I were greedy enough to allow this, before long I would be transformed into the grovelling person, with the spectre dictating terms to me. So, without bothering to reply, I walked away. However, the apparition did not go away and continued its vigil. I had heard that such beings could harm and even possess people during moments when they are depressed, angry, or under any emotional strain, making them vulnerable to such influences. Since these were common emotions at home with two teenage girls, I was afraid for my children.

I called up Gurunath to share this new development with him and ask him if he could suggest anything. He gave me specific sacred mantras and special rites to be performed on the following days. Every day, as I executed the rituals, the spirit continued to watch my actions, mournfully following me with its eyes. On the final day, as I completed the rituals, there was a blinding flash and the apparition dispersed in a burst of light as though released from an unfortunate state. The sweet feeling of an act well done enveloped me as I felt at peace with myself for having helped the spirit in distress.

At times, I have been instrumental in giving messages to my friends because of some clear insight that is communicated. One such incident happened with my friend Chand. As is her habit, Chand called one day requesting me to pray and send some energy for her mother who was unwell. When I sat down to meditate some time later, the message that her mother would not survive the night was communicated. I was forced by some inner urge to call her immediately with this insight, shocked at my certainty and my boldness. She was upset and angry at my prediction as her mother was not really very ill, so abruptly hung up the phone. Next morning, she called to say her mother had passed away that night and thanked me for helping prepare her for it. She could complete certain obligations to her mother, which she would not have been able to if it was not for the timely premonition.

A few years later when I was at her house, her mother's spirit appeared again to ask me to tell her daughter to stop grieving and allow her to move on. Despite many years having passed, my friend continued to mourn deeply for her mother and this seemed to be very painful for the soul, making it difficult for it to journey onwards to other planes. Many insights have come my way since then, about Chands and my relationship in past lives, which may have been a reason for this empathy for her situation.

Another incident occurred when I had gone to attend the ceremony marking the tenth day after the death of Jujhars friends father. As I sat immersed in the *kirtan* at the gurudwara gently following my breath, as is my habit. I saw the form of the father and felt his presence. Having met this friend only recently, I had met his father very occasionally and had not been well acquainted with him. As I watched, fascinated, the spirit led me to my friend's house and into a storeroom. There were many trunks and boxes lying there and, opening one, he showed me some papers. When I got home, I was in a dilemma, for this new friend was then a total non-believer and I did not know how he would react to information like this. I almost decided not to say anything but knowing that I had been entrusted with the information, I knew I had to do the right thing. So I called Jujhars' friend and recounted the whole episode at the gurudwara to him and, feeling instantly relieved of the burden, promptly forgot all about it. Ten years later, he recounted how he and his sister had looked everywhere for their father's will and other papers unsuccessfully and then remembering my vision, had then searched and found them in the trunk in the store. I wondered why he waited ten years to tell me this, sometimes it's just a reluctance of the mind to acknowledge that such things are possible. I too am amazed when such incidents occur, for there has to be some level in which we are all connected to some common pool of consciousness that allows these subtle messages to filter through. Maybe with practice the barrier that is between two different planes melts away, allowing these beings to communicate with ease.

Jujhar had lost both parents at an early age, his father in an accident a few months before he was born and his mother in a tragic family feud when he was five. She had been shot and killed by a family member and unfortunately, the family had conducted no proper funeral rites for her, quickly burning the body to hide the crime. After I met Gurunath, she started appearing to me; first at the family land in Uttar Pradesh and later at my home in Chandigarh. She appeared before both my daughters when they had gone to the ancestral farm for the festival of Holi with their cousins, unaccompanied by either Jujhar or me. During the stay there, as Rukmani was getting ready one evening in a room upstairs, while combing her hair near the window she saw a figure outside standing under a tree on the ground. She instinctively knew it was her grandmother, although we have no photographs of her. As she watched, the figure seemed to float up to come and stand outside the window. Rukmani too amazed to move, felt an outpouring of tender love coming from her, as she faded away. The same night, Sukhmani woke up to see a figure standing by the bedside. Unafraid, she did not feel threatened but, in her own words thought, that grandmother had just come to check on her two grandchildren. Her sister, now unaware, was sleeping by her side.

The appearances became more frequent, and my mother-in-law started insisting that I do something to release her from this painful existence of forty-five years in the nether world. My heart reached out to her and was saddened by her state. She had been in this condition for a long time and I could feel the weariness in her bearing. I asked Gurunath for advice and he said that whatever I may do, true solace would come only when her own children conduct the rites of passing. I kept pestering my husband and other family members, but my insistence was brushed aside as the ranting of a superstitious woman. The next time my mother-in-law appeared, I told her about my inability to help her and that she must persuade one of her children. After this episode, she vanished and I felt distressed that I had been powerless to help her.

A month later, as Jujhar and I were returning from Delhi after visiting his brother, without reason, he stopped the car by the side of the road and broke down. Weeping unashamedly, he confessed that he had been dreaming of his mother every day for the past one month. The dreams would be of scenes from his childhood, of being carried and cajoled by her, of her communicating her love and concern for him. He recalled how one day as he toddled down the stairs, a huge black snake lay on the step and she had quickly grabbed him and hugged him to her chest protectively. He had not thought of his mother for all these past many years, hiding the pain and isolation in some corner of his psyche.

After this significant event, he readily agreed to perform all the requisite rituals. I invited family members to participate in this ceremony, as the spirit wanted it to be a public function and not conducted secretly. Some approved and others refused, saying they did not believe in such phenomenon. I, nevertheless, carried on with the programme. I bought all the required items, bedding, clothes, utensils and other objects traditionally offered to help the soul to move on, after due consultation with her spirit that accompanied me now at all times. As the day of the ritual drew near, I sensed, in her, a tremendous fear of approaching death. I tried to console and support her as best as I could. The programme concluded well, with her spirit blossoming into a blaze of light as she was released. In the physical world, this was followed by unexpected thundershowers and lightning. It conveyed to us the appreciation of a job well done. After this, I could feel a palpable change in the energy patterns surrounding us, and the bestowing of unimaginable grace.

There must be something magical about the Sukhna Lake and its surrounding area, which has been the scene of many of my mystical experiences. One day, I was on my regular evening walk at the lake. It was two years since my mother had passed away when, during the walk, I suddenly felt a presence by my side and realised it was the figure of my mother. She walked silently for some distance and then, near the Peepul tree, led me down the steps to the bank of the lake and sat me down. She communicated without words, urging me to continue my work for my guru through teaching his practices and my writing. She also made clear that I was not to hold back my efforts by worrying about the girls, as she was looking after their interests. After this, she put her hand on my head in a blessing and placed a coconut on my lap. When she moved away, I saw standing behind her four more figures; all of them repeated the ritual of the blessing and the coconut. My mother then left, as if in a hurry to get about her work in other planes, followed by the others. It was uncanny how I felt the heaviness of the coconuts on my lap and the weight of their hands on my head. I did not know what to do with the astral coconuts, so I immersed them in the lake and completed my walk.

When I told Gurunath about this experience he said, "Yes, she came to give you special blessings. It is true that ancestors who have evolved keep watch over us. Did you feel the weight of the coconuts on your lap?" Then, in a lighter vein, "I don't know what these women from the South have with coconuts." But, the assurance that I did not have to keep a constant vigil over the future of my daughters palpably lifted a load off my shoulders, making me feel immediately lightened. Whenever the girls call now I say to them, "Do not worry, everything will be fine, grandma is looking after you!" Surprisingly, for two weeks before I had this vision; both the girls, Sukhmani in UK and Rukmani in Delhi, had been having regular dreams of their grandmother and remembering her fondly during the day. They told me this after I communicated my vision to them.

Over the years I formed a friendly connect with such spirits and they were like any other people around me. I would see family members who have not passed when I visited someone or stayed with them. Often the spirits would come and tell their tales to me as if looking for some company. I find them not that different from us and why should they be seeing they were us once.

One monsoon couple of years ago I had gone to Bir a small hill town in the Dhauladhar range in Himachal. I was staying in a house that overlooked the mountains on one side and an open pasture on the other. As I lay in bed that night, gazing out of my window I could see a whirling light formation, oh I thought inwardly a portal is opening. I must have dozed off looking at it when I felt a pull on the blanket I had taken over me. I pulled it back thinking it had got tucked into the mattress but there was a reverse tug. I opened my eyes to see a spirit standing over my bed pulling at my blanket. I looked crossly at him for waking me and pulled my blanket again, like a tug of war, but he wouldn't leave. So I remembered the chant that Gurunath had taught me for the spectre in my garden and chanted it, the moment I did it he dropped the blanket and was off into the portal of light outside in the field to be pulled into it. What stumped me here was the fact that the spirit knew I knew the chant that could release him. Mysterious are the ways of the universe.

The incidents are too many and cannot all be written about. But this one is of such great import that I have to chronicle it here. In December of 2015, we were at the Pune ashram for the winter camp. Gurunath had just recorded a talk on the journey of a soul after death and its subsequent reincarnation. It was a fascinating fifty-minute discourse and the information coming from a living master was very precious. It explained the mystical ritual of the *shraddh* ceremony of the Brahmins performed after death. Gurunath in his simple manner had articulated an ancient wisdom in current perspective. I came back determined to have a public viewing of this talk in Chandigarh. I got busy discussing this with local disciples and planning details of venue, promotion of the event etc. One morning as I was still in bed I felt a constant nudge against me like an insistent child pushing against a parent for some treat. I realised it to be a soul that wanted to see the film on Life after Death as the recording was now titled. I was bemused and informed the soul about the date and the venue. In the meantime I was concerned about how the general public will receive this recording. As disciples we are in tune with our masters' teachings but what about the common people would they be interested in this, I wanted to know. So we decided to organise a private viewing for a select group that included a few journalists and college professors. I shared the information about this new date and venue with the soul extending the invitation to attend. Light heartedly I told Babit my student and disciple of Gurunath, in whose house in the city we were showing the film to expect some unusual guests.

It was a large room where the television was placed and we sat down to view the film. After the film began I glanced to the side and imagine my surprise when I saw a group of at least seventy to ninety souls packed into the other side of the room. They were everywhere, floating on the ceiling, arrayed along the sofas, all wispy protoplasmic beings dutifully watching the film. It was interesting to see that they kept to a side of the room without encroaching upon us. The moment the film ended they disappeared in powders of light released from this intermittent state of existence. I shared this open eye vision later on phone with Gurunath who was in the midst of a German camp at the ashram and he made me repeat it so others could hear it over the speakerphone. For me this recording is as powerful as the performance of the brahminical ritual after death. I have seen it has the power to do what the ritual does, give a roadmap to the soul for its journey ahead. Most common question after seeing the talk is what about religions that don't have a ritual such as this does their soul not pass on. My understanding is that the ancient text chronicles the journey of the soul, which is the same for everyone after death. Having the text read out at death is like providing the facility of being handed a GPS but even without it the soul manoeuvres itself through the maze, as there are signs and guides along the way.

For me the most interesting part of the video was that sometime in the past the rishis had studied and chronicled a journey such as this of the soul, from death to rebirth.

The world of black magic and possessions

The topic of possession by spirits and black magic is a very contentious one as it is difficult to prove their existence logically, and talking about them often comes across as some crazy mumbo jumbo. Personally, I can only recount what my experiences are and leave it to the reader to form an opinion. An incident occurred very early in my practice of yogic sadhana. A young teenaged boy was brought to me. He seemed to be very charming and well behaved but his mother said that sometimes he would behave as if he was a totally different person. He was undergoing psychiatric treatment for his condition but, as in India it is customary to try everything else as well, she thought I might be able to help. I sat him down in front of me and, as I closed my eyes to concentrate, an apparition suddenly leapt angrily out of him with a growl as if to warn me away. The apparition had no shape or figure but was like a million particles of condensed black dust. I was overwhelmed by a vision of this boy as a child of four playing in a mango grove when the spirit had possessed him. His mother confirmed that he had fallen very ill at that time, and that it happened when they were living in a small town in a house next to a mango grove. I was not equipped to deal with it so I asked her to take the boy to Gurunath. It has been many years now but though she was familiar with Gurunath and was invited many times, she never visited him with her son. This boy, I later came to know, after going through a cycle of addiction and rehab many times passed away at a young age.

Another such incident, where I was witness to a possession, occurred while I was on a visit to a friend's place in New Delhi, when she received a telephone call in the midst of our chat. As she conversed on the phone, from my seat across the room, I saw a black apparition filter out of the receiver and stand next to her. The formation had a human shape, but consisted of the same black particles as I had seen in the boy. It felt as if this figure was leaning over, reaching into my friend's mind as she spoke. I instinctively knew that this spirit, which was standing next to her, in reality, possessed the body of the person she was speaking with. After she finished talking, I enquired about the person who had called and was surprised to hear the name of a well-known entity who we both knew indulged in tantric practices. He had readily admitted to my friend his desire to become famous and amass great wealth and had, in fact, asked her to join him at the initial stages of his career. Today, he was riding high on the pinnacle of a successful career, having achieved what he had set out to get. On that day, after witnessing the presence of the apparition, I understood that his body was being used by a very strong spirit of a long deceased tantric who had taken possession of his body to realise its own unfulfilled desires. Trapped inside was the weak spirit of the child, the original soul that had been stifled and never grew up since the possession. I saw this soul plaintively reaching out and crying for help but felt inadequate to assist. The spirit was using the life force present in the body of this person, quickly pushing him towards an early death.

The following incident of black magic was performed on us some years ago. One night, while sleeping, my eyes flew open suddenly and I saw a dense blanket made of spinning black particles descending on the bed and felt as if my breath had been sucked out with force. I realised that I was chanting a mantra that Gurunath had taught me for protection, when I had last met him. Jujhar was fast asleep next to me, unaware of my horror. Surprisingly, even in my terror, I remembered the symbols that accompanied the mantra taught by Gurunath. I made these hand movements, and kept repeating them until the blanket exploded and dissipated and, suddenly freed, I felt my lungs expand as the breath flowed back. Spots from the astral blanket floated over my bed for the next ten days. I sensed that this had been a black magic attack for death and it was only through the effort of the satguru that we were saved. When Gurunath had casually mentioned this technique of combating such attacks, I had wondered why he was interrupting his main topic that was being discussed to talk about these things but my brain had stored this information in the memory to be released even in sleep. I understood now that his message had specifically been for me.

While meditating later, I saw the face of the person, a family member, at whose request this act was commissioned. The face of the person who actually conducted the rituals was clouded. The vision was accompanied by the smell of blood that had been used in the rites for this attack. Next morning, my daughter Sukhmani recounted how she had woken up at the same time that night unable to breathe and with the feeling of someone sitting on her chest.

Some experiences were disturbing, like the one above, but others filled me with a sense of joy. During a yoga class I was conducting, I was overwhelmed by the vision of the wonderful form of God-intoxicated Chaitanya Mahaprabhu completely saturated in a state of divine bliss. The vaishnav saint was swaying in what seemed to be a deep trance-like state of ecstasy. The vision was accompanied by the heady fragrance of sandalwood. When I mentioned this casually, after the session was over, one of the students confessed that he was a devotee of this particular saint. In fact, at that moment, he said he was carrying in his pocket an article about Chaitanya Mahaprabhu that he had written for publication!

From my understanding of all these experiences, I could only conclude that somehow, during the course of my practice regimen, a time came when the boundaries demarcating individual personalities gradually began to dissolve. This probably enables a bridge to form between the consciousness of different individuals, allowing easier access and greater communication at a subtler level.

Many such incidents occurred regularly, helping me to understand the complex functioning of a universe at different vibrational frequencies. When an individual vibration synchronised with these manifold vibrations, I felt great leaps occurred, facilitating a clear vision of the phenomenon manifesting in other planes. For me, this happened spontaneously, and not because I was consciously trying to connect with these other realms.

Transformative spiritual experiences

Gurunath once asked me if I knew the difference between a mental experience and a spiritual one. When I shrugged in ignorance, he elaborated that a spiritual experience always directly transforms the disciple by giving a taste of the divine, filling the person with unexplainable ecstasy, while a mental experience, though subtler than a thought, is still a play of maya or illusion on the screen of the mind. Many of these mental experiences may be incidents pulled out from the memory of the sadhak from experiences of the past to be replayed in the present, akin to a rerun of an old television programme. This happens, I thought when the seeker reaches certain stages in the yoga practice and the centres in the brain start opening up. Gurunaths objective was not to discourage me about my numerous visions but to caution me to be aware and sensitive to the experiences. A mental experience may be very vivid and picturesque, of long duration and give great enjoyment. Nevertheless, though they help to strengthen the resolve to carry on with prescribed instructions from the master, they pale in front of the spiritual experience, which might be simple and last only a few seconds, but involves direct participation. Spiritual experiences deeply effect to transform the person experiencing and imparts insights and realisations of profound truth. The events mentioned here are mystical and every time I relive them, they retain this magical quality. It is very difficult to explain the experience of these experiences!

As I sat meditating late one night, I felt Gurunath blow forcefully into my right ear as he does during the initiation ceremony. Immediately, my consciousness exploded and atomised. I became a part of the galaxy and I saw the planets spinning lazily in and around me. I had heard that the human body carries a blueprint of the universe in it and both are part of one another, and I got a taste of it now.

Earlier, during my visit to the ashram, Gurunath had pointed a star out to me in the Orion's belt saying, "You have just seen Brahma." Don't know how but with my naked eye at that time I could see the star and the expanding stardust around it. Back home one night in my dream vision, I was outside the house looking up at the sky at the same star when suddenly my body and every fibre expanded, and again I underwent the sensation of being atomised – blown into smithereens – and I was part of the stars in that galaxy. As this feeling of expansion increased, I felt layers of gross material peeling off from my body and falling to the ground, and something extended out of me to become part of that galactic system. According to Gurunath, when the galaxy is born, it explodes and expands, and the planets and the solar systems are formed. This he explains is the phenomenon of Brahma. When this occurrence reaches the limits of expansion to stay constant, it is the character of Vishnu. Finally, when the galaxy implodes into the black hole pulling all the stars and solar systems with it, it is the phenomenon of Shiva.

The ashram has been the scene of many magical moments for me. During a visit there for *Mahashivratri* in 2004, Amandeep and I who were travelling together from Chandigarh reached the ashram late in the evening. The dormitories and all the rooms in the ashram were full as there was a visiting delegation of disciples from abroad. Seeking permission from Ayi, we were to stay in the Paran Kutir, the meditation hut made of bamboo and straw commonly used by students to meditate. Gurunath was away and, having decided to spend the better part of the night meditating, the two of us ate a very light supper.

After retiring to the meditation hut for the night, I thought of setting the mood for the meditation by chanting the special Gorakhsha Gayatri mantra as taught by Gurunath. Even known mantras flower into their potency after the guru gives them, which means the disciple hears it from the mouth of the master and has permission to chant it, with special instructions on its uses. Aman joined me with alacrity and we must have chanted the mantra for about fifteen minutes when I became gradually aware that my body was shaking. At first, I thought it was fatigue from the journey that was making me sway like this. Then I realised that it was not just my body but also the whole bed that was moving from side to side. Then I heard a strangled cry from Aman and, when I looked across at him, I saw his bed shaking too. It was not a gentle shaking but quite vigorous, making a rattling sound as the bed rocked on the ground. The tempo of our chanting increased proportionately with the increase in the movement of the beds. Strangely enough, neither of us thought of running out or shouting for help as there was no feeling of being threatened in any way. After some time, the shaking of the bed slowed and I lay down to sleep. My bed felt as though it was inclined at an angle and I had to hold on to its side, so as not to roll off. I kept meditating by gently observing my breath and finally, by about four in the morning, all activity ceased as the bed straightened and there was silence and blissful sleep. The next day we could not talk of anything else except this bizarre incident. Some believed us while others did not, until Gurunath came back and we excitedly told him all about it. He smilingly told us that Shakti had blessed us with a glimpse of her powers since we had so sincerely invoked her by chanting the mantra. The meditation hut was one of the earliest buildings at the ashram and had been used by Gurunath for intense meditation. In such places, the veil between the worlds is very fine so that one can easily flow from one dimension into the other.

After I returned, I continued with regular walks at the lake. I had grown especially fond of my walks, since it made me feel even more refreshed and rejuvenated to be consciously absorbing the vibrant energies in that place. One day as winter was slowly fading; I was rather irritable, as running errands for the household had made me late for the walk. Although it was getting dark, I decided to go to the lake anyway. I was walking back towards the dam end where I had parked my car when I sighted two orbs of light slowly moving across the lake. At first I thought they were birds reflecting the light from the golf range nearby but it was not so, for they were on a tangent away from the light and still shining brightly. They were too low to be satellites, and my body was telling me differently. I could feel a strange tension in me as I felt rooted to the spot. Then I felt my entire body saturated by a wave of cool energy flowing from the top of my head to the tips of my toes. The lights were fluid, like liquid mercury with a bluish tint, one of them somehow older than the other was. They travelled the whole breadth of the water body and then went behind the faraway hills.

When I discussed the vision with Gurunath, he enquired about them in detail. When I started telling him about the colour and texture, he told me that I had seen the sacred sight of two Nath yogis travelling together in their body of light. Later, I discovered a Shiva temple on top of a hill at the point where the lights originated. My discovery of the Shiva temple was a mystery at the time, until one day when I stood on top of the hill and realised that it overlooked the entire lake. It was almost as if higher forces who watched over me as I walked by the lake had magnetically drawn me there.

There were times during my personal sadhana when I was overtaken by an intense desire to meditate at different times in the night. At first, I used to startle Jujhar when he found me sitting up in bed at odd hours, but then he got so used to it that he used to be surprised if he found me sleeping. One such night around three in the morning, the phone rang twice with no response from the other side when I answered, those were the days of the old rotary dial phones. Since I was up, I thought I would meditate for a while.

After an hour of meditation, I lay down to sleep once again. As was my habit, I was gently concentrating on my breath as a prelude to deep sleep. All of a sudden a figure appeared by the side of my bed. I could see it was a yogi by his posture and general appearance. I tried getting up, but could not even lift or turn my head, as my body seemed to have turned to stone. When I say I could not move I mean I was not even conscious of breathing, nor was I able to twitch a muscle or blink an eye. I could only watch as this yogi gently pressed my left knee, at which a bolt of electric current flowed up my right side. Then he vanished as mysteriously as he had appeared, and I found that the movement of my limbs had returned spontaneously. I immediately thought it was some healing transmission as though I had been saved from some terrible illness. Next morning when I recounted the incident to Gurunath on the phone, he said that it was a surge of spiritual power given by one of his astral projections to help me in the days to come.

It was only when one calamity after another hit me and I remained unshaken that I realised the power of this mystical meeting. First, there was an income tax survey against us, brought about when Jujhar had offended someone 'powerful' by refusing special charges for their wedding function. Next, my mother had to undergo surgery and passed away after being hospitalised for over two months, the last fifteen days of which she was in a coma. Then the building at Panchvati was demolished and the business we were running so successfully came to a standstill, due to a policy change by the Administration. I remained steadfast through all these events. I knew then where the strength came from. That gentle touch had given to me a transmission of so much power that it allowed me to be detached and unharmed during this turmoil. Even now, I am moved beyond words when I consider the compassion of this being that had come forth to give me support at my time of need.

One early morning I was practicing my Kriya when I heard the Sanskrit chant of *mantra pushpam*, a *vedic* hymn broadcasted from what seemed to be a loudspeaker nearby. I was surprised as this is a typical mantra from the South that I had learnt as a child and I didn't know of any temple near me that would have it on a loudspeaker like this. I usually heard the prayers from the Gurudwara or the Mosque or the Shiva temple nearby. So enchanted I went out and tried to locate the source of this chanting. As I looked around I realised it was coming from everywhere, seemingly from the skies and the earth and also from inside me. It sounded like a group of rishis chanting. Humbled I went back to sit on my meditation mat and enjoy this mantra vibration. The chant continued for another fifteen minutes and at the end of it a voice boomed and said very authoritatively in Sanskrit, "*Brahmano, brahmana sthava,*" which I instantly understood to mean, "A Brahmin is one who is established in the Brahman." The caste system was something that never reared its head during my childhood and westerners are often surprised to hear that I was not aware of the caste system as a practice until I was in college. But that day all doubts were put to rest with this one statement and I knew that no one I knew was a Brahmin as none I knew were established in that supreme reality except Gurunath, who can even give us the glimpse of that reality that is within us.

※

Glimpse of Babaji at Baglamukhi temple

I was visiting the shrines of Baglamukhi and Jwaladevi in Himachal Pradesh with Jujhar and a friend. The evening before leaving for the trip, I had seen the vision of a person I identified as Babaji through some inborn perception. Dressed in bright yellow clothes, he was laughing as if daring me to recognise him. A sheaf of peacock feathers fanned out behind him. Though he was laughing, his eyes were full of compassion as he gazed gently at me. I knew Babaji was Gurunaths guru and, in this way, I was connected to this same lineage. I could not consult with Gurunath as he was away on his foreign tour. I made up my mind to pay attention to everything remotely or outrageously yellow during this tour. I was ready for Babaji in the most incongruous and flamboyant yellow. So imagine my incredulity when I reached the Baglamukhi temple the whole temple was painted yellow and all the priests were dressed in yellow robes. My mouth fell open with amazement at this sight and laughter bubbled inside uncontrollably at my predicament. Composing myself, I walked into the temple trying to be attentive and looking carefully at all the priests. In the inner sanctum, an old man who seemed to be in an acute stage of Parkinson's disease was sweeping the place. He was dressed in soiled white clothes and had difficulty in holding the broom due to the tremors. As I walked past he looked up at me, his whole body shaking with the effort. I took no notice and went ahead to offer my prayers to the deity.

I sat to meditate, after a while when I opened my eyes I observed the old man with Parkinson's sitting in the sanctum sanctorum of the temple completely steady with not a twitch. Miraculously there was no one else in the temple at this time. Then as I continued to watch, I saw upon the old man's visage the face of Babaji as I had seen in the vision, the same laughing countenance shining out at me. I wanted to shout out and announce the presence of Babaji but all I could do was watch, rooted to the spot, and struck dumb so that no words issued from my mouth. Then he summoned me by crooking his index finger with twinkling, intelligent eyes astounding me with the transformation from the person who was sweeping the place. I moved forward almost sliding towards him wordlessly, and took the *prasad* he was offering. He blessed the threads I had bought from the shop outside by anointing it with sacred water and *kumkum* colour. Not a word was uttered by either of us; I was dumbstruck anyways and was like in a daze. Was Babaji using the body of this old priest as a conduit to manifest? I did not know at that moment. I floated out of the temple in a daze, my feet barely touching the ground. It was only when we were well away from the temple I could speak and share this with my friend and Jujhar, who was driving us.

When I shared this encounter with Gurunath when he returned, he was elated. However, even six months later, I was still in a state of daze after the encounter, having yet to absorb the power of this meeting totally. The Baglamukhi temple is renowned for granting relief from any legal issues and since that day though we had to fight many legal battles including one where I had the false case framed against me, we as a family have been winning all our legal encounters.

Purusha and *Prakriti* **unveiled**

In 2011 I got an opportunity to visit Varanasi or Kashi as it is addressed in ancient texts, the oldest city in the world that some believe existed in previous world cycles. I had been to this city as a child but never got a chance to revisit until then. After being reintroduced to the path of Kriya Yoga I unlocked many memories from past lives in this city. I had often had visions of Lahiri Baba only later becoming conscious of who he was and his connection to our lineage. In my vision I am a young girl taking his blessings in a Bengali bridal dress. I also had visions of handing him his umbrella and his shoes as he leaves the house for a stroll. I had vivid recollection of the house and its inside so was keen to visit the old home. After much research we found an address and arrived at "Satyalok" which on Internet was given as the address for Lahiri Mahasayas' temple and samadhi. When I entered the space there was no nostalgia or feeling of déjà vu. I felt a bit flat no effervescence of excitement. The place was empty had only a caretaker who was very kind and let us in, it was the English date of Lahiri Mahasayas' samadhi not the actual *tithi*. The caretaker unveiled a big white statue of Babaji and we sat ourselves down in front of it. A friend from Bangalore and Aman had accompanied me; Aman has accompanied me on many of my trips.

I was gazing with a steady eye on the statue of Babaji while moving my kriya breath. Almost playfully I saw

Babajis' face changing to a female face, then again it would transform to the male. I later learnt the female face was that of Mataji, who is considered the female aspect of Babaji. But for me in that revelation they were not different or different aspects they were One. I watched fascinated at this play of oneness as realisation poured in. A very profound experience, it was a revelation of a deep truth that there was no duality in the Divine, who was neither male nor female and was both male and female and all other genders in between and beyond. In the divine all polarities of gender become indivisible, inclusive and merged and yet are none. One yet None, my mind dissolved.

The topic of patriarchal terms and behaviour deep-seated in our scriptures, sculpture and language is very close to my heart and I have an issue with the Lord God always referred to as a 'He' by all gurus' male and female. Once I was protesting because Gurunath while making a statement said man and I thought it should also include women. He looked at me and said, "Jyoti, you know the word man has come from the word *man*". *Man*, I knew in Sanskrit means the mind and it includes emotions. "Man," he continued to explain, "means the thinking principle and should apply equally to both men and women as at the level of the mind they are equal. But men at some point appropriated this title for themselves. So when I say man it includes both."

I understood the same has been done with the terms Purusha and Prakriti. Purusha, which means pure consciousness, has been appropriated to mean the cosmic male and Prakriti, which means creative energy became 'mother' nature. And how convenient to say Prakriti does all the work while Purusha is unmoving. Well we can see the result of this fallacious representation now when the Purusha laze in front of the television while the dishes pile up for Prakriti! Even more frustrating is the fact that some scholars categorize all animated life including the biological male as Shakti, keeping the male Shiva for the pristine divine. There are instances of men dressed like *gopis* dancing to the flute of male lord god Krishna, Sufis dancing as Heer to merge into the male god symbolised by Ranjha. I find a fundamental misconception in this perception and am yet to decide whether this is genuinely a (mis) conception or patriarchy taken to another level.

For me simply, Shiva and Shakti are the left and right hemispheres of the brain. Giving one the title of male and the other female as in the Ardhanareshwar concept is a presumptuous generalisation according to me; as many men are right brain oriented and many women left-brain. The removing of the schiz between the two hemispheres of the brain brings balance and prepares the practitioner for further spiritual journey. The external union of man and woman is but a symbol of this inner fusion that awakens new life.

Continuing on this topic with Gurunath at another discussion, he explained patiently, "The most marked difference between men and women is in the physical body. This is a biological requirement for the procreation of our race. In the emotional, mental and spiritual aspects they are alike. There's no difference." This explanation resonated very deeply with me, as I have no sense of my own gender not only when sitting in sadhana but even otherwise. When I teach I am not conscious of my students as male or female, neither do I see my master as a male; the guru essence for me has no gender and since my guru is divine for me, neither does the divine have a gender for me. "When you are teaching you are a soul teaching a soul," Gurunath always instructs acharyas who are embarking on their role as teachers. The practice brings similar difficulties and obstructions for both students and teachers according to their mental and emotional states unconcerned by what gender they may belong to.

The vision that day opened me in many levels unravelling layers of understanding of this phenomenon of Purusha and Prakriti over the ages. A gleaning of the truth from the maze of imposed traditional, social and cultural bias, which continues to this day seemingly without being questioned. Nature requires both the male and the female for evolution and so I observed do we in the practice of the Kriya, needing both polarities of Shiva and Shakti to transport us to merge into the singularity. Somehow I feel I am just a sliver away from realising this truth. This insight has contributed greatly to my practice of the Shiva Shakti Kriya enhancing my realisations and ability to communicate this understanding to my students. I know this is a drastic thought questioning an old system of understanding and I might be opening myself to ridicule and controversy and may be bombarded with volumes of scriptural anecdotes. But this was the core essence of the teaching that day. It's not the rant of a feminist as many people may choose to see this.

We sat for over an hour in front of what for me was the living statue of Babaji. But there was dissatisfaction in my heart as I kept feeling this was not the house I saw in my vision of Lahiri baba. The caretaker took me on a tour of the house, upstairs to show me the wooden sandals of Lahiri Mahasaya. When I told him about my vision and how I felt this was not the house he surprised me by saying that though old this was a reconstituted house and was not where Lahiri Mahasaya lived. He then offered to take us to the original house that was only opened on Gurupurnima. We walked through familiar pathways and the moment I saw the door to the house memories came flooding back. I had to wait for another four years before I could coincide my visit with Gurupurnima and enter the house from my vision. I was overtaken with nostalgia when I entered and recognised the house, the staircase, the patio and the terrace. It was an important homecoming but I left knowing I had been delivered into the hands of a living master in this life to continue my discipleship.

I was so enchanted with the city of *Kashi*, recognising it from many past lives spent there that I was overtaken by a desire to stay there for a few months. I started actively planning my move in my mind including renting a house, its location and so on. As I sat in this reverie on my bed facing the Ganga, a blue light appeared above my head to the right. The light was bright and pulsating and I 'heard' a voice tell me, "Go to California." The voice was not a language but a vibration that communicated this short cryptic message. Then the light expanded and showed me a vision of Kashi, the streets were lined with dead people and vultures were feeding on them, the walls of the buildings on the *ghat* were crawling with rats, there seemed to be some kind of epidemic and then slowly the whole city sank into the river. Even though the city was submerged I could feel the energy of the Kashi Vishwanath temple pulsating strongly from below as if not affected by it. The resonance of the communication was that this would happen since the behaviour of charlatans who fleece poor people who come from far and wide to this sacred city was corrupting the whole area. Dressed in robes and external marks of holy men they were polluting the Ganga and the hallowed essence of Kashi by their acts. Though when this was going to happen and how I would go to

California, in this life or next was not explained. This blue light, I want to call it divine but it was very matter of fact, was a presence. The light had no gender and I recognised no deity in it and the 'voice' as I said earlier was not a language and the communication was in some kind of wave.

※

Galactic and Planetary experiences

During this same visit to Kashi we were told to visit the famous Vishvanath temple and especially witness the *saptarishi* aarti in the evening. The saptarishis are the seven stars of the big dipper and in the Hindu tradition every human on earth can trace their genealogy to one of them. My family traces it back to Rishi Angiras and his descendant Rishi Bharadwaj, at least that's what I have been told by my father. Having no clue about this ceremony we purchased tickets, which was the only way we would be allowed inside as they restricted the number of people attending. At the event time we arrived and made our way in to the inner sanctum of the temple. There was quite a crowd but we found our way to the entrance and sat on the doorway with a clear view of the inside, a bribe to the pundit helped to get us the good seat. My friend from Bangalore kept insisting I ask one of the many priests who were in the process of beginning the ceremony, the meaning of the saptarishi aarti. The priests were all bare bodied and wearing many strings of rudraksha mala and looked quite fierce. In jest I told my friend I was not going to tap one of them on the shoulder to get their attention as who knows what their policy is about women touching them so lets just wait and see.

The Shiva mantra chanting started in earnest, very powerful it was all the priests chanting in unison with traditional timbre and cadence. There were as many lamps as priests and they started waving them, as the chants grew louder with more power. I was sitting quite relaxed when perchance I glanced upwards into the dark cavernous receding roof of the sanctum sanctorum. Imagine my surprise when I saw the open sky and star formations instead of the ceiling as if the top had opened up. Then as I kept watching I saw the seven rishis of the great dipper descend down to take the customary aarti of Kashi Vishwanath, just like devotees do. Each rishi came down, the most ancient first and though I could see the face old as parchment there was no body attached. And what was more; I was aware that they were aware that I could see them. My whole body shivered and went into goose bumps at this and I had to bow my head in reverence and I understood that during saptarishi aarti the rishis descended on earth to pay reverence to this shivaling, so what does it make this shivaling, I wondered, which is not even the original one that was uprooted and thrown into a well by a marauding Mughal emperor in 1669 CE.

I often wonder why I witness such manifestations, my nature being so irreverent. I am not pious or devout or religious and have an attitude of humour towards epic events. I never feel the desire to defend mythological figures in the religion I am born into or sympathise with or give excuses for what they supposedly did, gamble their wife, make them go through fire to prove their purity, abandoned them based on gossip or to selfishly find 'truth', adopt unfair war tactics, steal clothes of women etc etc etc. Yet I have had visions of all of them, Ram as *Ramachandra* with a moon on his forehead as I hiked up to Tunganath, Krishna in a very intimate dream that transported me physically almost within twenty four hours to *Gokul* and Vrindavan, manifestation of Shiva and Babaji and Hanuman all of them approaching with compassion and immense love with meaningful revelations.

Late one night I finished meditation at about three a.m. and had just laid down to rest when I was overcome by a great desire to go up on my terrace. Try as I may I couldn't resist this need to go out. So naturally I made my way up to the roof and as I came up I saw a brilliant star shining down from the sky. It was unusually close, so close I thought I could reach up and grab it. I was so fascinated that I kept walking looking up at the star and walked straight into an iron wire mesh I had placed to protect my havan-kund- a space to hold fire rites. I tripped and fell hard and a rusted iron rod from the mesh penetrated deep into the flesh on my thigh. The whole process from getting up from my bed to falling took barely few minutes. Now when I looked up the star had receded as if its job completed and I looked complainingly up to enquire why, I was pulled out for this when I was on my way to sleep like a good girl. Of course then I realised the planet to be Saturn, the point was not lost on me the iron rod, the hurt on my leg. These were all signs of Saturn, some great karma seemed to have been worked out, I thought with relief. The deep injury miraculously healed by the morning.

The experiences with Saturn were around the time in 2006 when I was leading a major farmer agitation against acquisition of their land by the local administration. I was making a lot of headway and was generally being a pain to many powerful lobbies. Some weeks after this incident I was arrested on a fabricated criminal case I was not jailed but released on bail the same day. The case went on for seven years till I was acquitted without prejudice. A few weeks after my arrest I was doing my morning practice when I heard a very clear voice that I recognised as Saturn's tell me to go and buy two blue sapphires and keep them in the cupboard. The instruction was so authoritative that I had no choice but to go and spend a wad of money I could ill afford at that time. So I went to a jeweller I knew who had genuine gemstones. The two sapphires in a way found their way into my palm, I recognised them as a couple, distinctively emitting male and female vibrations. As instructed I wrapped them in a soft cloth and kept them in my cupboard. Seven years passed, my court case was decided in my favour and then in 2013 I started getting an internal desire to wear the sapphires in a ring. I am not a fan of jewellery in the form of rings finding them very irritating but circumstances brought so many signs that I finally had them designed into a ring and started wearing it all the time. Yes I still have it though I wear it more intuitively now rather than everyday. I felt tangible changes in my life over the years since I bought them, a freeing of karmic debts so I can more freely move towards my spiritual destiny, including my divorce, which I see as a grace that liberated me from bondage. For me Saturn is one of the most compassionate of planets that metes out the karma that needs to be worked out if we are to progress.

"The sun walked upon this earth once," Gurunath would often say as he taught us the powerful solar practices. I always wondered how this was possible in logic till he explained how our limited consciousness is contained within our limited physical body. But with meditative practices as our consciousness starts to grow and the expanse of our influence to do service extends, the mass of the body that has to contain this expanded consciousness becomes proportionately larger. According to him the sun, the planets and the stars in the galactic systems are offices for the expanding consciousness and are occupied for a certain time by one till that consciousness evolves and another takes its place. Made me wonder if they had a head hunting and placement department!

"The universe is teeming with life," Gurunath replied once to a question about other life forms in the galaxy. "Don't be arrogant to think that you are the pinnacle of evolution. Evolution does not stop at the human level, it goes on to subtler beings who share this universe with us."

※

Krishna gives a task

Early one summer morning in 2006 I was awake but idling in bed, in that state of awake but not awake yet. In a dreamlike state I saw a young Krishna about twelve years old, selling ice cream in an old ice cream stand like we have in India, just a boxed refrigerator with an awning over it. The topography was a dusty muddy area with low trees scantily growing. I recognized the boy as Krishna though he was not sporting the usual mark of the peacock feather or the flute. In fact he was dressed in rather soiled clothes, a dhoti and a faded yellow sash around his waist. He was standing by his unsteady ice cream box on wheels, the wheels were misaligned and the awning on top was tilted to the side. Handwritten on the awning was Gokul Ice-Cream. Not a very pretty picture for the Lord of the Universe. He was looking at me and telling me to help advertise his ice cream. In my dream vision I started, as is my habit to plan an advertising campaign for him. I thought I will ask Rukmani, who was a graphic designer and would help create posters for Gurunath for our events in Chandigarh to help. I started visualising the colours to be used, the tag line and which media to advertise on. Then suddenly I realise all this is going to cost money so I tell Krishna that, at that he makes a sign to me to wait and crawls into a small house made of mud and thatch and comes out with wads of cash. While he is handing me this enormous amount of cash, I'm thinking what does he sell drugs? From where does he have all this money? At that moment my dream broke and I was fully awake. The message of the dream was not lost upon me, I realized it was a message to continue my work for my master sharing Kriya Yoga which is the ice cream and that I need not worry about money as I would be cared for. Maybe I had some subconscious worry about finances to continue guru's work, as most of the funds to organize events were from my own, siphoned off from the farm income.

But that was not the end, later the same morning Jujhar came to me and said that he had some bank work and has to go to Agra and as his brother in the army was posted in Mathura he was planning to stay there. At this I promptly cancelled all my classes and hopped into the car with him. So within a day of having the dream I was in Gokul and Mathura and Brindavan visiting the places where Krishna lived and loved.

The Judas message

A year after our earth peace temple was consecrated, one morning Gurunath asked all the disciples, there were very few of us at the ashram, to go to the temple and pray for whatever we desired. To me it seemed more than just an instruction as is given by priests in religious places to ask for material blessings for money, health and other external tools of happiness. I made my way up and sat down in front of the mercury shivaling. Wondering in my mind what I desire most. I realised I irritated and troubled my master a lot so was generally praying to be a better disciple. As my thoughts were forming I saw a figure loom on top of the shivaling and recognised it as Judas, don't ask me how, I just knew. Connected to his back almost like the other side of the coin was Jesus and they both looked like twins. Then Judas looking penetratingly at me said authoritatively, "You will be disciple to Gurunath as I was to Jesus." After this both figures dissolved slowly and disappeared. I completely freaked, as we all know the story of Judas and how he betrayed Jesus. I came down from the temple and my lips zipped, my mind in a turmoil wondering how I was going to betray my master. I had also felt a very close connection of Gurunath to both of them.

When Gurunath asked us about the meditation at the temple, I just said softly that I had seen one of the apostles of Jesus. Of course nothing is hidden from the master as I have come to know. So at lunchtime while I was pensively chewing on my food Gurunath looked directly at me and said, "Do you know Judas was the closest disciple of Jesus?" I looked up startled yet interested at the same time. "Jesus asked him to do what he knew none of his other disciples would do especially as for posterity it would make them the archetype of betrayal." I thought Gurunath in his compassion was saying it to make me feel better as his words did bring solace to my heart. This started me on a quest to know more about Judas and once surfing on the Internet I found a link to a page on National Geographic called The Gospel of Judas, a lost manuscript, a gospel recorded by the gnostic Christians. Dated the second century it included conversations between

Judas Iscariot and Jesus of Nazareth. Lost for seventeen hundred years it had recently been discovered and was being restored. The manuscripts in short revealed what Gurunath had told me that morning at the ashram, that Judas was acting on Jesus's request to betray him. I bought a copy of this manuscript and the DVD accompanying it as an offering to my guru on *gurupurnima* that year in 2008 when I was lucky to be in the United States to attend it.

My second encounter with Judas and Jesus was a few months later when I was visiting my daughter in London. I had a very lucid dream one night, me along with a group of ten more people were standing with a person who I recognised as Judas. We were waiting seaside on a deserted beach with a lighthouse. I watched as a ship pulled close by and Jesus steeped down from the ship. Jesus was dressed like a king; he was wearing flowing robes of some exquisite material and was adorned with jewels and a crown. When he came down Judas and him met each other warmly and side-by-side walked into the lighthouse. I was standing with the group outside and gazing at the door of the lighthouse when the lighthouse transformed into a blazing cross extending into the sky and all of us standing by were pulled into the cross. My eyes flew open and I woke with a feeling I cannot describe in words, my whole body bathed in light. Later when I asked Gurunath he said the cross was the Christos into which we had merged.

My intention while recounting the above incidences about Judas is not to create controversies or refute ideologies and belief systems it is just to record events as it happened to me; I really have no conflict with anyone who believes otherwise being firmly of the opinion that each one must learn from their own revelations.

After every such incidence, came a sense of exhilaration with the surcharge of energy that seemed to flow into me as an aftermath. The only way I can explain this is that, like nitrogen fixation during lightning, this inflow of energy seemed to infuse into me essential nutrients that enlivened the subtle nerves in the body and the brain. Simply put spiritual experiences appeared to perform the activity of *nadi shodan*, a clearing of the psychic nerves preparing the body for the incoming surge of divine energy whenever it may come. I realize there is close connection between the two, the divine energy within us mirroring the divine energy around us and the union will not happen unless our body is truly ready. By body I mean the entire five *koshas*. The resulting sensation of all these cumulative incidences was an unexplainable feeling of joy and bliss as if every cell in the body was alive.

CHAPTER 5

THE DISCIPLE'S PILGRIMAGE

Travelling with the master is an important part of the learning process for the disciple. Continuous dialogue and interaction, understanding every word and gesture of the master, can be very rewarding to an attentive pupil. During our travels, Gurunath is constantly instructing and guiding us. He builds our self-esteem, confidence and concentration, and if the ego rears its head in a disciple, he knows how to kill it gently. The conscientious student is the one who does not waste energy frivolously and gains the most from close association with the guru. This is real education.

"Movement, Mantra and Meditation are the three 'M's' of the practicing yogi," Gurunath would say. Yogis travel a lot so as not to be attached to the comforts of a particular place, as normally happens when one lives in the same place for a long time. Of course, the practicing householder cannot move about much since responsibilities committed to family and society needs to be followed through. Yet, the practicing householder sadhak is expected to live within the family and society without attachment to the comforts provided by them. The air conditioners and the washing machines, the car, air travel, the cosy bed and the warm quilt, the servants at our beck and call, the familiar support system, all these can become habits that are difficult to break when the time comes for rigorous sadhana. Even dwelling on sorrows and acquired habits of self-punishment can be an impediment. Gurunath does not advise us to shun the comforts of modern living but says that, like Janak, we should be able to walk away from it all at the instruction of the guru. Janak was a legendary king and father who was also a sage and philosopher. Legend has it that he could walk through his entire kingdom, passing all the allurements and riches of his court, the enticing semi-clad dancing girls, through his kingdom while carrying a bowl filled to the brim with oil and not spilling a drop. He is the example often quoted in scriptures for total detachment of the senses from objects of desire.

'Mantra' is every gesture and word of the master that helps us on our spiritual journey and 'Meditation' is the yogic discipline taught by them. Only by following these implicitly do we effortlessly make our way upstream towards the source from where we have come, which is the ultimate goal of yoga practice.

※

Experiencing Dreamweaver for the first time

Back in 2003, Gurunath was yet to name this Dreamweaver. This is a unique part of the camps with Gurunath where he enters the dream of the disciple and works out some of their karmas correcting the DNA structure and seamlessly weaving the tapestry without a glitch. At these moments the disciple may or may not be consciously aware of the healing. In Delhi for a weekend camp, we were told by Gurunath that he will be working on us that night and that we should remember any dream that we had. I went to bed excited with this new experience that we were going to be given.

The dream that night was so real that I actually felt it as a reality. Gurunaths room was on the second floor while my room was on the ground. The whole night I was filling a brass bowl of water from the tap outside my room and carrying it to Gurunaths room. As soon as I am outside the room I see the water is soiled so back I come down the stairs to rinse the bowl and fill it again; when I reach outside Gurunath' room again I find the water soiled and make the trip back again to rinse and refill the pot. This continued throughout the night at around five in the morning I make my way up again after I don't know how many trips up and down. The water was now clear and I hand the bowl to Gurunath who is standing at the open door of his room. The moment he takes the water from me both my hands up to the elbow feel as if shoved into a burning pyre without the accompanying sensation of burning. The skin on both my arms up to the elbow splits open and comes off like a glove. I woke up very clearly remembering every detail of the dream and feeling a pain on the legs as if from running up and down the stairs the whole night. When I recounted the dream to Gurunath the next morning, he said simply that I had worked out a lot of Karma towards him that night and was free of them.

❃

Incidents at Jwalaji and Gorakh Tibba

Early in my association with Gurunath, I accompanied him on a pilgrimage to Jwalaji, in Himachal Pradesh. Once a stronghold of the Nath yogis, today the temple of the Divine Mother *Jwaladevi* is more famous with pilgrims than *Gorakh Tibba*, the shrine dedicated to Gorakshanath. It was my first close encounter with the Nath yogis, ascetics of the Nath order, who are devotees of Guru Gorakshanath and follow a strong guru-disciple tradition.

One Master one disciple

The aarti, the traditional waving of lamps at the Gorakh Tibba, is conducted by these yogis and is accompanied by rhythmic beating of drums and special trumpets. The whole temple complex reverberates with the sound. While attending this function, Gurunath pointed out that the beat of the drums and trumpets facilitate the awakening of the chakras. He instructed us to close our eyes and listen to the reverberations of the music in various chakras in a systematic rhythm. Lost in this experience, I felt my body become an instrument reciprocating the music outside.

Before leaving on this trip, following Gurunaths instruction that disciples must have a mat to meditate upon which is not to be shared with others, I had enthusiastically purchased an expensive designer asan to begin my new role as a yogi! Yogis believe that a personal mat imbibes the positive vibrations of the sadhak, making it easier to flow into meditation every time the practitioner sits on it. I insisted on carrying mine everywhere, not knowing where a desire to meditate may overtake me. The apparent act of sitting importantly for meditation was, to me, more exciting than the actual time spent in meditation.

We arrived in the holy inner sanctum of Gorakh Tibba in the evening and, before the rituals began, Gurunath was explaining some point about the history of the place. In my excitement to hear him, I left my mat where I had spread it. As the crowd kept increasing I began to fret about my beautiful new mat. Scarcely paying heed to Gurunath, my thoughts turned obsessively to my misplaced asan. Then Gurunath interrupted his talk to look at me, sternly saying, "Now stop thinking about your asan. What I am saying is important so listen to me, and anyway your rug is safe! That Baba has kept it aside." One of the priests had caringly picked up my rug and put it safely near the feet of the idol.

Although this was an ordinary incident it made a deep impact on me. I felt how easily I fritter away my whole life on trivia that like the beautiful asan are only a means to higher things. Whenever my mind battles today with the petty travails of daily living, I say to myself 'Stop thinking about the asan and leave it at the feet of the Lord!' During this first trip with Gurunath to Jwalaji, he told me that when I reach a particular stage in my practice I should do some meditation at the Taradevi temple on top of the adjacent hill. Reading my mind, where I had immediately started planning a timetable, he was quick to point out that it might take me some time to reach that stage when I can receive the full potential grace of the place and its deity Tara.

What is not very well known is that the Taradevi temple was originally the temple of Taranath, a Nath yogi who had swallowed the flames of Jwalaji during a duel with the Devi. Stories about the Nath yogis are replete with incidents where the yogi has supposedly subjugated a powerful female deity. This is also symbolic of taming the feminine Kundalini Shakti. The recounting of incidents of conquering the feminine may find their roots in patriarchy; it's a possibility though the origin may have been more about acquiring spiritual prowess. However, the temple is now dedicated to Taradevi, a goddess revered in both Hinduism and Buddhism and is one of the ten aspects of the dasa mahavidyas. When visiting Jwalaji with Gurunath again after a couple of years, I remembered his previous instructions and thought that I would try to meditate for some time at the temple if the opportunity arose.

During the journey, the disciples had been pestering Gurunath to conduct a meditation at midnight at the esoteric Taradevi temple. Although he agreed at first, as the town drew near he said he could feel the presence of a very strong spirit that would harm the male among us and he would not jeopardise the lives of his disciples thus. The three days at Jwalaji were wonderful, with us meditating deep into the night. We stayed at an inexpensive lodge maintained for travellers by a group of Nath yogis; most of us felt part of this ancient sect and were at home with their rustic humour and direct ways. They recognised Gurunath as a satguru and gave the respect he deserved as a disciple of Guru Gorakshanath. On our last day there, after meditating at the Jwalaji temple, I could not see Gurunath anywhere. So, Aman and I, thinking that he must be at the Taradevi temple, hurried up the hill without informing anyone. Being my student and equally adventurous, Aman did not express any qualms about joining me in this venture. In my anxiety to be with the guru, I overlooked the warning by Gurunath not to go there. It was twelve o'clock, the sun was blazing down on the rocky path, and having taken off my shoes at the entrance of the temple below I walked up the rocky path, blistering my bare feet. There was no sign of Gurunath at the temple, but we decided to meditate there for a while. After about forty minutes, I felt that the quality of the meditation was not deep enough and I grew restless. Seeing a narrow mud path leading up the hill, we asked the priest where it led to and he told us that it led to an old Bhairon temple.

So, up the path Aman and I went boldly. After climbing up a few metres there was a sound of something being dragged or rolled down the hill. Aman stopped in his track and was ready to flee back down the path. I assured him that it was probably someone working on the hillside, or maybe a *langur*, and we should carry on. After a few more yards, the sound was repeated again and I was amused to see Aman's face drain of colour and turn completely white. Again, I brushed aside his fears, urging him to carry on with the climb. I must have taken just another step when I thought I heard Gurunaths voice bellowing at me to come back. I stopped in my tracks and the command was repeated again, this time very clearly. I communicated this to Aman who now seemed keen to return. After that, we ran helter-skelter down the hill like naughty children eager to obey after a spanking.

Gurunath was sitting with the other disciples in a circle around him when we entered the rest house, sheepishly. Looking sternly, he said without any preamble, "Didn't I tell you not to go there? How do you expect me to do any important spiritual work if I have to keep guard over disobedient disciples all the time?" Then his face softened as he smiled and said, "Jyoti, you are full of mischief. When will you grow up?" Gurunath explained that an aspect of a still-evolving goddess inhabited the hill we had been ascending; she blossomed on male energy, and would not have hesitated to entice Aman. In my selfishness to look for Gurunath, I had inadvertently put Aman to great danger by disobeying the guru's direct order.

Every time I have visited Jwalaji with Gurunath, there have always been some magical moments to affirm my belief in an old connection with this place. The title Jwalaji is from the word jwalamukhi literally meaning 'fire mouth' or a volcano; the hill on which the temple is situated emits flames and hence the name Jwalaji. The temple town is situated in the Shivalik foothills. It is believed that during the legendary dance of Shiva with the body of Sati, that was subsequently sliced by Vishnu to stop the destruction of the galaxies by an enraged Shiva, the Devi's tongue fell here and since then it has been a centre of cosmic power – a Shakti Peeth. People come here to worship and ask for wishes to be granted by the Devi. My understanding is that these power centres are places where large meteors hit and are embedded deep in the earth's crust emitting a vibration that connects us to the origin of our source. As Gurunath often says, "You are nothing but cosmic dust." Therefore when we sit in deep meditation in these spots our consciousness resonates with that of the universe and many secrets are revealed to the sensitized.

One evening, we were at the temple for the evening aarti, an exhilarating ritual when the deity is worshipped with chanting of sacred mantras, drum beats, and the whole atmosphere cleared with swinging lamps. We were walking in a row past the flames emerging from the hillside. I was right behind Gurunath when he lightly touched one of the flames, which immediately split into three with the centre one becoming electric blue – the mystical colour of Gorakshanath and Shiva. Gurunath turned back to see if I had seen it. He was delighted like a child. I too, with quick reflexes, put my finger on the blue flame and rubbed it on my third eye between the eyebrows. I then excitedly turned around to call the attention of the other disciples to this phenomenon but when they looked the flame had gone out completely. Aman right behind me, managed to get a glimpse of it.

※

In the Brahma temple at Pushkar

Another trip with Gurunath took us to Pushkar, situated in the desert territory of Rajasthan. I dragged my teenage daughters along, promising them accommodation in air-conditioned

The Disciple's Pilgrimage

Swiss tents, which I had mistakenly thought we were to be staying in. I also promised them the use of a swimming pool that looked lovely and blue in the brochure but turned out to be a green stagnant pool when we arrived there. The temperature was close to forty-five degrees, with sand blowing everywhere. It was so hot that if I peeled an orange it would dehydrate before I put it into my mouth. My girls, of course, immediately began to sulk and stopped talking to me. I did the best thing possible by ignoring them. But personally I loved it. Always a summer person, the heat seemed to dry up all the phlegm in me. A few of the others who had come along with us left the camp to stay at an air-conditioned resort nearby. The rest of us who stayed on cooled ourselves by lying on the damp grass in the sweltering afternoon heat and eating lots of raw onions with our meals, which, according to *ayurveda*, are very cooling. Both my daughters confined themselves to their tent and made their own plans for the next day. As we were to go to the Brahma temple in town they decided to trek up to the Savitri temple on top of an adjoining hill. They made arrangements for a ride to the bottom of the steep hill, and were to leave before us in the morning.

As was the norm, when we reached the Brahma temple, Gurunath first told us about the history of the temple and its mythology. When Gurunath speaks it is as if he was present at the point of time when the events actually took place. He does not speak from acquired knowledge but from direct experience. Among other things, he said that to humble the ego of Savitri, his wife as she arrogantly made the Gods' wait for her to arrive for an auspicious ceremony, Brahma had cursed her and put the condition that before entering her temple on top of the hill it would be imperative that the devotees first come to his own temple to pay respects. After spending a great morning meditating at the temple and then wandering in the bazaar, we returned to the camp.

Here I found the girls already back and a bit annoyed. Then the story tumbled out that they had reached the top of the isolated Savitri hill and were about to enter the deserted temple when they saw an absolutely naked man sitting on the steps of the main temple. Totally embarrassed, both of them had fled down the hill and had arrived just a while before us. Then, laughing, I told them about the curse of Brahma on his wife and that they should have first been to his temple before going to the other one. What better way to stop two determined young girls from entering the temple than to have a naked man reclining on the stairs? At this, both the girls burst out laughing, a bit hysterical after the day's events.

❈

Himalayan pilgrimage

My most memorable tours with Gurunath have been to the Himalayas. In March of the year 2001 I was instrumental in organizing the first Himalayan tour and though I have accompanied and been part of the organisation in many others, this first trip is etched in my memory. I felt lucky to be one of thirty disciples who were on that initial journey, some of whom came from as far away as America, Sweden, Switzerland and England. We were visiting some of the locations that were an important part of Gurunaths spiritual quest. The tour had started with the disciples' first coming to Chandigarh and a visit to the powerful Jwalaji temple in Himachal. The next leg of the tour took us to Rishikesh from where began the ascent into the Himalayas. The day in Rishikesh was spent roaming the markets with Gurunath and Ayi and in the evening we saw the enchanting Ganga aarti and floated diyas, the earthen oil lamps and flowers as an offering to fulfil our wishes. So beautiful was the sight of the *diyas* being carried away by the current that

The Disciple's Pilgrimage

I forgot to make a wish. Meditating that night I felt as if I was sitting immersed in the cool flowing waters of the Ganga that engulfed me in a loving embrace, even though we were a few kilometres away from the bank. Such was the power of her love. Was it a foresight of times to come when fifteen years hence sent by my guru, I would be a regular visiting teacher at an ashram by her side?

Our next stop was the confluence of the sacred rivers Mandakini and Alaknanda at Rudraprayag, where Gurunath had a deep and personal experience with Mahavatar Shiv Gorakshanath Babaji. Words cannot explain my feelings as I gazed at the spot on the confluence where Gurunath saw Babaji bathing. I was mesmerized and could palpably feel the magic. All of us had rooms facing the confluence and at night we were silhouettes as we sat meditating. With the sound of the confluence raging in my ears, the starry sky above, and the mountains around me, I understood the true meaning of pilgrimage was to be connected to a spot of special importance on the master's spiritual journey.

Early next morning we were excited as Gurunath was leading us to a secret spot that he used to visit. We walked along a path and came to the snake cave of Koteshwar a prehistoric cave that instantly transported me back to the age of mammoths and rivers of fire. But nothing had prepared me for the sandy white beach down below where flowed the majestic Alakhnanda. With a whoop and shout of joy we ran down to the beach like little kids exploring and climbing the huge boulders that lay strewn as if by a giant playing marbles. Doing Surya upasana at this spot, I inhaled deeply all the vibrations kept alive by innumerable selfless yogis who stop, rest and meditate charging the environment with their benedictions and blessings. The Vivar, a whirling meditation taught by Gurunath, became the whirling of the cosmos and there were many a clash of the titans as bodies fell without control on the sand and on each other. This was followed by a dip in the freezing waters of the tumultuous Alakhananda.

Next day, we visited the ancient temple town of Ukhimath, named after Usha, daughter of Banasur, who married Aniruddha, Krishna's grandson. The original temple though, believed to be at least ten thousand years old, is Onkareshwar, where the great legendary King Mahandata performed austere penance. Standing unmoving on one leg for twelve years, his single-pointed devotion pleased Shiva, who appeared in the form of the omkara to bless him. King Mahandata is believed to have burst out of his father's chest at the time of birth and this whole area was referred to as the Mahandati Kshetra – the realm of Mahandata. The incident of Mahandata's birth seemed to me like some extra-terrestrial delivery, and I wondered if such stories were actual galactic events turned into interesting tales by the ancient sages for us fledgling humans. Just as we explain profound scientific principles to children by simple story-telling tactics!

The temple is the winter abode of lord Shiva, as Kedarnath, who is worshipped here when the snow-bound temple in the higher reaches of the Himalayas becomes inaccessible each year in winter for pilgrims. The priest informed us we were lucky to visit as Lord Kedarnath was present and we could partake of the grace. The temple complex here also houses the marriage hall where Usha married Aniruddha about five thousand years ago.

After everyone retired for the night, three of us disciples decided to continue meditating around the fire for a while longer. I felt the silent peaks of Neelkanth, Tungnath and Chandrashila watching our endeavour dispassionately. I was filled with the silence of the night when, suddenly, I felt a presence and opened my eyes to see who was around. I was amazed to see a yogi standing silently a little distance away from the fire as if checking us out. I had not heard him approaching; the dry leaves on the path would have given him away. He seemed to have just materialised out of thin air. He was thin and very dark, dressed all in black with many rudraksh beads around his neck and arms. He wore a huge turban on his head. He took no note of me as he came close to the fire. In the light of the fire I realised that it was not a turban on his head but his dreadlocks wrapped around in such a manner as to give the impression of a colossal headgear. His movement was fluid and he just seemed to float towards the fire. He sat silently by the fire for a few moments to warm himself and then was gone, even as I continued watching him with fascination. Gurunath later explained how the Himalayan ranges are alive with the presence of many yogis who roam unhindered by the laws of physics, with most travellers being completely unaware of their passing.

The following day we went to Duggalbitta, where Gurunath planned to acquire some land for a Himalayan ashram. The valley was a gentle undulation after a severe climb. We stopped en-route to have a snow fight, flinging snowballs with glee on each other, Gurunath participated too and childlike joined us in the merriment. Looking at the gentle slopes of Dugalbitta Gurunaths eyes softened as he reminisced nostalgically, "When, as a young yogi, I reached here after an arduous trek, this place was welcoming like a mother's arms. I rested here for a while before moving higher to Kedarnath and Badrinath.

Disciples are discouraged to take random photographs of Gurunath as he sits or meditates, as it is distracting to others and to him. During that visit to Duggalbitta, as Gurunath sat in seclusion meditating, one of the young disciples very foolishly went and clicked some snaps, startling him with the flash. Gurunath opened his eyes and looked at her fixedly. The frightened girl ran away. Later, he gently explained to her why it is important to follow instructions and not be mischievous and make a nuisance of oneself. He explained that the satguru, while in deep meditation, may be in communication with other beings, or working at other astral planes, and disciples must respect the instructions for privacy at such times. Gurunath often reiterates the importance of paying attention to direct instructions of the master and following them implicitly. When the girl came to Chandigarh and developed the pictures, all the others except those of Gurunath meditating were there. The frames with him meditating were blank.

As we left Dugalbitta a storm was brewing and some of the American disciples were noticeably disturbed. They pointed out the bald tyres of our rickety bus and the slippery roads with thin ice on it and showed their consternation about hurrying back. Some of them were wearing expensive watches that could tell the altitude, the temperature and wind speed. Gurunath then taught us a simple trick, he said when yogis walk the Himalayas to ascertain whether a storm was heading towards them, they would just lick their finger and hold it up, whichever side the wind blew left or right the storm would also pass by in that direction. One only had to worry if the wind was dead centre! That got us all licking our finger and then sticking it up in the air to declare the storm was definitely not heading towards us.

The journey was nearing its end the last stop being Hardwar where we visited the twenty five thousand years old cave where Raja Bhartaharinath meditated. Gurunath discouraged me from buying a statue of Gorakhnath to which I was unusually attracted, saying I still had worldly duties to get over with. Six years later he specifically asked me to go and get the same idol for my new yoga centre, saying that with his blessings I could place it there.

❈

Discovering an ancient cave of Babaji

Acting upon Gurunaths desire to establish a Himalayan ashram at a comfortable height, a disciple from Delhi, had been reconnoitering the area around Kedarnath, Duggalbitta and Gupt Kashi. Soon after a camp in Chandigarh, I got a message from him saying he had identified certain plots and if I could drive up with Gurunath and check out the location, the deal could be finalised. I needed no more urging and Aman and I took turns driving Gurunath to arrive at Rudraprayag that same evening after a drive of nine hours. The trip went as planned and we spent a week travelling in the mountains with long stretches of meditation in the morning and nights. Aman and I often wonder what karma we must have accumulated to spend these ten days in the Himalayas practically on our own with Gurunath, walking the trails with him, meditating and sitting around a fire at night in Okimath.

I had picked up a copy of Uttarakhand Tourism's travel guide and, lazily flicking through it, I chanced upon a mention of an ancient cave of Babaji in Srinagar, which falls on the route from Rudraprayag to Rishikesh. I do not know what sparked off this desire but I felt a yearning to visit this cave. Like a child desiring something, I constantly kept thinking of this cave and kept repeating to Gurunath about stopping at this shrine on our way back. Gurunath pointed out that celibate Nath yogis manage many of these shrines, and they do not allow women to enter the inner sanctum. This set me off indignantly saying that considering men require women for all other activities, and since I had been cooking and looking after Gurunath like a true disciple for the past one week, I would like to see how anyone could keep me out of the temple!

While returning, I was annoyed that Gurunath seemed oblivious of where we were seemingly unconcerned we were crossing the town with the cave. Exasperated, I told Aman to stop and enquire about the location of the cave. Would you believe that nobody knew where it was? The town seemed to me to be populated with people who knew where every other temple was except this one. However, we kept driving back and forth and I was determined not to move further without locating this enigmatic cave of Babaji.

Gurunath, laughing mischievously, said, "I think Babaji is playing hide and seek with Jyoti He has lifted up the whole cave into another dimension."

In the end, we drove up to a temple by the side of the river and, while Gurunath went off for a stroll to the riverside, I went into the temple. As I bent to prostrate before the idol, an old wizened lady walked out from a nearby room. Her face was gentle and shining brightly. Almost in tears by now, I asked her if she knew where the cave of Babaji was, as no one in the town seemed to know. She smiled and said, "You have come in search of God, how will you not find Him? I know the way to the cave."

As we followed her directions, help came via other people and, at last, a small girl playing in the street escorted us to the mouth of this cave. There was no one guarding the entry and I happily crawled in behind Gurunath, for the roof was very low. The three of us sat for a while meditating. The cave smelt fresh and cool even though it was small and had a low roof. Sitting with Gurunath, I felt important, like a child who has accompanied her parent to meet another exalted member of the family. A meeting where children are to keep quiet while the grown-ups spoke on important subjects.

The lesson of this whole exercise was not missed by me I felt it showed me what determination to achieve a goal could do. In fact the whole exercise, in retrospect, seemed like a little game that was played on me to test my grit.

※

Raja Bhagirath at Kedar Ganga

The Himalayan tours as an annual feature were started in right earnest a couple of years after this around 2007. Every year after Mahashivaratri a group of disciples from all over the globe would make their way up these mountains with Gurunath. I was one amongst the first organisers and stories of these trips are replete with wondrous experiences for disciples and peppered with humorous incidents along the treacherous Himalayan highway. The number of disciples in the group

One Master one disciple

slowly increased as the disciple base of Gurunath went up over the years. One year we were a hundred and fifty people on that trip, three bus loads full and numerous private vehicles.

On one such tour Gurunath organised for us to first stop and take a dip at a waterfall that he said originated from Kedarnath and was called the Kedar Ganga. As Gurunath now travelled in a private vehicle, the bus with disciples would leave early and we would wait for him at any given destination. We disembarked at this scenic waterfall; the waterfall itself was powerful and in a distance huge boulders dotted the stream forming pools of clear cold water. As was customary as organisers we instructed the disciples to not go into the water until Gurunath arrived. As I sat relaxing after a morning of hectic activity organising the group, I became aware of a very ancient yogi figure floating above the mountain from where the waterfall was flowing. His eyes were very piercing, he had a flowing white beard and wore a turban and I thought he was a *khshetrapal* a guardian of that area who had come to stakeout the group. Gurunath arrived in some time and took his place on one of the boulders. Imagine my surprise when the figure quickly moved down and took blessings from Gurunath by prostrating at his feet. Gurunath too acknowledged him by blessing him. I was agog with excitement and wanted to question Gurunath about this incident and share it with the other disciples. I had to wait until the evening campfire to do so as we at this time made our way to take our place under the waterfall and get drenched in the icy waters.

That evening when I recounted my experience of the day another disciple from Scotland immediately said he saw the same incident but with closed eyes. Gurunath very casually mentioned the yogi was Raja Bhagirathi. It made me wonder at the fact that if the person who had been instrumental in bringing Ganga to earth came to be blessed by my guru who must my guru be? After a while, I stopped wondering about these magical moments and just felt awed and humbled to be touched by the grace of it all.

※

At the Kalimath vortex

The Himalayan tours were always filled with enigmatic experiences for me as if the very mountains were ready to impart their wisdom to a seeker. Once we were visiting the temple town of Kalimath a very powerful centre where Shakti in her avatar as kali had vanquished the demon Raktabeej, who had received a boon that in war when even a drop of his blood fell on the ground another raktabeej would sprout from it. So naturally his power knew no bounds and as is usual with absolute power he became absolutely invincible and a danger to all. So it came upon the mother in her Kali avatar to fight with him and before a drop of blood could fall on the ground she would lap it with her tongue and so the demon was finally overpowered. For me since childhood these stories depicted cosmic events of epic proportions that I feel were strung into stories for the limited human minds. We were a really large group of disciples that year almost touching a hundred and fifty. When we reached the temple there were big signboards that prohibited photography. Majority of the disciples were from abroad with a smattering of Indian origin people amongst them.

As I watched the priests' behaviour I started to get disgusted, while they were fawning on the 'white' people by allowing them to pause as long as they wanted in front of the *swayambhu* self-manifested deity, they hurried the 'brown' people along hardly giving them time to gaze at the idol. In fact I felt if the priests had a chance they would turn away from the idol of

One Master one disciple

mother and garland and do aarti of the foreign disciples. Their discriminatory fussing and fawning was unbearable to me and my patience blew a fuse when I saw them allow certain of the disciples to merrily take photographs while being rough with the others. I got so revolted with their behaviour that I turned the anger on the deity and sat down in a huff refusing to take *darshan* or go around the rest of the temple. I waited for everyone to finish and start the trek to the busses parked a little distance away. Making sure everyone was accounted for, I was one of the last to struggle along. Suddenly I felt a tug on my arm and saw a young boy priest pulling my hand, when I stopped and looked back at him, he thrust something into my palm and said in Hindi, "Didi, this is for you." Before I could react he ran away. I was surprised at this sudden gesture of the arrogant priest to send this young boy to me with a *prasad*. When I opened the palm of my hand to see what was inside laughter bubbled up inside me at the revelation. In my palm was a small packet of joss and written on the cover was *shiv mahima*, which meant Shiva's divine play. I understood that it was a playful message from the divine at my childish anger, that everything that happens is divine play.

In 2013 there was the great tragic flash flood in Uttarakhand, the area of our Himalayan sojourn that wiped out most of the roads we would travel on in the Himalayas. An example of how humans can pollute and endanger the delicate ecosystem of fragile places, these floods were an eye opener for many. Once upon a time only the very sincere made their way, often on foot, walking up the treacherous Himalayas to reach destinations guarded by the high mountains, snow and jungles. Today, tourists who want all the comfort of their home have replaced the humble pilgrims, and greed has overtaken virtue. Rampant building work, helicopter services for that quick blessing and pressure of human population culminated in a tragedy where many humans and animals lost their lives. This put an end to our travels to the higher regions and the Himalayan tour at the time of writing this was confined to Hardwar and Rishikesh. I no longer participate in the hectic organisational duties of the Himalayan tour, which is now handed over to younger disciples of Gurunath.

Two years ago Gurunath instructed me to start classes in Rishikesh, which is called the yoga capital of the world. Seekers from all over the world flock here to learn, steal, devour information and misinformation about this ancient yogic technique, many sincerely and many as a fad, many to further their careers back home in gyms and yoga studios others to move forward on the path of spirituality, many are there just for a respite from their humdrum lives back home and others to try drugs as a release. It's a melting pot with all forms of true and not so true gurus and disciples. But still a place where with clarity one can find true gnosis. So there I was back again to a start up work, which I really do enjoy, putting up my flyers and finding yoga studios that are friendly.

Here too luck was by my side when the Parmarth Niketan Ashram on the banks of the Ganga opened the doors of their ashram to Gurunath and my classes without reservations. An ashram that has been instrumental in holding the world famous International Yoga Festival, this was an ideal venue for the work given to me by Gurunath. I have been a regular visitor here holding classes in Kriya Yoga and other practices formulated by Gurunath and we have held two public satsangs and empowerments for Gurunath attended by thousands of Indian and international seekers. Coinciding with the International Yoga Fest it's a great awareness outreach where various strata of seekers get to meet the master. As the satsangs are free, open and easy to walk in we have had unprecedented success in introducing Gurunath to a diaspora of seekers in quest. This year I start with two-day workshops at the same venue. I can feel an evolutionary chapter in my responsibility as teacher flowering. Being at this space interacting with the volunteers and organisers who welcome everyone like it is their home gave me great lessons and insights on how to conduct myself and free myself from narrow restrictions and bias against other yoga paths and gurus. This was an important lesson to learn and I am forever thankful to Gurunath for making such myriads of opportunities come the way of an unruly disciple to learn life lessons.

Often, when I am at our ashram in Pune, I feel so thankful for this opportunity to be so close to a living master. Sitting with Gurunath under the thatched hut, I feel as if I have been doing this for many lifetimes, and am reminded of the *gurukuls* of ancient days. It may seem that I have spent many months with Gurunath at his ashram in those years between 2000 and 2005. However, if I count the number of days that I spend in his company each year it will not be more than twenty or twenty-five days. This includes a few days during a tour, a couple of days at the ashram, some in camps at Delhi or Chandigarh and the days during Mahashivratri at the ashram that I have made a point never to miss, urged by some inner intuition that understands the higher initiations that take place at such auspicious times.

In the ashram, we do not have a set timetable to meditate, to eat, sleep and so on. Gurunath believes in breaking the rigid patterns of linear thinking of his disciples. He also does not want us to be mindless slave of the sadhana, which according to him, has to be joyous, free and spontaneous. Freeing us as he says from deadlines, he humorously says, "Deadline, deadline, deadline, deadline," then after a dramatic pause he continues, "Dead."

"Fixity of purpose and flexibility of routine is what you should be guided by," says Gurunath. So, at the ashram, taking cue from the guru, the disciples may be sitting and talking at one time and then, in continuity, flow into the meditation with him. Or they may be sleeping, and be suddenly woken up for a very early morning meditation, that too after staying awake way past midnight.

On one such occasion I was at the ashram a day after Mahashivratri. Most of the disciples had already left and it was my last day there as well. He had just taken a disciple to task for missing a previous meditation session because he was out walking with his girlfriend. Gurunath told him that even if God asked to go for a walk with him he should say, "No, my guru is calling me for meditation." As I sat next to Gurunath, meditating with him, I felt as though he was a big flame and I was lighting a lamp within myself from this larger light and would carry this beacon within me. From that day, I realised I was a ray of my guru and my every moment would be dedicated to his work.

CHAPTER 6

THE FLOWING RIVER OF LIFE

As a child of six, angry with my mother for leaving me behind when she went on some errand, I had kicked a long glass window to be rewarded with a big cut on my Achilles tendon. The overzealous doctor, because I kept walking without rest and breaking the stitches, which were on a delicate spot on the ankle, had compounded the mistake by putting the leg of a growing child in a plaster for many weeks. This had left one of my legs slightly shorter than the other, which makes me limp while walking. In school, I remember feeling hurt when anyone pointed out this 'defect' in me. This usually happened whenever there was a quarrel and I had got the better of the argument. The opponent would then hit out verbally, with a jibe at my most vulnerable spot, literally my Achilles. I must have strongly resented this deformity, and felt embarrassed by it, but pushed it into some dark recess of my mind.

Since freeing oneself from past encumbrances is part of the cleansing process in yoga sadhana, when purification through prescribed practices started, this memory from a past life rose to the surface to reveal the reason for my handicap. I returned to an earlier period in ancient India where I saw myself as a young man of about twenty-two kicking and abusing a gentle saint sitting on the steps of the water tank of a temple. I was lashing out at him with my right leg; kicking him down the steps leading to a water reservoir. As I relived this experience, I could clearly see the eyes of the older man, full of compassion for me even as I cursed and hit out with unbridled anger. A group of people then caught and hit me till I was bruised and bleeding. Then while the others held me, a man came forward and, with the swipe of a long sword, cut my leg off completely. I recognised the temple subsequently as the Sun Temple at Modhera, Gujarat. It is interesting how I came about this information, one of my students who lives in Ahmedabad, visited this temple and brought along some photographs on her visit to Chandigarh. As I gazed at the pictures, I felt a strong sense of déjà vu. Later, as I kept recalling the details in the photograph, I was disturbed as though the picture was not complete. A vision of a pagoda kept recurring. My efforts to ignore all of it as a figment of imagination did not help. So I logged on to the net and searched for this site. And imagine my astonishment when the page opened to reveal the exact replica of the image of the temple pagoda in my mind. The photographs my student had taken were from a different angle and did not show this structure. I could pinpoint the exact location where I had been standing, towering belligerently over that kind soul.

This experience was the first of a series of recollections of how this one act of hitting a helpless person had led to me being without a leg in many past lives. Next, I saw myself as a soldier in World War I again without a right leg. I had been one-legged in many of my past lives, all due to the first instance. It was probably due to my later more humane acts in other lives, in which the hatred and anger had been diluted, that I had both legs and in this one and was let off with a minor blow. I felt tears of forgiveness and compassion for myself that washed away all accumulated grief of so many past lives. After these experiences, I went about for a few days feeling a lack of sensation in the area of my right leg and had to keep feeling the leg to reassure myself of its presence.

I have had visions of many of my past lives, due to the practice given by the guru. The practice seemed to have opened up pathways in the brain, allowing these memories to surface. It definitely helped me to have a perspective on my present life. The experiences did not follow any typical routine. They could come at any time, while driving, cooking, standing under the shower, or in the midst of lovemaking, and while meditating or immediately afterwards. For me it is not necessary to be in a deep trance to recall past life incidents. I do not know how the memory is triggered off but, generally, a vision would arise, take shape and lead to the whole revelation. I would liken it to looking into a pool of water watching as slowly the vision, at first distorted or unclear, would rise and subsequently become crystal clear. How could I make out that it was a scene from my past life and not a flight of fancy? I cannot really say except that there was a familiarity with the moment, a clear knowingness about the event unfolding before my inner eye – the recognition of the characters though they looked different and sometimes were of a different gender.

Past life regression is today believed by many to hold the key to solving all problems, from relationship to economic and behavioural. From my personal experiences, I feel that once the door to this portion of the brain is opened, memories that are unrelated to the primary problem may also come unbidden. If, at this point, the seeker has no support system it can push one to the brink of madness where the line dividing the past from the present can merge and overlap, making one bewildered. Hence, I consider it important that the person experimenting with regression must have the guidance of a master and a supporting practice to assist in dealing with the revelations that come.

Evolution of the soul

Over the past few years, I have experienced strong recollections of many of my past lives. Though they did not come in sequence, I can chronicle them to show the evolution of this one single soul, from a boulder to animal to the beastly individual kicking the old man, a Native American warrior fighting for his land, the dawning of love as a Sufi devotee and so on.

I start with this experience as I feel it to have been my beginning. This happened in 1997 just before I left for Australia and a few months before I met Gurunath. In this period I went through a stage of writing poetry and part of a poem is on the blurb of this book at the back. As I sat silently in a meditative state, I felt my whole being become dense and compact. I felt cool water flowing around me while the sense of depth was intense. I saw myself, as a huge boulder at the bottom of what I felt was an immense water body. The sensation was as if I was looking out at the immense water body. As I sat motionless, I could 'see' the fish swimming around me. The movement of the water felt heavy against the body.

One day going about my daily chores, the vision in my right eye felt impaired as if filmed over. Rubbing, squeezing and washing my eye did not help. I was further disturbed as, after a few days, the left eye too filmed over, distorting my vision completely. Gradually, my surroundings changed as I looked out through what felt like inhuman eyes placed closer to the ground. There was a dense forest around me and, through the trees and the shrubs I perceived a hut or room with a flickering lamp. However, I can tell you now, that they did not look like anything as seen with human eyes. The vision of the scene was somehow elongated and in smaller frames, as if being seen through a different lens. Recognition came only from some long forgotten awareness. I was conscious of low growling sounds that came from deep within me. I felt a searing pain and the right side of my face felt as if it was on fire. It took me some time to understand that I was a black panther prowling in a dense jungle, the right side of my face rotten and eaten away by maggots. The vision in my right eye remained blurred for some more days, and then magically cleared. In that vision even though besotted with pain I was trying to make my way to rather than away from the hut with the flame of a lamp.

※

Love and romance

Reliving past life incidents definitely helped me to understand and recognise the bonds that ran through many lives, connecting me to people I share a relationship with in this one.

As mentioned earlier, I have had much anguish and multifaceted difficulties in my marriage, which finally became so divisive, that it led me to separate from my children for a short while and move to Australia for four months. But later, when I saw how long and varied the links to my husband were in life after life, the troubles that arose in this one seemed not to matter in the larger scheme of things. I have recognised him as my cousin when we were both Native American men, as my friend in World War I, and even as my son in another life. Thus, for me, awareness of my past life connections has brought a great sense of depth and maturity to my relationship with him, stemming from recognising the link that has formed through previous lives. I have no knowledge as yet of my daughters being part of my earlier lives. Interestingly, though I have tried, I have not been able to see my past life relationship with some of my closest friends and students. So, that makes me wonder if the selection of what is to be revealed and what is not lies elsewhere.

We meet again and again in different relationships to complete our residual emotions and attachments with each other. This was particularly true of my one relationship, which had left a deep wound on me. In fact, it left me shattered when we had to separate, until I saw events in my past when I had been meeting this person in many lives with the same result. I had vivid memories of a country that I recognised as the area now adjoining Afghanistan and Iran. I could feel the sun beating down on the bare landscape and feel the longing as I waited for my lover. In continuation of this vision, he left on a journey to fight in some faraway foreign land and never returned, leaving me pining.

This whole drama was repeated again, in another lifetime, this time somewhere in Europe where we are travelling in a horse-drawn carriage. Suddenly, a group of people on horses stop the carriage and drag him out, separating us, leaving me with the pangs of separation. Since the seed of desire for one another remained embedded in both our subtle bodies, we would meet and then part ways either because of social or other compulsions. This had been happening for a few past lives – the seesaw of meeting and then the separation, pain and joy, grief and elation…. Talk about compulsive behaviour! In both lives I was a woman. These memories occurred during a period when I was reliving the pangs of separation in this life involuntarily. It was as if the memories were rising to the surface, to reveal a compulsive connection carried over lifetimes, until it lost its grip.

I realised that the lessons learnt from an ardent love later transferred to my spiritual quest. I understood deeply what the Sufis meant when they talk about *ishq-e-majazi*, passion in the physical that transforms into *ishq-e-haqiqi*, divine love. The longing for the beloved, the feeling of completion however momentary, the melting and merging are all duplicated infinitely for the divine. These experiences in the past served to open pathways within my own consciousness that helped me accept with grace the manifold gifts of love and magic

I received, once I set my foot on the spiritual path. Slowly, I could feel the knot loosening to free me from the bondage of this memory, past and present. The test of true sadhana is the ease with which we detach from all these entanglements and steadfastly move on the path shown by the master.

※

Native American, Sufi and other roles

My intuitive purchase of the picture of Sitting Bull – the Native American Warrior-Shaman, during my self-imposed sabbatical in Australia, was a faint reflection of this memory, which was revealed in full later. My interest in Native American shamanic rites, the visitation by the pair of wolves, and my fluency with the rituals, while attending the workshop by Sally Perry, I take as proof of this connection. I had taken to the rituals and rites performed by her with ease and, in fact, after the programme she had invited me to become part of the group. She had been impressed by my familiarity and the easy way I had flowed into the ceremony. I felt my association with the crystals too stemmed from this era.

Further corroboration came in the nature of a vision of my husband and me as warriors who rode and fought together for Sitting Bull. The memory that flashed is of us attending a meeting of warriors. We were both between eighteen and twenty years of age, in that revelation. The scenery was largely of a plain, but with some boulders scattered around. I saw Jujhar sitting on one such boulder, sharpening what looked like an arrow or spearhead. I was sitting in the opposite end of the circle. Our physical features were different but, without doubt, I recognised the soul. Even now, scenes and sounds from this era flash upon my inner eye – a glimpse of a village, the sound of barking dogs, of gazing at alien star formations in the night skies. Unfamiliar terrain, but strangely familiar!

I realised I have been a man in many of my past lives. So, when my shortcomings as a housewife are pointed out (my sewing and washing abilities are not that great), I say, "Please give me a break – I haven't had much practice being a woman." I wonder with my vision of Babaji/Mataji in Kashi whether I am in some small way chosen to bring to light this unwarranted gender divide and its fallacious adoption by society. I will wait for that to unfold.

While visiting my native village in Kerala with my father in 2013, I was in our old ancestral home and a series of revelations happened, I saw myself as one of my own ancestors a patriarch of the family, dark, tall and imposing. A curse on the family was also revealed at that time, a curse that was given by the tortured soul of a woman much subjugated and exploited by a man of my family. Her curse was on the daughters of the family, who would suffer in the hands of other men. When I look back on my immediate family this was truly played out all the daughters had sad lives, early widowhood, loss of property, exploitation by relatives, mistreatment by spouses and often, abject poverty. The daughters in law on the other hand were not badly off at all. I was told in that revelation that by my practice and dedication to my maser I will somehow help in releasing that curse.

Though I was always attracted to Sufi music and lifestyle, my interest deepened after I started seeing Persian or Arabic calligraphy as I meditated. Lines of writing would stream by, all somehow familiar, as if I ought to be able to read and understand the script. A face that had superimposed on Gurunaths during the Shivapat transmissions kept appearing during my meditation at this time. I would excitedly describe the features to Gurunath and he would then identify the

The Flowing River of life

person. I learnt that Gurunath had been a Sufi saint in the thirteenth century, whose dargah still exists in Delhi today and, like Rumi, Gurunath too was connected to the master dervish Shams-i-Tabrizi, in fact I learnt much later the connection was closer than that. I too, had been a member of that sect then, and the face that I saw was Gurunaths as had been in that life.

During the transmissions, I would predominantly see two faces of Gurunath; one was of this Sufi saint. It was Gurunath himself who cleared the mystery of the second person I would see. He revealed that I had met him in 30 B.C. when he had been a warrior saint. Continuing to talk about our past connections, Gurunath once revealed that he had also given me spiritual initiation in Ranikhet in present Uttarakhand in 740CE. He said I was from a renowned family in South India but married a prince against my family's wishes and was banished and ran away with him to his kingdom in Kashmir where I started practicing Kashmir Saivism. Trained in classical dance I developed a problem in my legs and was guided to Gurunath who initiated me into a spiritual practice. I understood then how we were connected from many different lives and why the bonding was so strong now. I wondered if the satguru, after initiating a disciple, becomes responsible for the faithfully practicing disciple's spiritual advancement. Is that why, often, the master and disciple move together from life to life?

Sometimes it would bother me that though Gurunath was so freely accessible yet an audience would pass him by without being affected and I asked Gurunath what I could do to help them more. Very kindly, Gurunath said, "Jyoti, you concentrate on your sadhana, we are there to lookout for them. Just as we found you they will also be found." He said windows of opportunity came to everyone, some take it some being batted about in life's tsunami let it pass. But the window keeps reappearing and at some point the soul will take the leap in this life or next, until then they are just working out their karma. There's nothing to worry about he said.

My Islamic connection predominated the past life recollections at one point taking me on my first foreign tour to Dubai UAE. As I was taking a class during my visit there, I had a vivid vision in which I saw one of the students of German nationality as my sister. Both of us were of Islamic faith in the vision and were in the midst of a scene of mayhem. There were war cries all around us and she was a younger sister who I was trying to protect in vain. After class, I communicated this to the student, thinking that as she herself was on the spiritual path she may be able to appreciate such connections. But it scared her, as she may have thought that an effort to forge a relationship based on the past was being made, and I have not heard from her since. I have met many brothers and sisters and even a daughter from my past and not always do I share this knowledge with them. As for me, I have no wish to renew old ties since the whole idea of yogic sadhana is to free oneself from existing bondage, not recreate a new one from the past.

※

Australia a country of origin

My association with Australia from the past is undeniable, I always feel like a child visiting her ancestral home when I am there. When I returned in 2011, sent by Gurunath to help sow the seeds of the practices of Siddhanath Yoga, I started seeing the native elders, the original people of the land. They were tall as trees and due to an earlier experience back in India I realized they were the keepers of the land. They kept pointing me towards the east directing me to visit the centre of this land, so to Uluru I must go. On that visit I also had the opportunity

The Flowing River of life

to visit ancient spots that are not accessible to tourists. I had immersions in sacred waterways and pools where mothers birthed their children in seclusion. When I was sitting in one such pool a deep connection formed with the *swadhishthan* chakra, the chakra of the womb as if I was connected deeply with this land by birth. It's difficult to explain in words the nuances of these experiences that penetrated many layers of understanding and often the flowering of the information took place in the future.

My friend and I arrived at the small airport at Ayers Rock as Uluru had been renamed, another attempt by the explorers and pioneers to piss and mark territory. We drove through exquisite scenery to reach our hotel. That night I sat feeling quite comfortable like a little girl in my pyjamas in bed. Spontaneously my friend and I took a post midnight drive parking the car with the lights off to take in the vast skyscape, millions of stars so close to the earth, a horizon that stretched from one end to the other and a silence that was so sweet. After we came back, my friend went to sleep but I was alert with my senses in a heightened state. As I went into a deepened state I saw descending upon the earth a blazing figure like a meteor, the figure was a fused male female figure one yet two. In their collective arms, holding close they were carrying what looked like embers that I 'recognised' as eggs of souls, like sparks of intelligence to populate our earth. There was no dating this image it seemed like a scene out of a pre era, millions of years old when the planets were molten globes of fire. It's interesting to note that the topography of Uluru is burnt red as if a great fire has scorched the molten earth leaving its signature here for posterity. As we went around the ancient rock formations I saw inscribed names such as Kalawati, names that are still used in India. There were many dreamtime stories that were attributed to Uluru and one stuck to me about a snake guarding her eggs.

I was also told during this visit that I will be instrumental in bridging the old wisdom with the modern, as much of the information of the elders has been lost without being passed on. As to when in this life or the next I have no clue.

I came back to Sydney the last leg of my journey, to conclude the classes I had to conduct. The day before I was to return we had organized an event on the beach at Bondi, my old jaunt. It was the Siddhanath Surya, the solar practice formulated by Gurunath. Many attended it and one of the students mother had accompanied him. While chatting later I told her about my visit to Uluru. She was quite taken aback as she heard of my experiences there and invited me home as she was working closely with aboriginal people and their art. As her home was close to where we were I took a detour accompanied by Altaf, a teacher and main organiser of the Australian events for Gurunaths work. As I entered her house a large painting adorning her wall on top of the stairs at the entrance captivated me. I was gazing at it when she explained it was a painting of the constellation of Pleiades. According to aboriginal legend the seven stars of Pleiades represented seven women who nurtured and protected a divine radiant being in Uluru and the painting was a portrayal of it. This was amazing as this legend resonated with our own Hindu legend of the six wives of the Krittika (Pleiades) constellation nurturing Kartikeya the son of Shiva born as a burning ember from the tapa of his parents. According to hindu mythology, the six stars of the constellation of Krittika are the wives of the six rishis of the big dipper. The seventh wife of Vasishth, Arundhati having stayed on with her husband and can be seen on a clear night by his side. Moreover I was born under the Krittika nakshatra, a system followed by Indian astrologers. There were too many overlapping coincidences to be coincidences.

Full of all this information I was wondering how I will keep it alive for Gurunath who I would be meeting only after a couple of months on his return from his foreign tour. I consciously tried to file all this information in my brain in a filing cabinet so Gurunath could pull it out when I met him. Just before I boarded the flight though I received information that Gurunaths father had passed away and he was cutting short his Europe tour returning for the final rites for his father. For the first time in many years we would have the Gurupurnima celebrations at the ashram in his presence. So there I was within a few days of returning to India in the presence of my master excitedly sharing with him every scrap of information. Gurunath laughingly said, "You know Jyoti, a time will come when we wont need this form of communication, one will be able to project from the shivanetra and others will be able to take cognizance from wherever they are." What a wonderful scene that created in my imagination.

One day last year I was in Rishikesh I had just concluded my Kriya initiations and was sitting by the side of the Ganga a treat I was greatly blessed to have in my visits to this city.

The famous Ganga aarti at Parmarth Niketan had just begun and I was taking some pictures for promotional material for Gurunaths forthcoming satsang at the same venue. I looked up to see the moon and thought it would make a great frame with the temple dome and the moon in it. It was still daylight the sun still not having set, and I clicked a couple of shots. I was not using any fancy camera but taking pictures with my humble phone, when I looked closely at the picture I saw what looked like a group of dots, I looked up immediately to see if there was anything above but couldn't see anything. Imagine my wonder when I recognized group of dots to be the constellation of Pleiades. Without a doubt I considered it a darshan of Krittika, surprised at the blessing I surely was.

 Guided by intuition and open eye visitations by elders I took many short and longer trips to destinations that along with bringing to light this beautiful country also made me whole. On one such break I visited Mt. Wollumbin. I was conducting classes in Byron Bay and felt this longing to visit this mountain whose name meant cloud-catcher. Our then local teacher accompanied me; she is not with us any longer having found an alternate path to follow. I had no desire to hike up the mountain to defeat or conquer it, all I wanted was to stay at the base of that sacred mountain and see the first rays of the sunlight caress the top of the mountain. We arrived in the evening and settled down into our small caravan residence. I opted to take the smaller of the room sparsely furnished compared to the more cosy larger bedroom. There was a magical feel to the whole place an undercurrent of mystique. I meditated deep into the night feeling a warmth and protection that comes in a safe sanctuary. I was very awake but lay down to relax and as I quietly settled I saw beings around me seemingly made of light, they took positions around me and as I watched incredulously, started taking out each organ in my body, cleaning it and putting it back into place gently. The whole procedure was filled with love and I felt completely safe with no trepidation whatsoever. In the morning I felt fresh like a child, the teacher who had accompanied me duly noted this.

One look at me in the morning and she exclaimed, "Jyoti, what happened to you? You look ten years younger." All I felt was a joy and elation beyond words.

※

Connection to the land of Punjab

In reality, this portion should come under the section on my spiritual experiences, but I am recounting it here because it led me to powerful past life recollections that showed how I was connected to this land, area and people. One day in March 2003, while meditating at Panchvati before its demolition, I had seen four tall figures, between fifty and seventy feet in height, standing watch from the forest. When I asked Gurunath about them he said they were the Kshetrapals or the guardians of this land. He indicated that I am connected to this area from a past life and asked me to perform some simple acts of puja to appease them.

A year later, one early morning before dawn, I was meditating facing the full moon and, as I relaxed, I felt the gentle healing caress of the moonbeams on my body. Smiling serenely, I opened my eyes to gaze at the moon and was startled to see a face appear on it. I recognised it to be that of Yogi Sri Chandra, Baba Siri Chand as he is known in Punjab, is the son of Guru Nanak and founder of the *Udaseen Sampradaya*. He is also said to be a ray of Babaji and, according to Gurunath, works closely with him in the Himalayas. The vision communicated to me that he wanted me to visit his *akhada* that very day. I got a bit flustered, as my whole day had already been planned, so I asked if I could come the next day. At this, the face slowly dissolved and merged back into the moon. I came down from my meditation and called Ms. Chand my friend who is a great devotee of Yogi Sri Chandra. She was shocked that I was not planning to go right away but was postponing the visit to the next day. She could not believe that after such a revelation I could be arrogant enough to request to come another day and not to go immediately. When she pointed it out in this manner, I too was amazed at my conduct. I drove to Kiratpur that same day and visited the Gurudwara, which seemed very ordinary, and was disappointed that no great revelation occurred there.

Many months after this incident, the same friend asked me to accompany her to a Gurudwara in Chandigarh. Not one for visiting religious places, I tried to wriggle out, but went with her as she had broken her arm and needed me to drive her. The energy there was very powerful and I could feel my body vibrating with the frequencies of the place.

Guided by an intuition, I visited the place once again, on a full moon day, to place a *roomala* on the altar. That day, the meditation was even more powerful. Late that night as I sat meditating at home I was assailed by visions of a camp with horses being fixed with shoes and Sikh warriors cleaning their weapons; the fragrance of wood fire strong in my nostrils. I could hear horses snorting and galloping and goats bleating, and my sense of smell was heightened. I could see huge cauldrons of food being prepared for great number of people. The site was the Gurudwara I had visited; I saw a well from which water was being drawn for the horse and for the community cooking. The whole scene resembled an army camp. Later, I was able to confirm that this was the route taken by the guerrilla army of the gurus on their way to fight the oppression of Muslim rulers. Guru Gobind Singh had visited this place and Baba Siri Chand had spent many years in deep penance here. Many of the later gurus had visited him to take his blessings and Guru Gobind Singh would often camp here during the war.

However, my excitement knew no bounds when I found the old well, which was filled and boarded up many years ago. It explained why a girl from Palakkad had to come all this way to marry a Sikh boy and become one with the people here! Is it coincidence that today, I actively participate in an organisation dedicated to farmers' rights in the city? The Chandigarh Farmers Action Group was formed to fight for protection of land rights and livelihood of farmers in the city and protect farmers from arbitrary acquisition laws. I understood later this was a throwback from that life of fighting for the land with the gurus. Many udasis answered the call of the Sikh gurus at that time for a concerted fight against the ruling Mughals efforts of forcible conversion of the masses to Islam.

I excitedly took Gurunath to this place when he was in Chandigarh next time for a satsang, and was amazed to see the face of Yogi Sri Chandra superimposing on him while we meditated there. At this, even this connection to Yogi Sri Chandra fell away as I was freed from this past life memory and my present guru was revealed to be my only guide. I felt I had formed an attachment to the past, and with this revelation I sensed immense lightening as if an encumbrance had fallen away. Whenever Gurunath visited Chandigarh he always made a call on this place. On one such visit when Gurunath was still planning the construction of the earth peace temple at the ashram, he was sitting in meditation here. Just before that he had expressed a desire to help construct a temple for Shri Chandra here with his idol. After he came out of the meditation he chuckled and said he had seen Yogi Sri Chandra who told him, "You look after the making of your temple and I will see to this one". By the time Gurunath visited next the Gurudwara dome was made and the *parikrama*, the outer corridor completed.

❋

Past as reason for the present

In the beginning, the remembered incidents had no relation to on going problems or circumstances but, lately, it is more immediate and specific. When I look for answers to situation in my life, they often lead to incidents stemming from the past. Many a time I have unintentionally become privy to knowledge from other people's past lives too.

One of my friends was troubled a great deal by her mother-in-law, who was nagging and demanding at all times. My friend was at the end of her tether. Eventually, the old lady passed away, and all the last rites were performed according to custom. Later, while meditating at my friend's place, it was revealed to me that her mother-in-law had been the daughter whom she had abandoned in a previous life. The daughter was reborn to be her mother-in-law, demanding the attention that she never had as a daughter. She had actually behaved as a cranky child but, though my friend had been very kind to her towards the end of her life, some old residue of karmic debt continued to linger. I knew she would be born once again in the same family as a grandchild, to complete that relationship. Thus it is that we complete our past life obligations through our present relationships.

Some time ago, Chand, who regularly tries to test my 'skills' and is always asking me to pray for someone or the other, called to say that her guru was hospitalised in intensive care and could I please pray for him. Later, when I sat to meditate, I was astonished at the vision of her guru in hospital surrounded by many astral figures, among which I recognised Shirdi Sai Baba and Jesus. All of them were transmitting white gold energy to the prone body on the hospital bed. I understood that Chands guru had been associated with all these masters and they were there to give their blessings. And above them all, towering immensely and filling the very sky was the figure of Yogi Sri Chand, aloof and full of compassion. In the following days, I was given some messages for her guru, a devotee of Yogi Sri Chand that she communicated to him. When Gurunath visited, he reiterated those messages, making me feel more confident about my intuition.

Though excited when I was told that such experiences were not ordinary, I was confused, as I had no grandiose opinion about my own spiritual attainments. So, when I had a chance, I asked Gurunath to explain these, as I surely was not lying about them. Smiling gently Gurunath explained, "With the grace of the Satguru and influenced by his words a disciple can have these flashes of events from their past lives but the disciple must remember that this is purely due to grace and must not let it inflate their ego. Besides it is always better to put our life and dedication into the practice and not be distracted by such phenomenon as they may be real or the product of an active imagination."

I have always asserted that just knowing the past is of no significance. But, when the past is revealed as a natural part of the sadhana, it has greater meaning as it unfolds, and helps remove obstacles on one's onward spiritual journey. The brain stores every gesture, thought, word, or deed and this is the basis of the theory of karma. When the mystery of the brain is finally solved, it may clarify how the soul carries the residue of these desires and is reborn, again and again, to satisfy them. Gurunath says the seeds of karma are embedded in the DNA and thus expresses itself in this life. An overall perspective of the past helps one to understand and conduct oneself better in the present. As the heart opens with love and compassion for all humanity without conditions, boundaries and limits, earth peace and evolution become possible.

Reaping what I have sown, I constantly remind myself of my free will to choose my actions today. The present is the result of the past but the future will be a result of present actions. Attempting to act with full awareness of the consequences of my actions, offers me a way to put an end to the repetitive patterns of behaviour that are carried forward from lifetime to lifetime. Therefore, I am greatly relieved that due to my practice of Kriya Yoga today, I can hope to burn the seeds of desires embedded in my memory, preventing them from sprouting again. The breath in the Kriya Yoga crashes like waves upon the rock of desires, and a process of loosening and dissolving of old karmic bondage begins at long last. This shaking off of age-old shackles eventually leads to liberation.

CHAPTER 7

THE HOME OF THE HAMSAS

The aura of the ashram increased palpably as we neared Khadakvasla on the outskirts of Pune. I could feel the power and strength of the place pulling at me like a magnet, though the ashram was still twenty kilometres away. Accompanied by my father and Aman, I had arrived in Pune early that year in 2005 to help Ayi with her arrangements for the Mahashivaratri camp. The forest ashram is set in the idyllic surroundings of the Sitamai valley. There is no motorable road, with only a rough track leading to it over the last two kilometres. As we walked up to the simple iron-gate, the feeling was of entering an otherworldly dimension of a different vibrational frequency. The ashram appeared to be shimmering like a mirage. There was no one around, with the daily help from the village yet to arrive, so we sat down in a thatched enclosure near the entrance to wait for Hanumanta, a trusted old caretaker of the ashram environs, to arrive with the keys. The silence was deep and I easily slipped into a meditative trance. The breath became calm, long and deep, the eyes closed and focused upwards, and time seemed to have stopped still.

It is very difficult to explain the ambience of the ashram. For this, imagine the Gurukuls of the rishis of yore. The ashram is nestled in the valley, as if in the arms of Sitamai herself, dotted with trees planted and tended by Ayi that, over the years, has grown into shady sanctuaries for different varieties of birds. A pair of ravens that nest here fearlessly approach us at mealtimes, cawing politely until their demand for food is met. Even their cawing seemed to have mellowed in the sweet and enchanting environment of the ashram.

Unlike the surrounding terrain that is dry and peppered with the hardy Kikar tree, the ashram has a lush mango orchard with the cottages nestling in the midst. Ayi has carefully chosen the design of the ashram, which is all mud and thatch. The floor in the sitting and dining area is earthen and is plastered with fresh cow dung daily. The smell of mango blossoms and wild flowers pervades the environment in a refreshing manner. When I had first visited the ashram in 1999 the buildings were sparse, only two that housed a maximum of fifteen people, and the mango trees still not fully-grown. This year we had a few cottages and accommodation for disciples had increased to thirty. Today the ashram premise has grown considerably and number of people who can stay at one time up to a hundred.

❈

The enigmatic Gurumata Shivangini

In ancient days when children were sent to *gurukuls* to study and receive knowledge, the guru, and his wife who was reverentially addressed as the Gurumata, resided there and students were given holistic education, spanning from spiritual to vocational, to prepare them for life's journey. When I first met Gurunaths wife Shivangini, I was unschooled in the proper etiquette and respect accorded to the guru's wife in an ashram.

All I remember was being enveloped in an unexplainable aura of love as she welcomed me into the ashram environs with a gentle smile. But gradually, as I visited the ashram every year and was witness to the interaction between Gurunath and her, I realised the central role she played in integrating the spiritual with the material. "It is only thanks to her that you have this beautiful sanctuary of the Siddhanath Forest Ashram," Gurunath would often say, interrupting a satsang as Ayi walked past. "I was a mad yogi totally committed to my yoga sadhana and bereft of any desires and needs; left alone I might have burnt myself in the heat generated by the intensity of my tapa. It is your Ayi who managed the ashram organisation and literally put her life on line to build this place brick by brick." At this, Ayi would blush and with mock disapproval ask Gurunath to continue with the satsang instead of praising her. "Now-now, your students haven't come here to listen to this," she would admonish him. Then Gurunath, eyes twinkling mischievously, would continue, "But don't forget I was the one who got the *bijli* and *paani*, electricity and water line," he translated for the non-Hindi speaking disciples. This form of loving exchanges between Guru and Gurumata are common in gurukul-style living where disciples are exposed to glimpses of the Satguru's personal life and relationships as they go about their ashram life.

Both of them, though steeped in spiritual sadhana, revert to practicality when called for. One instance that stands out in memory is the forging of the road to the ashram. Though armed with a court approval to be allowed access to the ashram, Gurunath and Ayi were facing a lot of dissent from a neighbour, who would not allow the road to come through occupied land. Gurunath tried to have a dialogue with him but when everything failed, one day he called for a bulldozer and within hours the road had been marked, overgrowth flattened and the path forged!

Ayi belongs to the Bhonsle family of the illustrious Chatrapati Shivaji and we are sometimes exposed to her warrior-like qualities when eyes flashing – she commands the workers to get a job done or chastises a disciple for mischief done. We have heard with awe the stories of how she walked the lonely forest path with her two children, armed with a sword and rifle to protect them, from the dangers of the jungle surrounding the ashram thirty years ago.

Usually reticent, Ayi seldom speaks of her spiritual attainments, content to let Gurunath, who is also her Satguru, to take the lead. But she listens with amusement as we, the disciples, excitedly discuss our own 'spiritual experiences' and 'visions'. Her silence reveals the maturity and depth of her own personal sadhana. Gurunath exemplifies her as the epitome of a 'perfected being' who has her roots set deep into the bowels of *samsara*, while her wings fly her swiftly towards Samadhi.

※

Settling into gurukul life

While my father busied himself with his daily prayers, Aman and I organised the rooms, making sure each had mattresses, mosquito nets, sheets and blankets. We made a chart assigning rooms and dormitory beds to the disciples – men, women and children. The ashram is rustic and has basic necessities, with no extra frills like television or telephones. The checklist made us ensure that all the toilets were clean and to see that the flushes worked. Each toilet and bath had to be equipped with buckets and mugs, brush and toilet cleaner. This reminded me of an invitation our ashram received, sometime ago, to be included in a spiritual tourism programme where mainly foreign tourists and well-heeled locals were to be brought, as part of their search for nirvana. When the organisers asked for a list of the comforts we could provide, we joked that there was just a western-style commode. Needless to say, no further request to be a part of that tour was forthcoming. Once at the ashram, most of the disciples slip easily into the ordinary and simple lifestyle observed here, forgetting all amenities that, in normal life, seem essential. But over the years the ashram has taken on a more luxurious ambience, with more modern amenities, a gym, caterers for extra help in the kitchen and this year a sacred swimming pool lovingly built by our master. Gurunath is an ace swimmer and for a long time had envisioned a swimming pool at the ashram and this year we saw it taking shape at a rapid pace personally supervised by Gurunath at every stage. Immersion in the lilac pool, which has the three peaks and the Earth peace temple overlooking it, is a divine treat.

On that day though we started early with chores in the kitchen, checking stored items and lists of ingredients that had arrived from town. There would be close to fifty people residing in the ashram for the next week and there would be a Bhandara, or the community lunch, on the occasion of Mahashivratri, attended by hundreds of local villagers and their children who are given regular lessons in yogic practice at the ashram. To avoid confusion, Ayi had decided the menu for each day, along with orders for daily purchase of perishable items like milk and vegetables. By ten in the morning, we had accomplished most of the work assigned to us, with help from the hired workers. Ayi was still in the city purchasing last minute items for the ashram and Gurunath was expected to arrive late at night.

As a treat for work done, I collected a heap of cold ash from the havan-kund where Gurunath performs sacred fire rituals, and made my way up to the quaint Shiva temple on the hill overlooking the ashram. There, behaving like a true yogi, I first bathed the Shivalinga with water, then smeared ash on it, and then proceeded to smear the ash on my body and hair. I then sat in the fiery sun in proper Nath tradition doing my Surya Yoga, a form of solar worship taught by Gurunath, absorbing the life-giving energy till every atom and molecule in the body is saturated in solar brilliance. This involves accessing and applying the very essence of the sun on our body, in a protective shield, to ward off negativities.

Gurunath had once mentioned how this practice had saved him, when a crowd of angry hoodlums attacked him with wooden batons and soda water bottles. The solar energy shield had deflected the missiles before they could reach him. This happened in Gwalior in 1975, when Gurunath went to help some friends evacuate squatters forcefully occupying their tenement. The squatters were refusing to leave even after being served a legal notice by the court. This whole incident was published in the local newspaper the next day, which reported how none of the many bottles thrown at him contacted his person, and how, in fact, he had caught hold of one, smilingly quaffed the drink and then, instead of throwing the bottle back at his adversaries in retaliation, had gently rolled it back!

I was like a child imitating a grown up, but at the same time fulfilling some inner yearning, and felt very special to be able to follow such age-old traditions of the exalted yogis.

One Master one disciple

Gurunath taught us that by surrendering to the sun as our Father and the earth as our Mother, we learn to connect to the universal child within, the inner child whose nature is that of eternal joy and bliss, uncorrupted by external conditioning. This is Gurunaths gift to those of his disciples who are battered and abused and come from disturbed or alienated families. When they connect to the primordial energy of the sun and the earth, the hurt within is healed, and the yearning for parental love is satisfied manifold.

By lunchtime, a few overseas disciples had arrived and the ashram bustled with activity. The women from the village had cooked a simple meal of rice, dal, bajra and jowar rotis and vegetables. Ayi had been busy earlier, and had prepared varieties of condiments to go with it, pickles and chutneys, pounded peanuts, coconut and curry leaves mixtures, that are all traditional Maharashtrian fare. Food was prepared on a wood fire in the traditional manner and it tasted divine.

The kitchen at the ashram is stocked with utensils that are centuries old; it invokes a memory of ashrams in the ancient days, where disciples would spend years living with the guru and his wife, learning important skills. Each disciple who came left with just dues, and so it is at our ashram. Gurunath gives freely of his transmissions, his love, wisdom, healing and admonishment too. The more receptive and open the disciple, the quicker the disciple's learning and transformation.

Ashram life revolves around the guru; disciples spend as much time as possible with him, imbibing his words, transmissions, and his very essence. The air is informal with no set routines for waking, sleeping and meditation. In fact, every moment is meditation while in the presence of the master. Normally, in the morning, the disciples busy themselves with the practice of Surya Yoga. But if Gurunath is sitting outside with his morning cup of tea, the disciples tend to cluster around him, eager to share in the dialogue, with practice put off for later. There is no emphasis on breakfast and many of us miss it altogether. It is only when Gurunath leaves for his morning sadhana that the disciples also disperse to bathe, do their own sadhana, and some head straight for the dining table for breakfast.

Normally, Gurunath emerges from his meditation around noon. He is in the habit of blowing on the conch shell, calling us for a group meditation in the temple. The disciples spread all over the ashram grounds meditate with an ear out for the sound of the conch. Even though this session involves group meditation, each sadhak feels as though alone doing personal sadhana in the master's presence. After this powerful sadhana, the organisational activities in various centres, problems faced by them, achievements, and future plans are discussed. Gurunath has established three centres in India at that time Pune, Delhi and Chandigarh. These centres hold classes, organise satsangs during Gurunaths regular visits, and carry out the task of spreading the message of Gurunath through the practice of *Hamsa Yoga* and *Mahavatar Babaji Kriya Yoga*. These meetings are generally conducted in the open thatched circular hut. Sometimes, the gatherings can get loud and nasty with accusations flying thick and fast between disciples. Voices of dissent on various policies are loud and undercurrents of ill feelings are brought into the open. Gurunath is, of course, totally unfazed and is able to bring order fairly quickly; at other times he is happy to contribute his own to the on-going melee amongst the disciples. These are our brainstorming sessions and usually, at the end of it, the disciples make a workable plan and everyone feels like they have been heard.

※

Healing touch of the guru

The very soil of the ashram has acquired healing properties, saturated with the rarefied vibrations of years of rigorous tapa by Gurunath. We are instructed to walk barefoot here, though many city-bred disciples find it very painful. Yet, those who do are rewarded by miraculous healings of chronic ailments.

In the year 2002 one of my students visiting the ashram for the first time had preceded it by a weeklong binge at Goa, abusing body and mind with drugs and other excesses in the guise of celebrating New Year Eve! He was meeting Gurunath for the first time too. When it was time for the initiation ceremony, Gurunath took one look at him and said, "He is not well; how can I initiate him?" At this, the youngster made a woebegone face, for he was a sincere boy who had been looking forward to this initiation. Gurunath looked pointedly at him, as though seeing beyond the obvious, and asked him to participate in the initiation ceremony.

The first initiation is a rite in which a satguru activates the Kundalini energy of the disciple to rise upwards, sparking off the long-drawn process of spiritual evolution. Over the years, there are many levels of initiation and empowerment that the disciple is guided through to demonstrate the integrity, trust and loyalty reposed by the disciple in the satguru, as a mark of complete surrender. Often masters take tests to check the disciples' steadfastness.

After Gurunath had initiated the student who had come after partying in Goa, his right eye started watering. Within minutes the colourless liquid oozing from his eye had turned creamy, then yellow, and then putrefying green. Many attending the camp wanted to take him to the doctor, worried that he would lose his eyesight. But Gurunath, unworried, nonchalantly advised him to walk barefoot at the ashram, and to pick up and remove any stone or rubble that hurt his foot. Though his eye kept up the continuous discharge, this boy continued to walk barefoot, crying out when a thorn or sharp rock hurt him, but also picking it up and putting it aside. By the third day, he was completely cleansed, the eye clear, and the toxins flushed out. I have seen this disciple in the course of my classes as a Bhil tribal hunter in a past life. He is the same boy who got a tap on the head when in doubt about the guru.

Many disciples, after the first night at the ashram, exclaim how an excruciating pain, an irritating rash, or a recurring symptom has miraculously vanished. This strengthened my certainty that the very environs of the ashram had miraculous healing properties that cured visitors even without their conscious desire or active participation.

As I mentioned earlier, our group consists of many new-age healers, and Gurunath is always trying to wean them away from the body to the soul and spirit. To make a point with them, he sometimes holds healing sessions during which he does... nothing. "The very presence of a master is healing," he'd say. "A satguru wastes no time in healing the body. Healing just happens when the disciple is with him in a receptive frame of mind."

During one such remarkable session in the ashram, I was sitting in a relaxed mood on the earthen floor of the hut while Gurunath was resting; when I slowly felt my body lose its shape and start melting. Then, the chakras started to rotate one by one, starting from the lowest and moving upwards, a whirling and spinning until my whole being spiralled upwards and I was released from my body. I could see the whole scene below, Gurunath reclining on his *asan* with eyes closed; all the other disciples in a variety of poses, and me flopped over like a rag doll. I could even see the cows grazing in the neighbouring fields and over the hills for miles around. This is what real healing feels like, I thought, where the self, separated from the body like a bird and released from a constricting cage, knows full freedom; later there was a feeling of renewal as if I had been born again. All through this strange out-of-body experience, Gurunath was resting peacefully having- a pre-lunch nap.

That the masters' ways are unpredictable I learnt in innumerable ways. Once for no reason at all Gurunath rebuked me in front of other disciples over something that I felt was not my fault at all. Feeling very hurt and slighted I was openly weeping but Gurunath showed no mercy and kept up his censure. Crying I went to Ayi and complained about how unfair it all was. As I was sitting there Gurunath came in as if nothing had happened. When Gurumata in turn now questioned him, he looked with compassion at me and said casually, "Oh she was developing some tumours so I removed it!" Through my tears I started laughing because now I had to thank him for making me cry so.

The energy of the ashram seeped as it is in the aura of the gurus' transmissions is a nectarine bowl of holistic healing. In the years when I was actively involved in the ashram organisations for close to fifteen years, there was an unusual symptom that would manifest which I only later identified as a regular occurrence. The moment I would board the flight to my onward journey to the ashram both my legs would swell as with fluid build up. Throughout my stay at the ashram this uncomfortable symptom would persist but as soon as it was time to leave the swelling would reduce considerably disappearing miraculously by the time I reached the airport to board my return flight. An avid traveller, flying long hours up to fourteen hours to meet my family abroad and to Australia for Guru's work, I never suffered from this swelling on any of these flights. This came to my notice after a couple of years that this only happened on my trips to the ashram. It felt like a reverse healing to me as usually the healing takes place when one is at the ashram and here my symptoms occurred when I was there, the ashram soil pulling out some psychological stress when I was there and for it to disappear when I returned. The moment I stopped actively organising events at the ashram the symptom disappeared, now during my stay at the ashram my ankles are naturally slim, whatever stress was present seems to have been cured entirely.

The year 2007 saw the consecration of the Earth Peace Temple at the ashram; Gurunath being a yogi from the Nath lineage had always spoken of his desire to establish a temple for *dhyan* with a consolidated mercury shivaling as the central point. The temple for me is a symbol of what the master does for the disciple. "The mind when not tuned is like liquid mercury," Gurunath had once said. "It is distracted and when you try to catch it, the mind escapes just like liquid mercury escapes capture and the mind is as poisonous as liquid mercury. The disciple with grace from the satguru and the practice given by them tunes and tames the mind to flow in a disciplined manner and the same poisonous mind turns to nectar just as the consolidated mercury."

Once while I was sitting in front of Gurunath, I saw his form turn into a cosmic one with all the galaxies and solar systems spinning lazily in his body and the same formation in the consolidated mercury shivaling in the earth peace temple. I realised then that Gurunath and the Shivaling were one and the same. For me there is no distinction between the two of them. In 2013 I sprained both my knees, being stubborn about not going to a doctor I was doing my own thing to heal them. Despite a lot of pain and barely able to walk I continued to keep up my work at the ashram. The pain in the knee and the odd posture had started to put a strain on my spine as well

One Master one disciple

which had increased over time and caused a distortion on my vertebrae. I could scarcely walk up the steps to the temple but would hobble my way up with a contorted spine very early in the morning before ashram chores started.

This had always been my habit at the ashram to squeeze my practice in between chores that end late at night and begin early next morning continuing without break throughout the day.

Entering the temple I sat to one side extending one leg, as I could not fold both of them together, taking care not to point it towards the guru in the form of the shivaling. Though meditation was a smooth flow, I had to keep switching legs in order to stay comfortable and irritation at this was slowly building up. I was not complaining or even asking for relief or healing but just being annoyed at the discomfort. Suddenly I heard a crackling sound like at a chiropractor and the spine miraculously straightened up with complete release of the pressure on it. I tested the spine by moving around to make sure it was not just momentary but the stress, it was gone! I understood the healing touch of the guru that had come from his form as the shivaling.

Though the pressure from the spine was released and the spine sprung back to its original good health, the pain on the knee was still present. I had of course shared my healing at the temple with Gurunath, who felt the healing happened because there was no desire for it. That afternoon I was sitting at the small dining area in Gurunaths residence at the ashram, writing up some ashram accounts. Gurunath who was resting came out and said, "Jyoti, something has happened to my feet do you mind massaging them a bit to straighten them?" I was quite elated at this task, as usually it's the boys who get to massage his feet. I had never attempted it before. So though my knees hurt I sat on the floor in front of him and prepared to massage the foot when he picked up his foot and put it on my knee. With every passing moment the pressure of his foot got heavier and excruciating pain shot through my knee. But I persevered and completed massaging both feet that he had placed so painfully on both my knees. Then lo and behold when I started to get up the pain in both my knees had vanished, while I was importantly massaging the masters feet he had healed me. Seeing me stand up with ease Gurunath laughed and said, "Jyoti you have healing in your hands." I instantly felt an outpouring of love and devotion to such a being that takes care to relieve a disciples' suffering in such a thoughtful way. These experiences are not mine alone, many of the boys who massage Gurunaths feet have shared that while they were at some reflexology point on his feet they would feel a corresponding healing of their organs.

But this was not the end of the narrative with my knee pain. Sometime later I was discussing my vision of him as a cosmic being and the fact that the same pattern of the cosmos was in the shivaling for they were one when Gurunath interpolated with humour, "What cosmic being Jyoti, here I am with aches and pains all over me, my back is hurting and my knees the doctors feel needs surgery and replacement." I was very nonchalant at this dismissing his complaints, egoistically saying that when we can heal ourselves I don't believe he cannot and he must be doing it purposely. That night while sleeping my whole body writhed in pain all my joints ached unbearably. I realised in that instant that it was the collective pain of the disciple that the guru bears without complaint just because of the love for us. With folded hands I requested that from that day onwards I will suffer my own calamities, I sincerely did not want to put the burden of my pain on my master. With the realisation the pain too disappeared. Gurunaths knees that the doctors were advising for surgery and replacement healed without any intervention; magical indeed are the ways of the guru and their lessons.

Experiencing ShivaShakti

After my experiment with the ash-smearing meditation on the day of arrival, I started envisioning Shivalings that were colossal like Mount Kailash itself, sometime covered with snow, sometime black granite, gold, or mercury, but all over-powering and huge. A great hunger and yearning to dissolve in them evoked an erotic yet cleansing sensation. I felt as if I was sitting atop a burning funeral pyre and melting into it. And yet, the feeling was refreshingly cool. The desire to shed all my clothes and remove the few pieces of jewellery I wore was strong; as if it was a prelude to splitting open my body from head to toe and dropping the carcass.

    I confessed to Ayi about it, for I felt the need for her motherly reassurance that I had done nothing wrong by bathing the Shivalinga and anointing it with ash. She smiled gently as I breathlessly repeated my experiences, and that very smile told me there was nothing to worry about. Like a child with her secret out, I instantly felt better. That year, Ayi presented me with a traditional gold bracelet with twenty-one little coins, each one embossed with the Devi figure.

    "Wear it on your left hand," she gently instructed. "This is to balance the Shiva and Shakti, the male and female energy in you, Jyoti, you still have many responsibilities towards your family and many years to go before complete renunciation and vairagya." Gurunath was more direct and succinct, "Along with the ash-smearing, you have to tend home and hearth, girl," he said. Gurunath being a householder yogi is always advising disciples to complete their education, not abrogate their duties towards society and family. When young disciples come and layabout at the ashram in pretext of being hard-core yogis, Gurunath tells them, "I will give you the first Kriya, get a job!"

This bracelet nicely balanced the one that I wore on the right hand – an *Om Namah Shivaya* bracelet given by Gurunath a few years ago. "Shiva and Shakti in my own body, the Ardhanareshwar? Hmm, as long as my right breast does not flatten," I could not help commenting frivolously, making them shake their head at my overactive imagination. "I know someone who wouldn't be too happy with that," I continued in the same vein. I must have been actually quite light-headed with all the events, to say this out aloud.

Could what I had experienced been visions of the final merging with Shiva? Or was it merely a deep-seated desire in me manifesting as the vision? I had not understood clearly the potency of the purposeful act of smearing the body with ashes in the holy temple on top of the hill, imbued as it was with power. The act seemed to have led to the sprouting of an old seed of renunciation latent in me. As I have mentioned earlier, I have lived many lives as a male sadhak in the past. By indulging in this act had I now unknowingly set off a course that would lead me away from my commitments to my family as mother, wife and daughter? These questions baffled me in the following days.

Whatever it may have been, the intervention by Ayi and Gurunath had been timely and necessary. I understood that the time was not yet ripe for my life to culminate in ascetic renunciation. In my innermost feelings, I was deeply touched by this gift from Gurunath and Ayi. Having lost my mother a year ago, it satisfied some deep-felt need in me for nourishment and brought home the importance and value of family concern. Today I have realized that detachment is not indifference, I don't have to turn away from or shun anything yet there is no clinging and there is unimaginable love for all. I don't search for a solitary cave but sitting in my bed at home I have the greatest of spiritual realisations due to the lessons imparted by my master.

※

Mahashivratri – the great night of Shiva at the old temple

As the day of Mahashivratri came close, all of us disciples settled into ashram routine, as if we had known no other, the energy of the ashram soothing our disturbances, and the constant practice refining our sensitivities. Home in Chandigarh seemed like far away in another lifetime, five days at the ashram more real than all the hustle and bustle of city living. Nights were spent around the fire listening to Gurunath; questions sometimes answered, unasked.

No campfire session is complete in India without the inimitable game of *antakshari*, a form of chain singing, where two groups compete with each other. One group has to start with the letter of the song the other finishes with, or else forfeit a turn. Even some of the foreign disciples participate repeated years of visiting bringing them into the fold of what has become a quintessential Indian custom. I remember an American disciple from across the seven seas actually quite aghast when the words of a newly released Hindi song "*bheegey honth tere… kabhi mere saath koi raat guzar, tujhe subah tak main karoon pyaar…*" which explicitly talks of "spending the night together, making love till dawn" were explained to him. He could not believe Indians could be so brazen, believing them to be coy and shy about such matters! And this in spite of carrying a miniature Kama Sutra for quick referral in his wallet, which we discovered by accident!

A day before Mahashivratri in the year 2001, the sun had just set and we sat in a circle around Gurunath. As I moved into deeper meditation I could feel my breath becoming finer, deeper and longer. Enjoying this moment, my eyes opened slightly and imagine my surprise when in the seat instead of Gurunath I saw a golden cobra. I closed and then opened my eyes again to make sure I was not hallucinating but there it was. Beautiful in its majesty, coiled with its head rearing up to where Gurunaths head should have been. As I kept looking I could see the golden figure of Gurunath and this snake superimposing upon each other. My body broke out in goose bumps and a feeling of exhilaration ran through. Then slowly the figure of Gurunath crystallised and he looked straight at me as he brought the meditation to an end. When I asked for his interpretation of this magnificent vision, he said that it was the vision of the awakened Kundalini Shakti of the guru. My God, I thought to myself, how am I to understand something profound like this? For a moment I felt helpless, unable to absorb this revelation by Gurunath, then the mind seemed to expand and fill with light, calming me.

Daytime on Mahashivratri is spent in preparation for the great night of Shiva. Many fast and others eat light food keeping the system clear for the surge of energy that would flow at the auspicious time, normally around midnight. Local disciples usually start trickling in by lunchtime and the numbers grow as the evening draws near. By late evening, the ashram reverberates with chants of Shiva coming from different gatherings of disciples but united in love and devotion for that mystic figure. The temple is decorated with rangoli and oil lamps twinkle from all corners of the ashram grounds.

Towards midnight, the disciples make their way to the Shiv temple on top of the hillock, silent figures moving in file in the dark night, up the rough-hewn steps. I felt the chants vibrating within me, one with my breath and heartbeat. We arrange ourselves in a circle around the temple, leaving a path for Gurunath to come up after his special yogic preparations. The very air feels refined and rarefied with all nature at a standstill as if waiting breathlessly for Mahashiva. The legend goes that on this auspicious day, Shiva and Parvati pass through our galaxy, and they specially bless all those involved in the practice of yoga at that moment. Their love for practicing yogis is well known. Gurunath explained this as two galaxies passing through each other and all the sentient beings on all the planets in these galaxies benefitting from the exchange.

The chants are now frenzied and many disciples are achieving an almost trance-like state when Gurunath comes up. I could see his body covered in a halo radiating an otherworldly blue light. He does the simple, familiar rite of bathing the Shivalinga and anointing it with bhang while chanting the mantras powerfully. The yogic rites are much more simple and direct than the ones done by priests, and so we move into our meditation quickly.

The significance of using cannabis for the anointment, according to Gurunath, is to communicate to the disciple yogis the extent of the highest state of *Kaivalya* or unbroken samadhi that *Sadashiva* is enjoying. The disciples partake of this as *Mahaprasad* and meditate to taste, in their limited way, a portion of that sublime state and use its quality to move to higher levels in sadhana. The key word here is to meditate, for if, after the intake, they were to fall in the gutter in a stupor, the whole exercise is negated as Gurunath instructed.

The very air seemed to crackle with electric static, the passing energy palpable to many. As I sat with eyes closed in anticipation, I wondered if it was my imagination or if I actually felt a cool wave of light-like particles pass through me, swaying my body and pushing it back. I do not know, but I was left with a feeling of being scraped clean from within. As the meditation ended, we did the traditional aarti and made our way down after individually taking blessings from Gurunath and the presiding Shivaling.

It was time, then, to drink the traditional Mahaprasad. I, along with some others, had looked on with interest as it was being prepared earlier in the evening by our usual team who traditionally make the prasad every year. I had watched with fascination, as the cannabis leaves had first been ground to a fine paste as the team chanted *Om Namah Shivaya*. The chanting continued throughout the whole preparation as this paste was mixed in milk to form a liquid consistency, then ground almonds followed by spices and sugar were thoroughly incorporated into it. The resulting product had a velvety greenish hue and smelt like freshly mown grass to me. Now, a lot of controversy has been created with this habit of imbibing what is seen as a drug, as prasad. But this tradition is carried out all over our country on this auspicious day and the keepers of the law too respect this centuries-old tradition. Even traditional Indian women like my mother, who have never tasted alcohol or any other intoxicants in the normal course of their life, would not hesitate to partake of this offering.

One Master one disciple

Before the *bhang* is distributed, Gurunath immerses a Shivaling of solidified mercury in it, chanting mantras in a ritual that has come down the ages from the ancient Nath yogis. Mercury is credited with the power of alchemy, turning base metal into gold and which, when imbibed, clears the psychic nerves helping in the process of *nadi shodan*; it is also used for rejuvenation and *kayakalp* by the yogis. Gurunath, at intervals, gives us mercury tea, which is a treat for us wannabe yogis who sip it very solemnly. Of course, these rituals are to be done in the presence and guidance of a realised master as mercury has other qualities and can be fatal if taken unsupervised. So, it comes with a warning tag – *Please do not try this at home.*

Gurunath led the chant as we formed a circle and were passed a small portion each of the prasad. He instructed that it was to be drunk slowly, and explained that it was to lower the mental prejudices and subconscious defence of the disciple, so the master can work more easily to remove obstacles hampering them on their spiritual path to realisation. Sometimes certain inhibitions can hold back the disciples from realising their true spiritual potential. The slowing of thought frequencies in the conscious and subconscious mind permits the disciple to move deep within and attempt to reach new heights in meditative practice. The sipping of the bhang made me feel steadier and steadier; as I began to see the auras in bright, dazzling colours around all the people collected in the enclosure. The physical feeling was of being gradually compacted, as if set in stone, immovable but completely alert.

This traditional *mahaprasad* of cannabis has now been discontinued for various reasons; one among them being it started attracting myriads of students who only came to partake of the intoxicant and not for the more precious teachings of the master, they had started creating an atmosphere not conducive to spiritual aspirations of others.

In one of the last years of this traditional prasad being offered at the ashram, I was sitting sipping the prasad slowly. It was the year the earth peace temple had been consecrated and truth to say all the disciples including me had gone a bit overboard with meditations upon the alchemical mercury. We would sit long hours in the earth peace temple, I had my personal mercury shivaling that never left my side. I think as a result of all this energy build up I had started feeling overly erotic, I watched this pure sexual energy building up in my *swadhishtan* chakra until it was a palpable throbbing, discomfiting yet enjoyable. I sat taking small sips of the prasad while participating in the group chanting being led by Gurunath. As I went deeper into my meditation I was aware of the gurus essence passing gently around the circle clearing the disciples chakras and psyche one by one. As this energy passed by me I reflexively held back this energy, whether due to an inbuilt inhibition about surrendering it to the master or the desire to savour it, I don't know. The gurus' energy however, passed by without hesitation, clearing the chakras of the disciples. The moment the illumining energy passed I was filled with regret for holding back instead of letting go but it was too late. I was filled with remorse the next day for my act of suppression as if I had missed an opportunity at some form of purification or transformation.

But that morning while all disciples were gathered at breakfast Gurunath gently looked at my woebegone face and said, "The energy that collects, when used in the act of sex is released outwards, and that which remains will be transformed to sacred spiritual energy and turned inwards by your practice. There's no need to worry." Gurunath explains the most complex spiritual truths in a simple manner even a child can understand.

The outcome of drinking bhang can never be predicted. I have attended many Mahashivratris at the ashram and each one has been different. Sometimes the whole scene is hilarious as people drop artificialities and become natural and spontaneous. Some would go into paroxysms of laughter, while others are unable to control their weeping. Still others play out their latent desires and fantasies. One such evening, a CEO from a Delhi firm insisted on giving us a presentation on some software programme while most of us were in fits of uncontrollable laughter for no apparent reason. Another woman, a teacher, insisted at the same time, on giving lessons in physics, though she was a language instructor. However, what she said sounded so logical that I found myself actually paying attention to her and trying to understand!

I especially remember one Mahashivratri, when the whole night seemed to have passed in trying to get people to go to their rooms and bed. I would lead one to the dorm and come back to see the previous disciple wandering outside. Afraid they might stray into the surrounding forest, I tried to persuade and cajole each one into going back to bed. Finally, exasperated, I asked Gurunath if everybody would be alright. He smiled gently and said, "Of course Jyoti, you can rest now." At that, I sat down for my meditation and the surrounding air immediately felt solidified and became motionless. I do not know how long I sat thus, but when at last I made my way to my bed there was someone else on it and I had to sleep under the mango tree outside. Through all this Gurunath is the most alert, his eyes piercing as he goes about doing his divine work on subtler planes, preparing his disciples to carry on Babaji's work. I always feel there is a subtle, higher level of awareness that is just beyond our reach, and if only we could tap into that state, we will know, more clearly, the purpose for which we are being groomed.

The next day, people emerge out of their rooms slowly. Some look sheepish, others gamely laugh at themselves, still others feign ignorance, and some are genuinely forgetful about the night's events. However, the day is busy as it is the day of the bhandara. All the neighbouring villagers are invited as also the children who regularly come to the ashram every Sunday for lessons in yoga. The ashram also looks after their education and daily needs. Ayi and her helpers lovingly serve all; we too pitch in serving the various items prepared for the feast. Then Gurunath, Ayi and the visiting teachers, distribute gifts to the children who are on their best behaviour, oiled hair shining, scrubbed squeaky clean by their mothers for this special occasion. The bhandara has now taken on epic proportions with thousands of children, villagers and guests arriving for this great feast and sharing of gifts.

In 2009 during Mahashivaratri celebrations, I was resting in my room in the afternoon when I heard a loud bellow. I thought it was a bull outside on the road, but when I looked out of the window I couldn't see anything. The bellow was repeated again and this time not knowing what force propelled me I ran helter-skelter out of my room in bare feet my hair dishevelled. I saw Gurunath and a group of disciples mostly boys standing near the gate bringing down a huge heavy crate from a truck. Lo and behold when the crate was opened out came a beautiful brass Nandi, sounds a bit bizarre but I'm certain what I heard was Nandi announcing his arrival. Gurunath was so excited he was helping to pull open the crate and a rusted nail jabbed him and drew blood. After much cajoling he was driven to get tetanus shot at the local doctors. There's a reason I am recounting this incident of the nail here.

That same evening one of the other disciples who was sharing the room with me came in to show me a small Bhagavad Gita very artistically bound with gold edging and looking very precious that Gurunath had gifted her out of his own collection. She was obviously very excited and feeling special. For an instant I felt a sharp sting of jealousy as I thought to myself, wow I have never received anything so special from him. Then as is my habit I just shook my head and perished the thought. Next morning I saw Gurunath out by the Nandi and went and stood nearby admiring the intricate handiwork on this very special piece of traditional art. Suddenly Gurunath bent down picked up something from the floor and handing it to me and said, "Here Jyoti, this is for you." And strode off. I was taken by surprise and looked down at my palm to see what he had handed me; it was a piece of rusted nail. I realised that the tip of it was tinged with dried blood. It was the nail that had stabbed him the day before. I felt a sob rising as I realised this was the answer to my childish envy at the gift he gave someone else. He was telling me that he was giving his lifeblood for me and I was grudging someone else their gift. How little and foolish I felt for the momentary slip of trust. I have kept this very precious gift safely as a reminder for what the true master does for us.

❊

Collecting spiritual treasures to take back

By evening, some of the disciples are already taking leave of Ayi and Gurunath while lucky ones like me have a few more days before leaving. I am happy and also just a bit ashamed about this selfish sentiment, for I look forward to this restful time at the ashram – before disciples start to arrive, and after they have all left. The next day I witness even more leave-taking, some tearful about having to depart and go back to stress filled lives. Ayi sees them off with gifts of little jars of their favourite pickle or some condiment prepared by her. My favourite is the aam ras, which means mango nectar, prepared from ripe mangoes from the ashram trees. Quite miraculously, she remembers what each person likes and appreciates. As the last stragglers leave, the ashram settles back into a serene silence albeit refreshed with all the recent activity. We go about the business of winding up, paying the grocer, the temporary help, clearing the dorms, and finishing other mundane chores.

On one such occasion, when most of the disciples had departed, I was fortunate to have a few more days' stay left. Late at night after a cup of tea, Gurunath retired to meditate in his secret den. I was wide-awake, since I can never sleep for more than two or three hours at the ashram. I sought permission to stay up and meditate in the *paran kutir* while he was meditating below the adjacent temple, in his underground room. I sat totally alive to my environment and utterly satisfied with myself at that moment. Suddenly, my eyes were drawn to a shaft of luminous light shooting out into the sky, from the basement where Gurunath was sitting in meditation. I thought that perhaps some divine being was entering the room in which Gurunath was, but then realised that it was Gurunath leaving. I had heard about the yogic astral travel so I waited until the shaft of light returned after what seemed a long time. Then I heard sounds of activity from the room down below. I heard the door open and Gurunath came out; he looked at me knowingly and retired to his room, while I sat with my eyes as round as saucers and my jaw hanging open in wonder at what I had just witnessed.

In February 2004 after Mahashivratri, I happened to be alone at the ashram with Ayi and Gurunath since the other remaining disciples had gone down to town. In the evening, I sat alone in the temple room near the entrance not doing anything in particular, just contemplating on how lucky I was. A large print of Shiva and Parvati dominated the front wall, above Babaji's alcove. Shiva as Adinath was regal and very masculine with his flowing beard and muscular body. He seemed to personify the Himalayan ranges to me; as for Parvati, how gentle she looked, like the Mandakini River. Her compassion and love seemed to gently flow and envelop me. Then something weird happened! As I gazed at the picture, I caught a glimpse of my husband Jujhar's face suddenly flash over that of Shiva. I blinked hard, startled and confused by the strange hallucination. So, of course, I trotted away to find Gurunath to demand an explanation from him.

"Yes," he explained, "every person will see the face of his or her spouse reflected on Shiva or Parvati, as they complement each other. This is the *leela* of *srishti*. Every man personifies Shiva and every woman Shakti, but you have to crystallise this latent nature in you. The two energies are present in each individual too, the external union of man and woman symbolising the ultimate union of the energies within one's own body." How easy it is to understand deep yogic truths when explained so simply by the master.

His eyes twinkled as he continued with humour, "How do you know when your husband stands there demanding something that it's not Shiva himself?"

"Do you remember when we visited Jwalaji I had told you, at Mother's altar, that if you look with reverence, you will see the face of your own mother juxtapose on the Divine Mother's countenance?" he reminded. Then I remembered the dissolving of the Divine Mother's face into my own mother's for a split second. How could I have forgotten that powerful experience? I had been so moved by it then. I immediately decided to be more loving and caring at home when I got back. Whenever I get short-tempered, upset, or exasperated with Jujhar's behaviour, I recall that superimposition on Shiva's face, and am instantly lightened, relieved of all negativity.

※

Dasamdvar sanctuary at dale farms

I came home from that trip in 2004, greatly energised and rejuvenated after my sojourn at the ashram. A small desire blossomed in me to create some space like the ashram on my farm. I knew just the right location for it. Ever since the demolition of Panchvati, I had felt the need for a room to practice yoga and take classes. I would have to tread carefully, for money was scarce. So I did what I do best – be stubborn and insist on having my way. After heated arguments and shouting matches sprinkled with subtle emotional tactics, I got what I desired, a separate room on the roof for my meditation.

From the beginning, everything moved smoothly, as the masons and the labourers were the ones who seemed to find me rather than the other way around. A friend designed the room, bringing a special craftsman to make a traditional domed roof without using any iron or shuttering. As he worked on the roof, it felt as if it was being held up by sheer divine will. The room gives the impression of being of mud and thatch, with a sprinkling of straw to create an authentic ashram effect.

The room felt blessed, the air charged with the energy of the guru. We started regular practice there and when Gurunath visited after a few months, the energy multiplied with powerful meditations and group activities. I had a regular stream of students coming to meditate here and the room came to be known as the temple room. By mere chance, the room has nine windows and one door, the nine windows signifying the nine openings in the human body with the tenth door or dasamdvar, symbolising the entry point of spiritual light into us or the exit point for the realised soul to move on. Open to the elements yet protected from them, I have had some awesome meditations there during full-blown thunderstorms and lightning, in the blazing afternoon sun and on full moon nights.

On Guru Purnima day of 2005, I was frustrated, as many disciples were not going to be able to make it. For me, nothing was more important than this full moon day, which was the annual occasion to profess undying love for the guru. It was late as we assembled for the moon meditation for earth peace.

As the few disciples gathered, I became aware of a presence in the room, and I was startled to see a light shimmering beside Gurunaths large photograph on the wall. The vision slowly cleared to reveal Ayi. She was resplendent in all her finery, the jewels she wore throwing off sparkling light. Gurunath was blazing in his starkness, to which she was a contrast, and yet she complemented his simplicity with her plenitude.

Gurunath has mentioned in his book Wings to Freedom, how he had fought using psychic weapons powered with mantras, a shakti called Yogini Velsa. At the time, he was a staunch, celibate yogi and was incensed by the advances of this Yogini Shakti, the powerful female yogi who was testing him. He lost the fight to her but pleased her with his steadfastness and courage. She had prophesied his marriage to Ayi, further adding that after their children were settled, with children of their own, his wife Shivangini would join him in sadhana, so her latent Shakti would fully blossom and propel her to great spiritual heights. Then I noticed that, by some quirk of divine inspiration, we were sitting in a formation that Gurunath makes us adopt during our powerful Kundalini *yagna* at the ashram, the women to the left in a half circle starting from Ayi and the men to the right completing the circle at Gurunath. This was a special fire rite ceremony that Gurunath would sometimes lead after a lot of cajoling and beseeching from us and after we like children would go and ask Ayi to convince him. Gurunath prescribes the direct path of Kriya Yoga to his disciples' as it is simple without discrimination. That evening I felt my body vibrating with the chants, which spontaneously emerged from my mouth. All of us were chanting in unison, and the powerful energy of Shiva and Shakti started spinning around the circle. This transmission went on for more than half an hour, after which we sat meditating in silence.

Now, the temple room feels more blessed and complete. Infused with Ayi's Shakti, it has truly become a part of the mother ashram in Pune. Since then, the room has developed gradually to become more and more sacred, witnessing many initiations by Gurunath during his annual visits, and numerous students who come to learn and practice their sadhana. From a stark, bare room the space has now acquired terracotta flooring and earthy blinds, everything seeming to happen on its own. It is as if the seed that I carried has germinated and taken root to become a centre to spread the work of Gurunath.

This year despite my estrangement from Jujhar we are both in the process of putting in more rooms and an external community kitchen and extra showers. Since I have students who come from all over to learn the practices of the Siddhanath lineage and as our community in Chandigarh is slowly expanding this space is taking shape as an oasis. The poultry now non-operational has given us the foundation of the construction. I was quite amazed as I in my typical nature did not have a desire or expect Jujhar to even consider setting up such an infrastructure. When Gurunath visited Chandigarh this year after a gap of ten years he was pleasantly surprised at the way this space was coming up and said that it was Guga Chohan who was overseeing this activity. Guga Chohan was the disciple of Gorakhnath whose *vibhuti* in Gwalior Gurunaths mother would mix with water and drink during the period of gestation before Gurunath was born. As it happens he is also Jujhars family kula guru, this fact was also brought to light first by Gurunath when he heard that Jujhar's family surname was Bachal and that they had migrated from Rajasthan. There was also an incident of a photograph I had of Gorakhnath that I kept in Gurunaths room when he was visiting us, only to be told that the other figure in the picture was none other than Guga Chohan. When I visited my in laws ancestral home, for the first time imagine my elation when I found the temple of Guga with the feet of Gorakhnath in the outskirts of their village. How interesting are the ways of destiny to be married into such a family who were themselves unaware of the connection.

Another interesting anecdote is about the name of our farm and its connection with Gurunath. Since Jujhar also studied in Sherwood College, he named the farm Dale Farms after the house that he was head boy of, Allen-a-Dale. When Gurunath visited us the first time in 2000 he surprised us by saying his house too was Allen-a-dale, and confidently he said this is my space! With all these blessing and signs is it any wonder that this space is taking on a life of its own. Developments happening as if by some divine intervention while I stand aside like a bystander.

My centre called āyu is dedicated to teaching and practicing the teachings of Gurunath and is slowly gaining recognition in the city and its surroundings with a very stable foundation of strong disciples of Gurunath. Every full moon we sit for a long silent meditation of four hours at night deepening sadhana and taking the many benefits of the transmissions of Gurunath at the temple room, where his seat has been laid since fifteen years and his presence is beyond doubt, felt by all who meditate here.

CHAPTER 8

AROUND THE CAMPFIRE

The campfire goshtis are a common custom in the guru-disciple life in India. As with other vernacular words there is no English equivalent to describe these discussions or question and answer sessions. It is an ancient tradition of the master and disciples sitting around a fire. These sessions can carry on until late at night with chanting giving way to meditative silence and questions from disciples leading to the master removing doubts and fears. Ribald jokes peppered with expressive gaalis are not unheard of either at these intimate sessions. In fact I learnt to use all the rustic swear words with abandon, after entering the yogic path.

On one such evening at the ashram, I watched, mesmerised, as the embers from the fire crackled and sparked. The fragrance of the wood smoke was strangely nostalgic and the silence palpable as we waited for Gurunath to join us in our late-night meditation. Gurunath often comes out even after retiring to his room and the veteran disciples who know this wait with anticipation for these very personal moments spent with him around the fire. The aura was easy and relaxed as

Around the Campfire

some disciples meditated while others chatted softly, and yet others sprawled dreamily on their mats.

The light breeze stirred the flames of the fire and they danced as Shivraj, Gurunath's son and disciple of Gayan Saraswati Kishori Amonkar, spontaneously rendered Adi Shankaracharya's Nirvanshatak to a tune he had composed. Shivraj sings only when the mood overtakes him. I was moved by the words and the melody, "...I am born neither of the father nor the mother, I am not the friend or the guru or disciple, I am not the food or the person satiating hunger, neither am I the earth, fire, or wind. I am none of the emotions and passions inherent in man; I am neither the mind nor the intelligence, neither a sinner nor a doer of good deeds....I am the exact image of Shiva... I am the exact image of Shiva..." The music tugged at my heart and tears welled up in my eyes. Shivraj's music is a great inspiration in the nights around the fire. My being resonated with the music and, accompanied by the meditative and rarefied atmosphere of the ashram, it transported me to an altered state of mind.

The campfire plays an important role during all Hamsa gatherings. Whenever we are together the day is not complete without this time spent around the fire. *Dhuni* – traditionally the fire of the Nath yogis, *havan* – sacrificial fire rite, campfire, a jolly bonfire, the activity is addressed by all these names though traditionally and technically they are all different depending on the purpose and identified by the shape and materials used. However, here the visitor may easily find the campfire and the havan addressed as dhuni. At the ashram, we do not yet have the traditional dhuni, commonplace to Nath habitats. It entails a great responsibility, as the fire in the dhuni needs to be constantly kept alive and not allowed to die out. Some dhunis like the one in Jwalaji are burning since two thousand years. But Gurunath has taught us that everything external is internal it's the fire rite in the spine that has to be kept alive. He calls Kriya Yoga the *pran apan yagnya*.

However, the *havan* used to be held often at the ashram. This is a purification ritual, which Gurunath conducts accompanied by Ayi, to invoke the Kundalini Shakti. Sacrificial offerings are made of rice, clarified butter and sometimes coconuts, limes or the Bael fruit. The formation of the circle is special and Gurunath directs us on how to sit. The energy released is very powerful and I carry the vibration of the mantras chanted within me, long after coming back home to Chandigarh.

Sitting by the bonfire, I become like a child listening to tales narrated by Gurunath who, like a master storyteller, can transport us back to the era in which the event took place. These amazing tales of Himalayan saints send a wave of exhilaration through me no matter how many times I hear them. When Gurunath describes these events, I feel connected to these ancient sages through him. Often, Gurunath picks up disturbances in the disciple's mind and offers solutions unasked. At other times, insistent questioning by a disciple may be ignored and bring forth no answers from him.

In our ignorance, spearheaded by our ego, we often ask frivolous questions of the master, though the answer given may be unexpected and profound. During our stay at Jwalaji, we were sitting around the campfire when a disciple asked Gurunath to tell each one of us our weaknesses and how we should overcome them. I thought he would point out bad habits such as smoking and drinking or maybe lack of will power or other such personal limitations. However, I was completely bowled over and moved to tears when he replied simply that he was our weakness and, therefore, our weakness would be our strength.

Around the Campfire

Questions that come from a deep yearning to know are the ones that most easily elicit a reply, and woe betide the disciple who asks a question flippantly to show off personal intellectual knowledge. I am one of those who contribute least in the goshti. Somehow, in the presence of Gurunath I have no questions. Seemingly at a loss for intelligent queries, I often feel dumb.

When Gurunath answers questions about deep yogic practice he takes you into the process. A true masters voice carries life force energy, every word is like a directed missile that can heal, enlighten or resurrect the disciple. Many mature disciples often wait for such questions to be effortlessly transported to another realm of awareness. My favourite is one question that is often asked by an intellectual audience about the various levels of samadhi. Every time Gurunath explains the various levels I experience the states that he describes so the moment this question is asked I sit quickly in a receptive mode to receive the wisdom and to experience it. My joy knows no bounds when I hear this magic question, "Nath, how many states of samadhi are there?"

❈

The enigma of Nath yogis

I have heard the following tales, anecdotes and stories many a time during innumerable nights spent by the fireside with Gurunath. Every time it is as fresh and exhilarating to hear the sagas of these ancient beings the path breakers of the techniques we were practicing.

A photograph of Raja Sundernath, an ancient Nath yogi, sitting cross-legged in a state of samadhi adorns our temple room at the ashram in Pune. He is bent slightly under the weight of the snow fallen on him, his elbow resting on his knee and his dreadlocks dusted with snow falling to the side. According to Gurunath, this majestic figure in the picture embodies for him, the antiquity of our country and the spiritual wealth that yogis of Sundernath's stature are silently contributing to us. Most of us have gazed at the picture with awe, one of the grandmasters of the Nath yogis. The picture is so life-like that I childishly wondered how I would feel if he just opened his eyes and looked at me, for I could palpably feel the compassion stored in them.

Late one night, we were sitting around the campfire and nobody wanted to be the first to get up and retire to bed, thereby breaking the magic of the evening. The logs of wood were smouldering and a disciple gently added a few more logs to rekindle the fire. Gurunath was talking about his association with Raja Sundernath whom he had met in the Himalayas during his days of tapa.

"Do you know that some of the sadhanas that you practice of the Hamsa Yoga were communicated to me by him?" He asked, looking around at us gently. My mind boggled at the thought of how tangible the thread was that connected us to these Himalayan masters who are said to be hundreds of years old. With a faraway look in his eyes, as if recollecting the past, Gurunath recounted the following incident, which was a turning point in the age-old Nath tradition of taking part in the Maha Kumbhmela at the Prayag in Allahabad.

"It was the Nath yogis who rightfully took the first bath during Kumbhmela at the confluence; this tradition had been established since thousands of years," he said. "But every year, bickering and petty fights would start among the akhadas of various sects of yogis, as to who would bathe next. During one such Kumbh, as Sundernath was sitting and meditating, a fight broke out and, in the melee, someone accidentally hit an axe on the meditating yogi, splitting his head. At that, Raja Sundernath calmly got up, unmindful of his brain spilling out. He declared that from today the Nath yogis would not take part in the Kumbh and, collecting himself, he just rose up into the sky in his physical body, and left for the Himalayas where he is meditating to this day. So even today, in obedience to that diktat, the Nath yogis as a group do not take part in the Kumbh. They may visit incognito or in their individual capacity but as a sect they are supposed to stay away."

We want to know more, so we look expectantly at Gurunath, silently extolling him to continue. "But do you think he was left in peace there?" Gurunath asked in an exasperated tone, as if feeling the irritation of these Himalayan sages. "No, even in the Himalayas, Raja Sundernath was not left in peace," Gurunath continued. "For, while meditating, sitting motionless in Badrinath for many years, he became covered in snow and looked like a stone sculpture. Some children found this frozen figure shrouded in snow and, out of curiosity, placed a burning piece of charcoal on his thigh, which sunk deep in. Thus disturbed from his deep samadhi, he has now moved higher into the mountains in search of solitude."

My imagination flew with this thought and I saw pictures of yogis frozen in snow meditating, in caves all over the Himalayan ranges. The sudden bursting of a log into sparks interrupted my reverie and I saw some disciples stretch and shuffle before they moved into the dorms to catch a little sleep before day dawned.

With the pressure of population, yogis are being pushed further into the higher reaches of the Himalayas where they meditate for the wellbeing and proper evolution of our young universe. Raja Sundernath is said to roam the Himalayas and, to avoid disturbance, transform himself into a tiger when confronted by village folk or travellers. When Gurunath was in this area with the directors and crew of his film Wings to Freedom, he was overtaken by a desire to meet his mentor Sundernath, and mentally asked for permission to come pay his respects. The denial came as one word "No," accompanied by a shaking head and finger. He did not want to be discovered by a crowd; if Gurunath was to come alone he was welcome. There was no mincing of words or attempt to be polite. The genuine Nath yogis are known for their fiery temperament and no-nonsense attitude. They are the embodiment of compassion, sharing their spiritual wealth with others, but have no time for social niceties. Though Gurunath is in communication with Raja Sundernath on the astral plane, like a child, he desired to visit him physically in his abode in the Himalayan cave, and was sorely disappointed that he could not.

This fiery trait is visible in the ascetic of the Nath tradition even today. While visiting Jwalaji with Gurunath, our entire group stayed at a guesthouse established and run by a group of Nath yogis. They were hard practitioners of tough yoga sadhana. One of these yogis would come to the guesthouse every morning, driving really fast on his scooter in the bitter cold, bare-bodied, but for a thin cotton cloth tied around his waist and dreadlocks flying in the wind, while we sat huddled around the fire with hot cups of tea to warm us on the chilly winter morning. One of our American disciples in true western attitude of charity, taking pity on him, asked me to interpret for her as she offered him an expensive shawl to keep warm. He gave her a piercing look and said to me, "Tell her that I am wearing this cotton cloth because of her. Otherwise, I roam naked in the woods with ash smeared on my body." He had no need for her sympathy or generosity.

At night we would sit around the large lifelike statue of Matsyendranath ensconced in a niche, to whom the yogi caretakers of the guesthouse were dedicated. The statue was wrapped tightly up to the shoulder in a light ochre colour cloth, the hallmark colour of the Nath yogis. On both shoulders of Mastyendranath were two lotuses facing up. It was then that Gurunath revealed that the lotuses symbolised different universes and that below the cloth wrapped around Matsyendranath the stems of the two lotus join in front of the navel forming a channel that reveals the secret wormhole path these great beings take to travel from one universe to the other. Like a child I wondered what it would be like to traverse this route, how amazing to exit from one universe to emerge in another. How wonderful to be privy to these secrets shared in hushed tones sitting with a group of ascetics while the dhuni crackled gently.

❋

Gurunath introduces Lalla Jogeswari

"Bhavati, Bhiksham Dehi," is the clarion call, the stentorian voice of yogis asking for alms at the door, said Gurunath. According to him, when a Nath yogi calls out thus for alms at your doorstep, it is not begging but the demand of the bhikshu's right to food from society. It is considered their right because they dedicate their lives to the search for God and their meditation helps society to evolve. Householders with responsibilities participate symbolically in this journey by giving alms to make the journey of the yogis less taxing. According to their guru's instruction, these bhikshus can make this act either more or less difficult. Some cry out only at one house, others at three or more. Some do not use a receptacle, accepting only what they can hold in both hands, and others in a single palm. Of course, there are charlatans and crooks and petty thieves taking advantage of this custom, but, when on the path, one hopes to develop the wisdom to distinguish between them and act accordingly. I pray for this intuition, for I do not relish the thought of being the one to shoo away any of these stalwarts from my doorstep.

Once when in Mumbai a friend had mentioned the name Lalla, her name had immediately invoked the image of a naked stark ascetic in front of a colossal Shivaling upon my inner eye. The power of that flashing image had left me momentarily stunned. At the next opportunity, I had questioned Gurunath about her. He answered that Lalla was a Shivbhakta who remained outside the purview of societal norms and roamed in the Kashmir valley. She wore no clothes and the reason she gave was that since no man she knew was a 'man', she was not coy of them.

One day, as she attended a village wedding, from outside came the sound of a mendicant crying out in a commanding voice Bhavati, Bhiksham Dehi. To the amazement of everyone present, Lalla ran and jumped into the burning furnace on which the meal was cooking. A while later, she emerged from it unharmed, dressed in a beautiful sari, embellished with golden threads and was resplendent with her jewellery sparkling. Covering her head coyly, she bent down to touch the feet of the alms seeker who was none other than lord Shiva!

My interest in Kashmir Saivism has a feeling of familiarity not arising out of any connect from this life. But whenever I have read any texts pertaining to that era, I have felt a saturation beyond explanation. My understanding that Gurus come to guide disciples in every life was reiterated when browsing the Shiva Sutras, an important text of Kashmir Saivism I realised that Gurunath had already familiarised me with the precepts of the text in this life without referring to them. But Lalleswari was ever present in the periphery teasing me with a glimpse of sometimes her poetry and sometimes with stories recited in groups.

So when I had a chance to be in Srinagar, as usual accompanied by Aman and Babit, I was overtaken with a desire to find the temple that Lalleshwari did sadhana in. Research did nothing; just pointed us to a mosque built in her name much later, while I knew she was a shiva bhakt. When I asked a friend who has been closely studying Lalla, she said the temple was deep in a terror-infected area near Srinagar and the army did not let anyone go there. But of course once I make up my mind I feel the universe, read guru's grace, comes out in support. I smartly roped in our driver who was a local to take us there, he turned out to be as adventurous as me, Aman and Babit didn't need any convincing, they were in the car in a flash.

Except for a general direction we had no clue how far or how deep into Kashmir we would be going. We started right in earnest though making our way towards our self-imposed destination. Our driver stopped at every diversion talking to the locals and sometimes going in one direction then turning around with new inputs to follow another lead. Throughout the journey there was a feeling of exhilaration, no despondency and definitely no doubt that we will make it. Finally after a couple of hours we reached what looked like a bus stand of a hamlet and tucked in behind it was the shiva temple where Lalla had practiced austere penance. The temple was her Guru Siddha Srikanth's and was dilapidated and locked. But the temple priest lived close by and we went and procured the keys to the temple from him. He was so happy that some devotees had made this trip to the temple that he left saying we could spend as much time as we wanted and invited us for a cup of tea later to his house.

Our elation knew no bounds as we sat inside the temple meditating like yogis. We first washed the shivaling with water then lit some lamps that the priest had kindly provided. I was overtaken by a desire to shed my clothes and sit starkly naked, as Lalla must have done. Next day we were back in Chandigarh and heard there had been a bomb blast near the bus stand at Pampore, the village we had visited. But throughout our journey to the temple not once did we feel threatened or anxious.

※

Day trips around the ashram

It was a pleasant breezy evening and we were walking in the forest surrounding the ashram. We disciples, along with the master, had been shooed out of the ashram premises by Ayi who needed some respite from the incessant demands of the visiting Hamsas. Many of the disciples were carrying dandas, long wooden batons, hitting them on the ground as they walked to scare away wild animals. I felt like an erstwhile yogi with my hair flying in the breeze, busily on my way to the next destination!

When we came to a clearing, Gurunath indicated that we sit and relax for a while since there were still some daylight hours and the ashram was near. We needed no coaxing as collectively we sank to the ground; some of the disciples sprawled gazing at the sky, others sat with pensive eyes looking at the distant mountains, and there was a feeling of ease and peace with

Around the Campfire

oneself. Gurunath was telling us about an incident when his friend and he had trekked up to a faraway peak which he pointed out to us. They sat to meditate outside the mouth of a cave after ascertaining that it was empty. As they sat with eyes closed, his friend heard a snorting sound and, thinking it to be the growl of a panther, started running helter-skelter down the hill, leaving his shoes behind. When, swearing and cursing, Gurunath had caught up with him and enquired about what had happened, the friend breathlessly explained that he had heard the panther. Gurunath told him that the sound had been him clearing his throat of some irritation. At that, both of them had broken into paroxysms of laughter just as we did now.

As the laughter petered out, one of the disciples, suddenly serious, asked Gurunath how much meditation is required to achieve a state of samadhi and nirvana? As an answer, Gurunath recounted this following incident about Tapasviji Maharaj, with a mischievous smile. Tapasviji Maharaj was from Punjab and had walked the length and breadth of ancient India. He lived to the age of over three hundred years. Meditating fifteen to twenty hours a day, for so many hundred years, he had an intense longing to meet Shiva. With this one-pointed thought, he trekked up Kailash Parvat in the Himalayas. As he neared the top, he saw a being of great stature walking towards him. This person was tall with matted hair and ash smeared on his body, which was shining with a divine blue light. Tapasviji immediately fell at his feet, not believing his good fortune to be face to face with his beloved lord. Then the great sage spoke, "I am Durvasa," he said, "there is yet time for you to meet Shiva, so go back and come later." So Tapasviji made his way back to the plains. Apparently, he did have his experience of Shiva in later years but his physical body did not survive the experience for long after that. It is said that a meeting with these great beings is akin to passing a surge of a million volts of electric current through the body. Gurunath describes the lustre of the divine energy in the following words: "If, at one moment, time and place, the sunburst of countless suns occurs then this would scarce express thy shadow. Oh lord, what must be thy light?" At this, my mind stops functioning since this picture is too dazzling to be visualised or absorbed mentally.

The constant rigours of yoga sadhana prepare the yogi to endure such encounters. Gurunath says that when we start practicing for fifteen to seventeen hours a day, the big guys would start to notice that a youngster is striving to meditate. That was not to say that our effort now would not bear fruit, since it was a preparation for longer hours of sadhana. Since this is an ever-evolving path, there are various levels to be reached involving different measures of practice. Gurunaths love and compassion for the disciples is always apparent, his encouraging words driving us on. Once he was telling us how a true guru to lead the disciples to light has to be at least three hundred million years more evolved than the disciples. At our incredulous face he immediately followed it by saying, "But I can hear all of you breathing down my neck, saying hey guru wait for us. We are catching up." That of course left us all smiling widely.

Then, as the shadows were lengthening in the setting sun, we got up to make our way back to the ashram. Walking silently, I renewed my resolve to continue and increase sadhana. The forest came alive with the sound of insects interspersed with the distant call of jackals, as we hurried back towards the welcoming sight of the twinkling ashram lights.

To break the monotony of daily ashram life and also because as we didn't have a generator then and the ashram would have no electricity on a certain day of the week, Ayi sometimes organised a day tour and picnic to nearby ancient temples for

Around the Campfire

the disciples. Many of these temples have special significance for us as Gurunath has performed intense sadhana here. On one such tour, we were at the Saswad temple near Pune. The temple has a powerful Shivaling and a huge Nandi bull outside. We were sitting outside the temple after a morning meditation session and waiting for the food we had brought along with us to be served. The sun felt pleasant in the winter afternoon, and the smell of the packets of food being opened was tantalising. Gazing at the Nandi standing guard, Gurunath smiled and said, "Will you believe me if I told you that this Nandi once got up from its place?" Seeing our disbelieving look, he told us about this incident, which is part of the legend at the Saswad temple.

It happened, Gurunath said, when a group of Nath yogis were camped here for the night. After their supper, the yogis were enjoying a shared *chillum* by the fire. This attracted other devotees visiting the temple, who collected around the fire to hear the yogis exchanging tales, and some to try their luck at getting a puff on their pipe. We were sitting at the same spot a few decades later.

At the gathering, one of the devotees had loudly started questioning the truth of magical incidents and lamenting that such events did not occur anymore. Plaintively, he was complaining about the absence of yogis of great calibre in this age. So, one among the visiting group of yogis raised his hand and told him *"Chup,"* to shut him up in the inimitable direct style of the Nath sect, and pointing at the stone bull, commanded it to get up. While everyone watched in amazement, the bull rose from its place. Then the yogi ordered the bull to graze on the grass surrounding the temple, so it ambled out into the meadow and chomped on the grass with its stony jaw. When it had finished, the yogi instructed the bull to come and crap in front of the suspicious devotee. When the bull evacuated its bowels, the dung was pure gold dust. The suspicious devotee was shivering and chattering in fear as he fell at the feet of the yogi and begged for forgiveness. Gurunaths recounting was so realistic and my imagination so vivid, that I could see the Nandi carved out of the gigantic black boulder get up and do as the yogi commanded.

※

Emulating the Nath yogis

Our group consists of many who practice new-age healing techniques and Gurunath watches their attempts at healing with amusement. Once, seeing a disciple missing sadhana to give healing to another disciple with a headache, he recalled this tale of a Nath yogi gloriously drunk in his love for the divine, walking down the street of an Indian town. A dead body was lying outside the cremation ground. As the yogi walked past, his toe brushed against the cloth with which the body was covered and the man sprang up alive. However, the yogi unmindful of, and uncaring for, such miracles walked on. As for the healed, Gurunath felt that if he had utilised this new lease of life in pursuit of the divine, it was a life saved. But, if he went back to his old ways of immersing himself in the external world then it was a wasted life anyway. Gurunaths examples are to guide us in a direction away from the body towards the soul. Though in his presence blocked arteries have opened, knee and joint pains have vanished, tumours and stones have dissolved, yet he is a yogi satguru who gives secondary place to healing of what he calls the "apparent self" – the body.

The yogis of the Nath tradition too attempt to prolong their life in a healthy body, but only to pursue their single aim of merging with Shiva in this lifetime. Staying in cool climates to discourage the decomposition and decay of the body, they practice rigorously for this one goal of self-realisation. Some, when they reach a debilitating age, go into solitude and perform the process of *kayakalp* or rejuvenation. The secret practices include special diet, treatments with herbs, imbibing mercury and other alchemical substances, and rigorous yoga practices. The results of these are a reversal of the decaying process of the body, and the yogi emerges in a younger body ready to continue with the sadhana. Every act they commit is to push them towards the goal of self-realisation using the physical body as a vehicle to realise this end.

I realised that with Gurunaths guidance, we, his disciples, were all following lifestyles that were most certainly leading us on this path. For instance, Gurunath is constantly monitoring my meditative practice; close association with him has influenced my food habits. I now eat mostly organically-grown fare, keeping the stomach clear with light, easily digestible food, and am conscious of the bodily requirements of nutrients guided not by medical reports but an inner sense of equilibrium. For many of us, Hatha Yoga practices are a part of daily routine along with the solar meditations. The master's transmissions and his introducing us to the usage of mercury under his strict supervision, all work at reversing the ageing process of the body. We are duplicating in our life the conduct of the ancient yogis of our country. Most of us are gradually becoming fearless in our opinions, conduct and, above all, detached from the result of all these activities. In my case, concern for the environment makes me follow natural organic living; resisting ills in society translates into fighting for farmers' rights.

These habits flowed naturally, were not cultivated and, as befits a yogi, there are no fanaticism about adhering to them at the cost of the yoga practice. That single-pointed focus reserved only for the yoga sadhana, everything else is secondary. This realisation seemed to wipe away the passing of thousands of years, making the yogic lifestyle immediate in the presence of a master.

As novitiates, many of us in the group are enamoured by the stature of the Nath yogis and try to emulate them more in the physical, since that is noticeable. Some of the disciples try to form dreadlocks by leaving their hair unwashed and rubbing ash on it. Others think smoking the chillum and saying *"Bum Bholey"* is cool and they have arrived on the yogic path to nirvana. Many of them visibly sport tattoos, r*udraksha*, and ornaments of precious stones just for effect, and yet others put on an arrogant attitude. Gurunath guides each disciple, whenever necessary, away from acquired habits and he does this with ease, with a unique personal relationship with each individual sadhak. If asked every disciple will have a personal incident to retell that is unique to them and Gurunath.

It was inevitable that interest in the Nath yogic traditions would kindle our curiosity about samshan sadhana. The yogis of the Nath tradition commonly meditate in cremation grounds mainly to conquer their fears and to test the skills acquired through rigorous sadhana. Gurunath, in his younger days, had indulged in many such practices and would often tell us about the pros and cons of tantra sadhana. He disclosed how, while meditating in such scary conditions, rabid dogs, apparitions of scary ghouls and seductive women, would visit the yogis. Throughout all of which, the yogi had to meditate with equanimity. He cautions disciples who are attracted towards such practices due to their sexual overtones. Though attractive to the physical, to be spiritually effective, this path requires immense purity in action, word and deed on the part of the adherent. Impurities in thought and even momentary absent-mindedness in performing exacting rituals can lead to harsh retribution.

Gurunath advocates the path of Hamsa Yoga, which includes Surya Yoga and Kriya Yoga, to his disciples as a complete discipline that will lead them relentlessly towards spiritual evolution. These practices avoid the perils that lurk on the path of the more harsh practices of Tantra Yoga and being the lightning path are speedier than the latter.

One day, during the course of discussion of cremation ground sadhana, he told us about a hilarious incident that happened when his friend and he had decided to meditate in a local cremation ground. They had sat in deep meditation until three in the morning, at which time, they had emerged from the grounds to come face to face with two men. Suddenly confronted by two figures clad in loincloths, with red eyes and ash-smeared bodies outside a lonely cremation ground, these men had screamed "Bhoot, bhoot," and run off, dropping whatever they were carrying in their hands. Gurunath and his friend picked up the dropped objects, which turned out to be jewellery and cash, and it became apparent to them that the persons who ran away were thieves who, after looting, were on their way back to their quarters. Gurunath and his friend went to the nearest police station to hand the loot in so it could be returned to the owners. The police however took one look at their appearance and instead of believing them, put them in the lock up as suspects! Gurunath's father had to bail them out in the early morning hours.

By nature a bit impatient, my attention is normally on getting on with the job with scant attention to details. Gurunath, quite meticulous himself, is always correcting me and sometimes gets quite exasperated with my carelessness with the fine points. Once, after a dynamic morning meditation, we were sitting in the thatched hut outside the ashram kitchen and discussing organisational matters, which included the printing of brochures. I had made a few mistakes while editing and some other 'faults' in design had been pointed out which, I felt, were just a matter of choice. I was sulking as I felt that the criticisms by other members were quite unfair. Gurunath's eyes twinkled as he looked at my woebegone face at his reprimand and said, "You better watch out or your state will be like Handiparagnath." At my sudden look of interest, he continued to explain that this yogi was part of the group that moved about with Babaji and the siddhas, cooking for them during their travels. Careless by nature, Paragnath had served rice that was not cooked properly to the siddhas. Therefore, as punishment, Babaji hung a handi, a mud utensil used to cook rice, around his neck to remind him to be more careful. He started his own sect later and all his disciples suspend this handi around their necks. To this day, you find yogis of the Handiparagnath sect roaming with this earthen burden around their neck.

Being one of the first to start organising satsangs for Gurunath in India, I have always just gone ahead and done things without consultation. I had no desire to waste time in meetings, which only seemed to delay all projects and often delivered no results. Raising my own funds to print literature and advertising the events with help from students and friends, I felt self-sufficient and not answerable to anyone, except Gurunath. This is one habit that is still prevalent in me.

Although I was at the receiving end many times for my haste in getting things done, I overheard Gurunath once telling a disciple on the phone, "You should be like Jyoti," he said to the disciple who was complaining about his displeasure at her for some errand she had botched. "The guru can kick her or give her a bouquet or a pat on the back. She carries on relentlessly." I smiled secretly at these words and they strengthened my resolve to work with more care, giving Gurunath less reason for irritation at my work.

Around the Campfire

A few weeks before the following incident in 2015, I was at the ashram for a camp and all of us disciples were sitting around Gurunath during breakfast. Disciples were asking various questions and Gurunath in his inimitable style enlightened them as only a true master could. I was in a very comfortable and satisfied space at that time with my life very peaceful and seemingly going according to plan. It was so smooth that I was feeling restless at the status quo and that was my question to Gurunath. I asked, "If a disciple is feeling very comfortable with life and its circumstances moving smoothly without a ripple, do we need some kind of shake up for spiritual evolution to accelerate?" At this Gurunath just looked at me and did not answer the question but moved on to the next query.

Later that year, Gurunath over time became especially harsh towards me in public, always being critical and admonishing me in front of my students form India and Australia while praising all the other teachers for their work. Nothing I did seemed to make him happy and I was at the end of my tether when a particular issue blew completely out of proportion and I got so hurt and angry that I did not return Gurunaths calls, messaged him I was very upset and didn't want to talk and switched off my phone. That night I developed shivers and started running a fever, for five days I was lying in bed burning but I did not consult a doctor. I kept putting cold compresses on my forehead and writhed in bed. I knew this was more than a fever, I felt as if pulled from the body, the body became like a shell while I was out roaming the galaxies. My fever was off the charts yet I persisted in taking no medicine. On the fifth day the fever broke and I emerged with clarity as from a near death experience. Sixth day in the morning I called Gurunath, he immediately picked up the phone and said gladly, "Oh, Jyoti I have been praying that please don't let her break, I hope I haven't given her a smack she can't handle." The moment I heard Gurunaths voice I was filled with gratitude and also grateful for the wisdom to understand the masters ways. Also I realised I had gotten the question to my earlier question about status quo; that shake-ups by the master does accelerate evolution.

This constant guidance from a living master forms the backbone of a disciple's life. Answering a question about detachment while we were relaxing after lunch, Gurunath told us this incident that happened one day as Lahiri Mahasaya was listening to Sri Yukteshwar reading from the scriptures. A boy interrupted them with the news that Lahiri Mahasaya's daughter had just passed away. Sri Yukteshwar stopped reading, but Lahiriji said, "This coming and going is a continuous process, please carry on reading." So Yukteshwar carried on while Lahiriji sat in blissful silence. Lahiri Mahasaya is an example of a realised person living within the confines of family and society, yet untouched by it all. He lived the ordinary life of a householder but his aura spread throughout the galaxies, explained Gurunath. Every incident became an inspiration to better my way of being and, just as he does with me, Gurunath guides other disciples too, personally, in the same manner.

※

Mystical Babaji – the great liberator

I was driving to Delhi once with Rukmani when, following a truck on the highway, I saw written in Hindi on the back, "*Guru Gorakshanath ke cheley, firtain hain akeley*" literally it means, "Guru Gorakshanath's disciples roam alone." The Nath yogis, followers of Guru Gorakshanath, carry no excess baggage. Such simple words etched on a dirty mud-encrusted body of a truck, written by a rustic truck driver, with such a profound meaning. It reiterated Gurunaths point that the spirit of Babaji is present in every grain of sand in our country, I feel it even more so in Punjab than in the east, west or the south where I had spent considerable amount of time in my younger days. Everywhere we went in the Himalayas, in little temples and caves all over the hills, Babaji was ever-present.

During our first visit to Jwalaji, at the guesthouse, we were exposed first hand to the ascetic lifestyle of the yogis staying there. Their down-to-earth humour and simple lifestyle was an inspiration to many of us from very privileged backgrounds. No job was lowly for them, from cleaning the toilets to serving the guests, in this case us. Nevertheless, through it all there was a sense of dignity; though they served, I realised they were not servile.

In the central sanctum of the Gorakh Tibba, there is a receptacle where one can see water boiling. If you dip your hand in it the water is cold, but if you tie some raw rice in a cloth and immerse it, it gets cooked. The yogi priest threw in a lighted match and the flames leapt out of the water, aided by the gaseous fumes of this volcanic phenomenon. We got special treatment as guests of the Nath yogis and thus managed to spend a great amount of time in the inner sanctum of Gorakh Tibba. In the afternoon, we sat around here sipping the sweet tea served by the very young Naths of the temple. All of them had their ears pierced and wore huge rings of bone in them – the identity of the Nath yogis. Some of them sat with us, fascinated by Gurunath's presence and personality. We asked Gurunath to tell us about the history of the place that was depicted on the temple walls in paintings.

According to legend, Babaji was performing severe penance here when Shiva and Parvati passed by. Parvati, who knew how fond Shiva was of meditating yogis, wanted to test this young boy who was seriously and effectively practicing the most rigorous of yoga disciplines. Shiva, knowing well that Babaji was a part of him, kept trying to dissuade her but to no avail. The Divine Mother was stubborn in her resolve, so Shiva playfully kept a condition of his own. If the yogi recognised her, she would have to cook, clean and serve him for a year, to which stipulation she readily agreed. So, mischievously dressed as a nubile nymphet, she set out to seduce this young yogi. The moment she stepped into the cave, Babaji looked up and said, "Come Mother, you are welcome into my abode." He got up and prostrated in front of a surprised Parvati recognising her for who she was, and so it came about that the Mother of the Universe, to keep her side of the promise, had to serve this ascetic for the duration of one year of her calendar.

While she was cleaning and cooking for this ascetic, it happened that one day there was no rice for lunch, so Mother took her problem to Babaji. He promised to go beg for alms but instructed her to put the water to boil, as he was hungry and wanted no time wasted when he returned, saying this he left. Aeons passed and he did not show up for a couple of thousand human years (which apparently translates into a few days in the divine calendar), Mother went to Shiva since she was afraid that all the water would boil away before Babaji came back. Shiva gave her some ash and asked her to drop it in the boiling water to prevent it from evaporating. It is believed that many million years have passed since then and Babaji has not yet returned, and the water is still boiling without evaporating in the small reservoir in the temple. Gurunath says, the day Babaji comes back will be the end of a cycle of Yugas. According to him, the reason that Babaji is staying away is to allow the compassionate Mother to do her work of awakening her children to bring them to the path of light. These stories fill me with awe. At one level, I am thrilled like a child at such a fantastic story, and at another level, my mind boggles to work out the mathematics of these millions of human years as compared to the divine calendar.

"Babaji appears again and again, down the ages, to keep alive the human search and movement towards final redemption," answered Gurunath in reply to a disciple's question about the real Babaji. We were now back at the guesthouse, where the young yogis had organised a small fire in the compound. An idol of Matsyendranath loomed large in the open temple in front. The atmosphere was serene and, except for the sound of the crackling fire, there was silence all around. Gurunath was telling us more about Babaji. "His ray has manifested in many saints and sages over the years." Then he continued with the popular story of Babaji as Gorakshanath, disciple of Matsyendranath. It is one that is often repeated by the Nath yogis of today, and one can find many variations and dialectic differences depending on the locale.

Gorakshanath was Matsyendranath's disciple, but mystically he is also the Guru. Matsyendranath had prayed to Shiva, his Guru, to give him a disciple who would be greater than him. To honour this promise Shiva had manifested as Gorakshanath. The traditional recitals tell of Matsyendranath giving some holy ash to enable a barren woman to have a child. The hapless woman instead of eating the ash had thrown it in the dung heap. After twelve years, Matsyendranath had returned to the village and realising what the woman had done had called out the boy's name and a twelve-year old had risen from the dung heap. Matsyendranath then took the boy, *Gorakh*, with him as a disciple.

Later, Matsyendranath, in accordance with a karmic debt, got enmeshed in the enjoyment of material and physical pleasures in Alkapuri as King of Nepal. Gorakshanath, it is said, was dismayed to realise that his Guru of yesteryears had forgotten his own divine nature and in order to remind

Macchinder of this stature, Gorakshanath made his way towards the hill kingdom. Even before his arrival, the drums beating in the King's court announced his coming. "Jago Macchinder, Gorakh aaya – wake up Macchinder, Gorakh has come," beat the drums continuously, while Matsyendranath was blissful in the company of his Queens, his two sons and the riches of his kingdom.

Finally, Gorakh arrived in the King's court and managed to tear his erstwhile guru away from the distraction of the material world and convinced him to accompany him into the jungles. But when Matsyendranath appeared at the gates of the kingdom, he was laden with gold and precious jewels that he could not bear to leave behind. Gorakshanath, to demonstrate the futility and worthlessness of these articles, urinated on a boulder lying by the side. To the wonder of everyone present, the boulder turned to gold. Properly chastised, Matsyendranath left behind his possessions but still wanted to take his children along. At this, Gorakh acquiesced for they had a higher purpose to fulfil.

Matsyendranath stopped en route, overtaken by a desire to meditate, and made his camp; he implored Gorakshanath to carry on, taking his two sons with him. As Gorakh moved about, the children would pester him to stop, either because they were hungry or because they wanted to relieve themselves. Finally, fed up, Gorakshanath gave strict instructions that there would be no food served nor stops made for bowel movements.

According to Gurunath and the *Nath Sampradaya*, these two children of Matsyendranath started the two tenets of Jainism – the *Shwetambar* and *Digambar*. During the same travels, it is said that Gorakshanath, lost in the trance of samadhi, washed the clothes along with the children inside the clothes, beating them to a pulp on the boulder by the river and put the remains out to dry. Of course, he brought them back to life later, symbolising the tradition of the guru giving new birth to the disciple. Each story of Babaji seemed to bring me closer to the mysterious being that was sometimes so tangible you could almost touch him and at other times, like the hint of a whisper, he passed you by.

※

With Gurunath and Babaji in Rudraprayag

During the Himalayan trip in 2001, when I was in Rudraprayag with Gurunath, the guesthouse where we stayed overlooked the confluence and a big bonfire was organised by the side of the river for the visitors. The Alaknanda and the Mandakini merge at Rudraprayag, and the sound of the water is loud and roaring on the Alaknanda side, while the Mandakini flows gently on. During our usual after-dinner gathering by the fireside, Gurunath commented that the Mandakini is said to represent our galactic neighbour – the Andromeda galaxy. Babaji's followers of the Nath Sampradaya believe that everything in the galaxy is replicated in the body. The physical body of man carries the blueprint of the vast universe. "You are nothing but cosmic dust, you are made of the universe, and the universe is within you. Samadhi is a realization of this eternal Truth," Gurunath explained, as we sat and watched the embers glow in the campfire by the side of the river.

The stars were bright in the clear sky and the air crisp. I gazed at the gap between the faraway mountains, from where the blue light representing Babaji had come towards Gurunath in what seemed like another age. The fire crackled and I saw sparks reflected in Gurunaths eyes and suddenly I was overcome by a sense of otherworldliness, as if time had stopped and I could, at that moment, be anywhere in the galaxy not a twenty-first century child but immortal, frozen in time.

Gurunath was in an almost trance-like state now when we asked him to narrate his meeting with the divine Babaji, there was a faraway look in his eyes as he relived the experience, "I had camped at Rudraprayag for some days and was intensely practicing my sadhana."

"That night was a full moon night," he continued in the same nostalgic tone, "as I sat by the Mandakini river I felt as if the two rivers were flowing through me and up my spine and meeting in my third eye."

"I had been in a meditative state for all these days as if preparing for this great happening," Gurunath continued, and the very air around us seemed to have stilled as if holding its breath in anticipation. "I was oblivious to my surroundings and entered a steady state of meditation. The outer and the inner became one, the trees, the mountains, the snow were all inside me; a sense of being turned inside out."

I could feel my own breath lengthening as Gurunath continued, "In that mystical hour of the night, I saw coming towards me from above the majestic mountains a revolving light, bright yet soft, and this lilac, indigo, blue light moved towards me. The whole area bathed in this light, the mountains, the trees, the rivers; the light flooded my body in its radiance and, madly drunk, I floated effortlessly in this ecstasy. I expanded out of my body to partake of this essence, finally becoming one with it in an egoless state where the light and I were one. And all nature and creation stood silent as if bowing to the presence of Babaji for this was He in his formless state of light."

There was complete silence as we waited for Gurunath to go on; even the flames of the fire held steady. "The centre of this light became whiter and brighter and then there was a blinding flash." I winced as Gurunath accompanied this with a clap of his hands. "The splendour of this flash reverberated deep within me and I blanked out. I don't know how long I was in this state but when I came to I saw the figure of Babaji bathing in the centre of the confluence. I gazed at him as he bathed and every pore in my body was saturated with his love. Even as I watched, he came up to where I was sitting and led me up to a hut on the hillside." At this, Gurunath gestured up the hill some distance away.

"Then, very simply, he sat by my side and smiling, picked up the seed of a tree lying there and said to me, 'Break this seed'. I did so. 'Look in the centre', he said, and when I did I saw an empty space, a hollow space in the centre. Then he picked up an onion that was lying there and said, 'Peel it', and so I did. As I peeled the onion it was like the peeling of delusive layers off my mind. I reached the last layer and he asked, 'What is left?' I said 'Nothing'. He smiled and said, 'My son, the truth of truths is that when the layers of maya or delusion are peeled off one is left with Pure Consciousness which is Nothing in the material world. But from this Nothing, that is Pure Consciousness, does all of Creation arise'. With this, he laughed and I passed out." All of us were so engrossed in this recounting, that the fire had burned low and Gurunath directed one of the disciples to add more wood to it. After the fire was tended, he continued, "It was after this experience that I was able to give the Shivapat transmissions to all sincere seekers of truth. Often, argumentatively, people ask me how it is possible to create something out of nothing, since science believes that one can only create something out of something else."

"Then I always answer", said Gurunath "That's why He is God and we are mortals."

Rudraprayag, according to mythology, is where lord Shiva revealed and taught Narada the complete musical ragas that are recorded in the *Bhakti Sutras*, an ancient vedic text. The temple commemorating this event is now dilapidated and has been relegated to second place, by a new temple that has been built recently with steps leading down to the confluence.

Gurunath often addresses Babaji as *Mahabinishkaran*, who was ready to evolve and merge into Infinite Consciousness but agreed, when beseeched, to remain in the physical to guide and inspire humankind. Thus, he sacrificed this great step in evolution to remain here and wait for us all to evolve at which moment; he will also finally relinquish his physical form.

"So hurry up with your practice," Gurunath motivates us lovingly. "Are you going to make Babaji wait forever? Though at the plane he is in, time and space has dissolved, a blink of his eye is a hundred years on this earth!"

I can understand this breakdown of time and space in a minuscule manner when I meditate. Earlier, twenty minutes used to seem like an hour, but now hours seem like minutes, sometimes! So, I suppose in a larger frame a hundred years can seem like time taken to blink once.

❈

The Neelkanteshwar-Badrinath experience

During one of Gurunath's visits to Chandigarh, we had a powerful havan at Panchvati attended by all the members. All of us formed a chain around the havan-kund and sat stacked one behind the other. As mentioned earlier, Gurunath makes the devotees form a chain around the havan-kund for the powerful Kundalini Shakti, facilitated by him and released during the invocation to flow through them. Since there were many new members, the formation was not perfect. However, it was an education, as everyone solemnly repeated the mantras chanted by Gurunath and followed his instructions. We all got to make our individual wishes and offer the mixture of rice and ghee to the fire.

Much later, after a light supper, we continued the evening gathered around the bonfire. It was Gurunaths last day here and so nobody wanted to waste a minute away from him. From the seven to the seventy-year olds, everyone was hoping the magical night would never end. One of the disciples wanted to hear about Gurunaths experience when he met Babaji at Jhilmili gufa in Badrinath. Though many of us had heard this recounted many times, I was all agog and ready once again. Quickly, Aman got up to replenish the fire with more wood, while another disciple edged closer to Gurunath, so as not to miss a word. We waited breathlessly for him to begin.

"This was in the year 1967," started Gurunath. "I was walking up to Badrinath from Rudraprayag. The whole journey was replete with the nostalgia of past life memories. It was as if I was entering a heavenly sphere, a different dimension, as I walked up the path, which was becoming steeper and steeper. But my desire to reach this cave was very strong, connected to it as I was from a past life." Gurunath stopped as some latecomers joined in and everyone shifted to allow them space to settle in. The crisp night air was cold and we huddled closer to the fire, as Gurunath continued, "Yes, my desire to reach the cave was strong, prompting me to keep on walking. As I reached the top I could see the entire Himalayan range and it reminded me of the poem of Kalidasa, where he likens the white peaks of the mountains to the laughter of Shiva."

I was listening to him but, at the same time, my eyes were fascinated with the fire changing the colour of Gurunath's skin to burnished gold. And was it my imagination or did I see bright blue motes flying around him in varying patterns?

"I was exhausted after the climb and lay down to rest for a while. The sun went behind some clouds, throwing the whole area into shadow." Gurunath's voice was now soft and I strained my ear to hear his words.

"Then, with my eyes closed, I felt the light reappear and thought the sun had come out again. But it was not so, for the whole area started filling with a great shimmering light. The aura of this light was immense; it seemed to fill the entire universe." Gurunath smiled gently and said, "I thought it was not proper for me to be on my back so I rolled on to my stomach and did sashtanga pranam."

"Who are you?' I asked wonderstruck, and the answer seemed to reverberate from all around, 'Whoever you think me to be, that I am to thee'. At this, my mind expanded without boundary, and I saw him from my past life association, my lips forming the words as I articulated, 'Shiv Goraksha Babaji'. And his words, 'Tathastu, Tathastu, Tathastu' rang out and resonated in every fibre of my being and in the surrounding mountains."

I felt a shiver and goose bumps appeared on my skin as Gurunath, now lost in memory, continued, "Then I felt a cold current flowing down from my head to the toes and a warm current flowing up. This was repeated – a nadi shodan – purifying of the psychic nerves that I intuitively understood was a way of preparing me to receive an inflow of higher spiritual energy. I had already been meditating for ten to twelve hours a day and yet more purification was taking place in preparation for higher samadhi. After this, I moved out of my physical body and expanded into my emotional body.

Breaking all barriers of time and space, I was just absorbed by this bliss and light as I expanded further into my mental body."

As Gurunath paused, I saw his aura expanding even now, as he relived the experience. The whole area of Panchvati seemed to be lighting up with an otherworldly light. Without looking, I was conscious of everyone gazing reverently at Gurunath transported to the vision of that event. "Then, the mental body expanded into Soul Consciousness and I was in my *Anandamaya kosha*. My crystal soul dissolved and expanded into an awareness that was boundless."

Gurunath looked around at our rapt faces and said, "I am trying to explain in human words my experience of the divine which is an impossible task. What can I say, I felt as if a gentle series of implosions were taking place, implosions to expand my being."

"All at once the trees, the birds, the clouds, the sky, the planets, the stars, and the galaxies were I and breathing my *prana*. It was only in this expanded state that I could understand and take in the messages given by this Nameless Being whom the world knows as Babaji. It was as if my whole being was being rocked by photons of light particles that carried these encapsulated messages, which got embedded in my memory. Messages for serving humanity, messages about my past, about my future, messages that were received without the mind being involved, in my super-consciousness to be recalled later. He cannot be understood or described, only experienced, you know," explained Gurunath in simplicity.

"How did Babaji look?" whispered a disciple, still enamoured by the physical entity. Smilingly, Gurunath obliged her.

"It's very difficult to describe his form," said Gurunath, "I was dumbfounded by his spiritual majesty. His hair, that touched his heels, was ablaze with a radiant fire. His body appeared wet from the bath in the Alaknanda River, yet was dry and there was a subtle fragrance emanating from his deathless, immortal body. Dressed in blackbuck skin, his feet did not touch the ground. I gazed into his compassionate eyes and was lost." And so were all of us so lost in the story that we did not realise that Gurunath had got up and left before any of us could take his leave.

After a while, the disciples too left in ones and twos taking this experience home as part of them. A few of us who were spending the night in tents in Panchvati kept sitting around the fire, quietly listening to the sounds of the surrounding forest. Then I got up and dampened the fire with some water lying nearby. The fire sizzled and smoked as it went out and all of us retired for a few hours of rest.

CHAPTER 9

PERSONAL SADHANA AND INNER TRANSFORMATION

With regular sadhana and dedication to the guru, I worked out a daily routine. I understood the importance of personal practice. In the early days, when I was just initiated, I found myself talking to everybody and anybody who would listen, about the glorious path that I had discovered. I realised later, that talk was easy but commitment to the practice more difficult to sustain.

"Your body is a temple," instructed Gurunath. "The external rituals represent what is already present internally. The rite of ringing the bell or blowing the conch, the offering of flowers and incense, are duplicated by the sadhak by chanting the 'Om', offering the lotus of our chakras, and burning in the practice of the spiritual sadhana given by the guru to release the fragrance for all humanity."

The guru-shishya mudra, a special hand posture that is a hallmark of Gurunath's teaching, transforms the body into a temple. The fingers form a steeple on top of the head, enabling the divine light to flow through and flood the practitioner.

With constant practice, the disciple realises the body as a sacred shrine, inhabited by the divine soul and the pristine spirit within the casing of the soul animating us. "Bathing in the Amrit sarovar is symbolic of being saturated in the amrit, the nectar flowing inside you. The Ganga flows within you," says Gurunath. Thus, he actualises all external, figurative practice for the disciples.

"This is Kundalini Yoga, energy in motion. A process of converting breath into life force and realising the physical body as a light body," Gurunath said, succinctly explaining the scientific practice of Kriya Yoga.

In the past, it was a practice intended only for souls who were already well on their way practicing ten to twelve hours everyday, said Gurunath to an incredulous group who were collectively probably practicing as much. A great meeting was thus convened, attended by *Indra*, the *brahmarishis*, the *Navnath* and other stalwarts, to debate whether such a worthy practice should be revealed to the human race that may not honour the potency of this technique. Lahiri Mahasaya is credited with intervening for us mortals and influenced the decision to allow this evolutionary technique to be taught to humans for speedier progression of their soul. Babaji then entrusted him to bring this practice to earth much like Prometheus who wrested fire from the gods and gave it to mortals. Like a child I loved hearing these legendary incidents that Gurunath recounted almost as if it happened yesterday.

At first, it was very difficult for me to sit even for twenty minutes of meditation. I would keep fidgeting and cocking an eye at the clock every few minutes. I did not realise how my restlessness, even though I made no sound, was a disturbance for the more experienced disciples. While meditating, the veteran sadhak becomes sensitive to the surrounding energy frequencies. With constant practice, I learnt to become more still. The physical body is trained with asans and the mind with pranayama to be steady. "Both complement one another and are essential for the sadhak who is learning to meditate," taught Gurunath.

One day, I was tired but had a powerful desire to do some Kriya, as we refer to this meditation in short, but physically felt unable to sit up. Then, sometime during the night, I found myself sitting and meditating, and was startled to see my physical body lie resting in front. It was uncanny; the body was getting the rest it desired while the spirit was completing the practice.

※

Slow ripening of the spirit

I had an opportunity to go to Pune in December 2002, without prior notice, and learnt that Gurunath and Ayi were at the ashram. I reached the ashram after dark, walking without fear as the rickshaw driver refused to venture on the unlit path to the ashram. I was delighted to realise that there was no one else at the ashram besides Gurunath, Ayi and a disciple from Australia. Now was the opportunity for me to get the full blast of the guru's powers without it being necessary to share it with anyone else, I thought. I was excited and considered not wasting any time sleeping but meditating the whole night.

Before supper, Gurunath instructed the other disciple and me to meditate for some time. I thought here was my opportunity and that I would sit and not get up for supper, impressing Gurunath with my fervour and steadfastness. When I sat in the Paran Kutir, I just could not concentrate... my mind was running in all directions and the thoughts continued relentlessly without mercy... people I had not thought of in years now appeared in never-ending rows. It was horrible and I was disgusted with myself. Though I heard Gurunath emerging from his den, I stubbornly sat there fuming. After a while, Gurunath called out to me to come and have food. I was almost in tears and tried to hide it as best as I could.

During supper, Gurunath talked of various things, asking the other disciple about Australia. Suddenly he looked at me and said, "Jyoti, you know, even the effort to sit for meditation is part of the meditation. No matter that your mind is wandering, you are like a child learning a new skill; it will come." I was deeply touched when I understood how nothing was hidden from him and his kind words made me realise the extent of his compassion for me. I slept like a child that night.

With time, my bond to the master was crystallising. I felt the guru as part of me, the essence present in me at all times. I improved as a person. It was as if all my rough edges were being filed and smoothed. Issues that would previously drive me to the brink of emotional outburst now left me calm. Of course, there were times I slipped badly but it was becoming easier to regain balance and to centre myself. It was painful at first as I learnt to unlearn many strong opinions and relax a rigid mind-set.

I could see my own behaviour, a lot of it rather ugly. There were glimpses of strong negative emotions, greed and jealousy, lust and envy, even pure hate. Slowly, as the witness perception in me developed, I became more natural, more innocent and childlike, as my artificiality was slowly stripped away. This is still an on-going process. Layer by layer, I am being cleansed. I am living the householder life mother, daughter and to a great extent some duties of a wife even after the divorce, alongside the life of an evolving sadhak committed to a fixed set of sadhana. Both these aspects of my life, I feel, enhance and complement one another without dichotomy. For the first time I could truly say that I was happy with all the circumstances of my life. With the children away and married now and the divorce more and more I am free to pursue the life of a sadhak.

❈

Deepening connections with the guru

On Gurunaths birthday, May 10, it is the habit of all disciples to wish him by phone or in person, wherever he may be. In fact, there is a certain amount of competition among the disciples to see who would wish him first, however childish this may sound. On one such occasion in 2002, he was to be in the Himalayas filming for his documentary and I called to wish him in advance, but he instructed me to do so on the actual day, by connecting to him. I had no idea what I was to do, for he had taught us no symbols or mantras to enable me to do so, this was pre golden gate bridge connection. Anyway, on the specified morning I sat down, mentally brought his picture before me, and sent him the wishes. I was sitting thus, when suddenly, the room filled with the aroma of roasted *chivda*, beaten rice crispies, flavoured with curry leaves and spices. My mouth was full of its salty taste and my belly felt satiated. It was definitely an acknowledgement and a blessing. I came to know later from Ayi that this was one of Gurunaths favourite snacks.

This phenomenon of tasting what Gurunath had eaten happened once again while I was on the phone talking to him. The mouth-watering aroma and taste of spicy rice biryani suddenly overwhelmed me and Gurunath asked, "Jyoti, did you get it?" Ayi had cooked rice biryani and Gurunath and some of his disciples were having lunch when I had called. I was in Chandigarh and the lunch was taking place in Pune, nearly eight hundred and sixty miles away!

This increasing connection with the guru became apparent when, once at the ashram, Gurunath was teaching us a mudra that accompanied a particular mantra. Again, I was amazed to realise that I had already been practicing it even without being taught this method. I was spluttering with surprise when Gurunath looked at me to simply remark, "You know that's because you are connected to me." Though it made me feel special, I knew that the master gives equally to all and there is no division in the master's attention. The master never withholds compassion or wisdom from some, while giving it to others. The pupils need to clean up their act and become receptive to the free-flowing transmissions.

The true guru guides the sincere disciple in every step of their practice, the call of the disciple is never unheard by them. One evening in 2009 well after I was established in my practice I was at the club with some friends. I was quite sure of my mental and emotional steadiness by now and thought that no incident could shake me. In the course of the evening I met an old friend with whom I have been estranged for many years who the moment she met me made a statement that in an instant shook me to the core with the same patterns of behaviour and my mind went into turmoil. Returning home that night I was disgusted with myself, it was as if all my practice of so many years were for naught. In tears at my weakness and lapse I was also berating myself.

That night as I slept I saw Sri Yukteswar Giri in my dream vision, he transformed into Gurunath and then back into Yukteswar. Now many disciples have seen Gurunath as Yukteswar Giri and identify Gurunath as a reincarnation of Sri Yukteswar, for me though this was a first time. Throughout the dream vision this kept happening this transition from one master to the other while they were both teaching me a lesson on how to withdraw my attention from the disturbing incident that had happened earlier that evening. It was like a physical withdrawal of energy, in the course of the night they showed me many images from my past that were disturbing and lovingly instructed me on how to withdraw from each scene. The dream went on for a very long time with very many episodes from the past being replayed in a loop and I was instructed how to consciously pull back my attachment from them. Every time I was unsuccessful in detachment they would sweetly bring the memory back till I succeeded. I woke up feeling very light as if having dropped a big load of baggage understanding how it's me who was giving power to these bondages and how I can consciously disengage from them. Truly a master's degree course on advance *pratyahar* I was tutored in that night! Once again an overwhelming feeling of gratitude engulfed me that the master cares so much for their disciples that they come in an instant at their cry. For the first time I truly understood the connection between Gurunath and Yukteswar Giri too.

As my intuition improved I came to understand more the relevance of a living master. The human awareness, as I understood, is reaching further and wider, with new inventions and breakthroughs happening daily. Since the practice of Kriya Yoga is a science of evolution, I presumed it has to be kept updated and in harmony with the developing cerebral system of the human race. My impression is that, as the human brain evolves rapidly, the old method of practice becomes less effective. Living masters are repeatedly sent by Babaji to make the practice more dynamic and appropriate for modern times. So disciples who connect with the living masters rather than existing organisations are the ones who have been with the masters in their previous lives. True integrity, for me is to the master who is living and present, though I agree we in all probability have been with the previous masters too, proof of that is because here we are practicing the same Kriya under the tutelage of this master. Often disciples will say they are Babaji's disciples or Yoganandas while never having met them in this life. I feel its easy to claim discipleship of masters gone but very difficult to be a disciple of a living master in close proximity, the chiselling, the polishing, the burning in tapa and the wisdom to know the difference between a true master and a pretentious one has to be endured for being fashioned into a true disciple of a true living master.

Disciples must understand that the master/gurus instructions override those of a teacher at any given time, however senior that teacher maybe, however exalted. Students must make this direct connection with the living master who is a rarity. This is possible even if the disciples are not able to physically meet the master due to various constraints, physical or financial. Local junior, senior and very senior teachers are there to help but the master's one word even if entirely contradictory to what the teacher says is the right instruction for them. I and many other disciples are witness to the fact that the master conveys this very personal message to you even in an audience of hundreds. The disciple's only need to be attentive, a dull and blunt intellect are not a tool conducive for cutting the bonds of illusion. "The only sin of the mind," Gurunath often repeats, "is not to have paid enough attention."

※

Physical and mental transformations

Along with the increase in visions and supernatural incidents that have been mentioned throughout the book, I underwent other physical experiences as well. There were days when my body felt so heavy that I could hardly drag myself around; this was often followed by weeks of feeling so light that I felt I could fly. One day, I heard a loud knocking sound and almost jumped out of my skin with the realisation that it was coming from inside me. I had just heard my heartbeat, from within, and almost immediately heard another sound that I identified as the sound of blood flowing in my veins.

It was all very puzzling and yet exciting. *Bandhas* – yogic locks that streamlined and controlled the flow of energy – and mudras occurred involuntarily, as though my body had its own agenda. While watching television, I could suddenly be over-taken by a desire to do certain asanas, and during meditation other bandhas would occur automatically, moving and channelling the life force into different parts of the body.

To the astonishment of my workers at the farm, I would go out into the lawn and do a series of forward rolls, whooping like a child. I heard the sound of crickets, bells pealing, whistles and gongs. The breath became dynamic, the outcome was a tremendous sense of power – physical as well as mental – and underlying all this was utter fearlessness. My voice took on a different timbre, my eyes are changing colour. I felt ready to face any challenge that life may throw up and, as the reader already knows, life gave me many opportunities to test this by and by. Every state of psychological or mental clarity was preceded by a physical experience of some magnitude. Though the result may not have been visible instantly, as time passed, I could notice the changes within me.

Once, I was sitting in meditation and I heard a sound like an electronic vibration, as if a million insects were buzzing in my head. Then, a black cloud lifted from the top of my head pulling out a shadow from within and, along with the buzzing sound, the dark cloud too went up and away. I felt instantly lighter. I realised later that my thinking had become much simpler and more straightforward and what I had actually witnessed was my being relieved of the mental baggage that was hindering further progress in my sadhana. This is the time when I was freed of many of my childhood inhibitions. The bottled-up feelings about not being hugged as a child, my mother not allowing me to receive my prize, my guilt about embezzling that money in school, and other such suppressed imprints, all seemed to disappear after this experience. The mind started to get crystal clear and life without subterfuge.

I can almost pinpoint the moment when I first vividly experienced the process of *pratyahar* – a reversal of energy. It was late at night and I was practicing the Jyoti mudra taught by Gurunath when I felt, or rather saw, the nerves in my body with an electro-magnetic, bluish current visibly flowing in them. An uncanny feeling of the current pausing and then flowing back towards the spine followed this. The sensation was like a cool gel flowing in my nerves. Filled with what seemed to me like a blissful sensation, I floated along joyfully.

Pratyahar is a stage in yoga during which the energy that is utilised in satisfying the desires of the five senses of sight, smell, hearing, touch and taste, gets inverted. From moving outwards, towards the external objects of the desire, this energy is re-routed, facilitating the sadhak to move towards the final stages of yoga – *dharana, dhyana and samadhi*.

Personal Sadhana and Inner Transformation

These spiritual experiences could sometimes come at odd moments. The actualisation of a practice is not a respecter of place; steadfastness in practice can unveil the result at any moment. I remember the first time I heard the full force of the Om, I was in a taxi driving to Dalhousie, a hill town to meet with a friend. The driver had stopped for a cup of tea and breakfast; I had refused any and was waiting in the car outside the quaint *dhaba* on the highway. I felt a sort of squeezing of my innards especially my brain and a sound that is indescribable. It was beautiful and felt as if I was being pulled outwards and inwards at the same time. The closest I can explain it is the sensation of labour during birth and it came exactly like that in intervals, not continuously. There was a squeeze and the accompanying deep sonic boom. The sound and the pressure carried on and I had not yet realised what it was. In what was an 'aha' moment my intellect recorded it as the sound of the Om that Gurunath calls the birthing hum of creation. The moment the 'mind' understood the phenomena ceased as mysteriously. Just recalling that instance sends the vibrations coursing through my body now.

Practicing the Jyoti mudra regularly I had started forming the circle and could see the star sometimes nebulous, sometimes pulsating. One day in the morning as I sat on the pot I rubbed my eyes and wow, the star appeared, clear and brilliant to stay suspended in my forehead in front of my inner eye. I couldn't but help break out in laughter at this inopportune time for it to appear. Jyoti Mudra is a yogic technique and key to Kriya Yoga; it facilitates seeing ourselves as the divine light spirit.

I would excitedly share all my experiences with Gurunath, asking him for interpretations. He would smile and say, "You are being rewarded. These are the fruits of your labour." This was regardless of whether the experience was pleasant or painful!

Visions of other masters and their lessons

At a particular phase during my practice I started seeing visions of Ramakrishna Paramahamsa and Lahiri Mahasaya more frequently. Whenever I sat for meditation, either one or the other would appear, smiling serenely. I was at a loss to understand what they wanted, so one day I mentally prostrated in front of them and with folded hands requested they tell me, through my living guru, what it was they wanted of me. After that, the visions faded away and stopped altogether. The only way I can explain this manifestation is that they were a mental projection from some past life connection that appeared to be removed forever, once I ascertained my steadfast faith in my guru.

Around this time, a friend of mine in Chandigarh requested that I meet this Satya Sai Baba *bhakta*. She was a woman from the Netherlands, whom Baba spoke with telepathically, in Dutch. On the appointed day, I went for coffee to my friend's house where two women were present. The Dutch woman told me that when my friend had called to invite her to the get-together, Baba had spoken to her saying that she was about to meet a woman of wisdom. As was her habit, she had written all this down in her diary. With a start, I realised that she was indicating that I was that woman of wisdom... oops! Baba had also told her to communicate to me that I was welcome to come to Whitefield and not to think of him as a charlatan. Although confused, I answered that I had never thought about Sai Baba, though I had dreamt about him a couple of times many years ago. As for coming to Whitefield, I clarified that I already had a guru and was initiated into a practice that I was very happy following. In fact, both of us left feeling dissatisfied with the meeting. I was wondering about what the message could have been, for surely I did not want to leave my guru for another. Later at home as I sat watching TV with my daughter, the whole room filled with the smell of vibhuti, the essence of Sai Baba, which both of us smelled. I felt strongly that the earlier message was a test to see how strong my ties to Gurunath were – whether I would jump onto another bandwagon if I were invited. Therefore, I assumed the latter blessing came in the form of the *vibhuti* because I had passed the test in my steadfastness to the guru. Every event seemed to teach a lesson. I knew, intellectually, that there were many paths, which led to the same goal of self- realisation. However, it took a visit to Pondicherry to bring this home to me. I was down South for a cousin's wedding and was in Pondicherry for a couple of days. I took the opportunity to visit Auroville and meditate at the *Matri Mandir*, the temple dedicated to the Mother, disciple of Sri Aurobindo, the moving spirit behind this unique international community. They allowed tourists to meditate there in the evening for an hour.

The temple was constructed to replicate a vortex of energy moving up, and the focal point was a large crystal ball that channelized solar energy into the temple. The energy produced by the crystal was beautiful, and I immediately felt calm and peaceful. As I sat meditating, I felt Mother's energy in blue and pink clouds swirling about me, the healing presence relaxing. Unintentionally, my mind recalled Gurunath, and the clouds dissipated and a fire blazed and enveloped me. I felt instantly cleansed. I understood, then, how disciples have to choose the path they must follow. The gentler path suited some and others the full blaze of yogic sadhana – though eventually both have to merge – yogic sadhana tempered with devotion and devotion fired with yogic sadhana, both leading to right action.

Ma excuses herself

Once a student visited Anandomoyee Ma's ashram in Kolkatta and brought me a beautiful picture of hers from there. Ma was looking lovely and her love pouring out of the framed picture. I took it from the student and put it alongside Gurunaths picture on my altar. I went about busy with the days work and forgot all about it except to feel the radiant love flowing from it. That night Ma came in my dream and very lovingly and simply said, "Please remove me from the altar, there is no space in your altar for anyone else except your Guru." So that morning I took her picture down and returned it to the student with thanks.

The feeling of relief I got at this was quite liberating as if freed from any compulsions. It is interesting that without active desire I have had experiences with many deities and visions of many masters yet I have never felt the need to identify with them; their message for me has always been that my guru is Gurunath as if reiterating a truth and imprinting it in my consciousness indelibly.

※

Buddha helps in the final bag drop

I am ever grateful for the messages that come to me whether brought forth by my mind or real contact by the great masters I don't know. I have more than a sneaky suspicion that it is Gurunath who makes possible these incoming messages to train me. Otherwise who am I to have such intimate contact with all these masters and divine beings and be recipient of their messages, I wonder.

Personal Sadhana and Inner Transformation

The final freeing of my attachment to any external form of worship came when I visited The Great *Stupa* of Universal Compassion in Bendigo, Australia. This had been on the cards for a couple of years when I visited Ballarat, but for some reason or another Susan our local teacher and I could not make it. Finally last year in 2018 we made the trip, Susan had spoken to the Rinpoche in charge about my visit and our keenness to hold classes or a retreat on my next visit, at their centre. The area where the stupa was situated was a large tract of land donated by a family. They were setting up an inter-faith area outside the stupa representing all religions and that was one area of discussion they wanted to have with me. They were confused with the number of Hindu gods and were not sure which deity they must have as representing all Hindus. This was one of the spaces that was left empty, for a Ganesh or a Krishna, they were still making up their mind. I saw a Sikh Ek Omkar and a statue of St. Francis of Asisi, which was apparently the first statue to be commissioned and placed. They had even imported bodhi trees from India that I wondered how they were going to perform in the chilling cold winter of Bendigo. It worried me that they may not survive, at the same time it amused me the length people will go to duplicate enlightenment spots of others. But they were putting a lot of thought and care into tending to the young plants.

During the discussion with the lady in charge I suggested a shivaling as representing hindu religious faith as that for me was a symbol of the brahmand, the universe with what Gurunath says, "The centre everywhere and the circumference nowhere." That to me seemed a very apt representation of Hinduism and its philosophy. As I was discussing this I started planning in my mind about raising some funds from the australian students, mostly one or two and thought I could also chip in for it. We would need a pump for continuous flow of water on the linga,

I thought, my mind going into details of sourcing it in Australia and other logistics.

Then we decided to go into the Stupa and take darshan of the very precious Jade Buddha, one of its kind as the uncut Jade was found in Canada and after the idol was made, it circumambulated the world collecting blessings before finally making its way here to the *stupa*. When I walked into the large hall, the statue of Buddha overpowered the space but equally strong was another statue by its side of Padmasambhav who beckoned me with a strong impulse. After bowing to both I sat in front of the Buddha and within a second a strong direct message issued from there. "Nothing doing," the Buddha said, very clearly referring to my plan for the shivaling outside. "This is not your work, your work is beyond the external," Buddha clarified. The preciseness of the message stunned me, it was clear and it was exact, no room for any doubt. I was to waste no time on this inter-faith business. In a flash the Buddha enlightened me that every religion is a bondage. The last vestiges of attachment dropped off.

Being me, I came out thinking humorously, wow, Buddha just saved us some money!

Being steadfast in practice

I was unreasonably enamoured by the word *sthitapragnya*, a word I had learnt from the Bhagavad Gita, meaning 'undaunted by external circumstances whether good or bad'. Before long, my own personal test on this score came during the course of seven months between December 2002 and June 2003. I thought the circumstances were very unjust as they unfolded in my life at a time when I was better than I had ever been as a person, involved seriously in a chosen spiritual path.

As mentioned earlier, first we had the income tax survey, and then my mother was taken ill and passed away after over two months of hospitalisation, the last fifteen days of which she spent in a coma. She had suffered from mild chest pains and was admitted for surgery from which she never recovered. She had been extremely spiritual, spending long hours in devotional practice at the local *Murugan* temple, and her pain and trauma during her last moments seemed undeserved. Then came the unwarranted demolition of Panchvati due to policy matters, and business losses followed as everything ground to a standstill. In these seven months, my life seemed to have taken a sudden turn for the worse.

At this time, a few of my friends and even some pupils asked me why such misfortune was occurring in my life in spite of all my spiritual sadhana. Some even questioned the role of Gurunath. "What is the use of a guru," they asked crudely, "who cannot stop such painful events from occurring in the lives of his sincere disciples?" I reminded them of the incident when Gurunath, during one of our camps, assured us that for the sincere practitioner he will be there even at the time of death. He would not let them die in darkness; he would be there to lead them into the light, he had promised. This was true in the case of my mother who was a sincere disciple. A devout traditional lady she was steeped in her puja especially of the *sri yantra* and Adi Shankaracharya's *saundarya lahiri*, but after initiation into Kriya Yoga she reduced all other external worship and flowed into the practice with ease. Gurunath visited her in the hospital during what later proved to be her last days. Throughout the time she was in a coma he guided me with the prayers to be said for her, and assured me that she would be released from the pain, either by complete recovery or by release from the body. As predicted by him, on the last day of the prayers her soul moved out, freed from the shackles of her body. I grieved for my mother as a daughter but also learnt to happily let go of her.

A few weeks after she passed our business was wrecked. When I called to tell Gurunath of the demolition of Panchvati, all he said was, "Jyoti, your husband and you have dropped a big load of karmic debt, just get up, dust yourself, and carry on." That is exactly what I did.

However hard it was to come to terms with the new circumstances of life, his words served to fill me with an internal strength. He also reminded me of what he had said when he invested in me the rank of senior Hamsacharya. "A Hamsacharya serves the human race by selflessly teaching sincere pupils the ways and means to realise themselves," he had said. "You need steadfastness not to cow down or turn back. Though everything seems against you, you must know that all is working for your ultimate good. Refuse in your mind to be disturbed by apparent injustice, for you are reaping the fruits of your past karmas. Never mind if your body is naked and shivering, you must not leave your soul naked and shivering." Gurunath always instructs us that we should not lament when we lose our 'something'; it's our 'Nothing' that we must not lose.

This was one of the important lessons that I learnt from Gurunath. Because of this revealing message and guidance, I was happy to note that, throughout these events, I remained steadfast in my sadhana, my sorrow minimal and disturbance nil. It has helped me in the intervening fifteen years up to writing this revised version too, continuing to be unshaken by all that has come my way. Now that I know I could be unwavering in times of sorrow, I wondered if I could maintain this equanimity in times of great joy and success.

Dropping excess baggage

As in all traditional Indian homes, mine too had a corner devoted to idols of various gods and goddesses. One day, when

I was meditating in front of the altar in the pre-dawn hours, I was inspired by an inner urge to get rid of all the excess paraphernalia of worship. After daybreak, I gathered all the idols together: Shiva, Durga, Ganesh, and various other good-luck charms collected over the years from various sources, pundits and babas. I drove to the Gagghar, a small rivulet flowing near the city, and lovingly immersed all of them. I came back feeling much lightened and uncomplicated. Now I meditate only on the picture of Gurunath. I started the New Year with more focus and clarity. In my temple room at Chandigarh,

I have a large photograph of Gurunath; as I meditate, through my inner eye, I see a vast space opening behind this picture leading to galaxies beyond. As universes form and dissolve, the absolute silence of the void is loud in my ears. I feel content to sit in front of my guru's picture and experience these visions through him. They seem to unfold a vista of possibilities that sincere practice will bring my way.

Tara comes home

I had completely forgotten the earlier instruction of Gurunath in Jwalaji that at some point in my sadhana I would have to meditate at the Taradevi temple in Jwalaji. Busy with my schedule at home, at the ashram, travelling to Australia to teach, undivided attention on Gurunath this was nowhere in my mind. In 2015 on my birthday I had the usual group of friends and students come over to enjoy some cake coffee and wine. It's an open house and people walk in from 4pm onwards to 10pm. No invitation is really sent out, so one student brought along another someone whom I had not met for a while. He handed me a present stating he had bought it in Bhutan few years back and did not know whom to give it and thought I might like it. After everyone left I opened the packet and imagine my surprise when out stepped a statue of Tara! I was immediately reminded of Gurunaths statement close to fourteen years ago and at the same time had to suppress a smile as I thought Tara must have realised this girl doesn't remember so I better show up at her house. So there she was and she chose her own space right on my bedside table.

Not much for external puja when she directed me to light a lamp in front of her I did so without much ado. A few nights after that I was sleeping and heard a sharp sound penetrate my left ear. I woke up realising it was a beej mantra initiation by Tara via a seed sound. Though she is placed on my right side during the course of the night I had twisted around and had my left ear towards her. This was unusual for me as I usually lie flat on my back at night and don't move much. I did not perceive much happening after this except plans started moving right along with help coming from unexpected sources for Gurunaths work as if now I had some extra help, a smoothening of an already pretty smooth path but even little concerns being taken care of.

By end 2016 she was well entrenched in my home, though I did not do any external prayer everyday I would at intervals light a lamp and sometimes offer flowers and incense often anointing her with a perfume, which she really liked. At about this time two of my very close students and steady disciples of Gurunath, Aman and Babit had been pestering me to hold a havan on my rooftop since a couple of years but I had not been in the mood. But that December something came over me and I said lets do it before the end of this year. We met late at night after ten and did a havan with eleven coconuts each.

Personal Sadhana and Inner Transformation

While the havan was in progress I got this exquisite feeling of purity emanating from the three of us. It was as if we were without any blemish, a humorous thought knowing what a load of crap we talked all the time; nevertheless that feeling of purity persisted and grew. As we finished the *havan* the smoke from the oblations rose up almost like a person, a swirling white form that rose without disintegrating unlike smoke that usually does and floated up in a column into the sky. When we finished I felt as if we had accomplished a long pending collective offering.

Next morning I was casually sitting on my bed, I had just lit the lamp in front of Gurunath and then Tara, her spot was not on the altar with him but on the table by my bed. Suddenly a deep reverie overtook me. A feeling of peace and sweet innocence, accompanied by a sense of unblemished purity settled on me. I relaxed and eased into this state. My eyes were half opened and I became aware of a strong flow of energy from Tara and then watched amazed as a powdery white figure rose up from her and towered way above. There was great love and compassion emanating from this figure. She was all white, loose white cloth wrapped around her, loose white hair, aged but young. The figure was akin to the white smoke that had arisen from the fire during our havan at night. I found myself whispering the word *dhumavati* not knowing what I was saying.

The secret gayatri

To keep count in some of the practices that need a ratio of breath I used to chant the *Rudra gayatri*, preferring it to the more traditional *gayatri* of Rishi Vishwamitra. Gurunath had enlivened and given us the Rudra gayatri free of the baggage of do's and don'ts that burdens the other gayatri due to traditional patriarchal usage, which according to Gurunath were in all probability never imposed by Rishi Vishwamitra. One morning as I was intently completing my practice I noticed that instead of the Rudra Gayatri I was chanting another mantra a *gayatri* for Satgurunath Siddhanath. This mantra flowed with ease from some deep receptacle of my psyche and I felt a comfort and sense of belonging, unlike when I chant the other mantras. As mentioned earlier, I had been introduced to mantras since childhood and grew up chanting the *Vishnu Sahasranama, Mahishasuramardini Stotra*, the various chants given by Adi Shankaracharya, chants and mantras from the vedas, and even today they are memorised and as we say I can chant them 'by heart' without conscious effort, though I am glad to say the memory is slowly fading.

Though inspiring and full of wisdom I never felt an obligation to chant them and had stopped completely as a teenager. I was drawn more to the simple practices given by Gurunath, which were much deeper and transformative. Gurunath once, when a disciple asked which was superior, had pointed out that Lahiri Mahasaya had been chanting the gayatri till he met Babaji and was given the Kriya Yoga.

There's a lot of mysticism covering the gayatri. For me gayatri was a mantra to facilitate progress along a path, a song whose wellspring is within pretty much like the *geeta*. In my understanding these are personal, private and are revealed as a result of personal effort bestowed by the benevolence of the master. Released at a relevant time for the disciple's onward progress, these are specifically aligned with the individual to whom it is revealed. A bit like when we unlock gifts in a computer game to get to the next level. Personally I felt relieved that I do not any more have to chant a 'borrowed' gayatri with its accompanying baggage but could now use one that seemingly flowered within due to the grace of the satguru. I took permission from Gurunath to use this personal mantra that I feel has more power, as it is personal. All other mantras fell away gradually to be replaced by this. As it is personal it cannot be shared with others.

Selfishly, I once asked Gurunath if I would be connected to him from the moment of birth in my next life. He looked directly at me and said, "Jyoti, do you want to be so small that you won't let your guru evolve and move on to the next plane? You will all be gurus and satgurus in your own right in future lives. Do not be attached to the physical body of the guru. I have and will always be there for you." In a flash I understood that this connection is eternal and his spiritual energy will always guide and communicate with me in this life, regardless of whether the physical body is present or not. In the next I am assured I will be guided once again to the living master.

※

Here and now

It has been twenty-one years since I first met Gurunath. There is nothing to say anymore. I feel a sense of great satisfaction, untouched by the circumstances surrounding me. Though externally living life normally there's a joy that wells from within for no apparent reason, and a general sense of contentment with all life as it is. A deep surrender to circumstances that takes me as if cradled in its arms. Gurunaths saying, "Do not depend on externals for your happiness" is becoming a reality. Not even concerned anymore that in my next life I must not forget the spiritual lessons of this one for I have personally experienced how the enlightened master unerringly finds the slumbering disciple.

One late night as I sat I felt a stillness come over me as if in deep space or deep under the ocean, an oceanic stillness while through the bubble of my still mind I became aware of a vaster stillness almost within my reach, for a long moment we gazed at each other through the clear film of my mind. I do not know what this was but there was a feeling of exquisite tenderness and love in that stillness; an alertness in our exchange full of an intelligence beyond thought. And then it retreated as if there was time yet for that merging, not gone but just on the edge of my consciousness while I continue with the chores that need to be done daily. I felt a familiarity with that energy similar to the one with my master. They are the same, I realised

In 1997, few months before I met Gurunath I had written a poem scant understanding the real import of it.

> "Fearless and free I move,
> I was here when the earth spun as a ball of fire,
> Through the ice ages I watched;
> Fishes kissed me as I sat —a rock at the bottom of the sea.
> I crawled with the amphibians.
> The early birds that took flight; I flew with them.
> I have felt the thrill of the hunter; the sheer panic of the hunted has been mine. Through the ages, I have been oppressor and the oppressed.
>
> Today a dewdrop is waiting to fall into the ocean."

I guess the ocean just moved a little closer to the drop, due to the grace of a living master.

CHAPTER 10

KRIYA YOGA THE ANTIDOTE

Without the master, the student and the practice are like a lamp filled with oil with a wick ready to be lighted. No doubt through years or lifetimes of intense discipline and personal effort the student may be able to bring a flicker to the wick, but the appearance of the satguru makes lighting the lamp effortless. Blessed is the disciple who is unerringly guided to the true master lifetime after lifetime. Incessantly over the past twenty-one years of association with Gurunath I have realized that he is the catalyst for what he calls the alchemy of total transformation in his disciples. The physical body of the master is a receptacle for this inner essential master who wields the secret key.

The master holds the *rasayan*, the essential spiritual nutrient that make possible the evolution of the disciple's soul and what's astonishing is that the masters cannot dispense or withhold this at whim from the disciples. The disciples without any expectation of entitlement gain access to it by their dedication and integrity to the practice and to the guru. This happens according to me, only in an environment of purity of intention and purpose of the disciple, which determines the degree of access. It is actually very humbling to realize the gravity of the service the master does holding this immense energy within this limited human body ready for access by a disciple when ready. In the physical body, masters reflect human fragilities to connect with the disciples at a human level while at same instant merged in the bliss of divine consciousness communicate the same to disciples ready for it; a constant shift that I'm sure is not very easy and the fact they do it for us to evolve is very awe-inspiring. Understanding these nuances in the master disciple bond is a learning process of great import and comes as the sadhak progresses on the shown path.

On my third visit to Kashi end July 2015, it was the monsoon season and the Ganga was in full spate. I had planned my visit especially with Gurupurnima to be able to visit Lahiri Baba's original home. The Ganga was majestically full, a pregnant womb carrying the prayers of the devotees bathing in her. Sitting by her side evoked memories of many past lives spent frolicking with her on these very *ghats*. A familiarity with her ebbs and flows, that could not have come from the visits of this lifetime. As I sat thus enchanted, in my room overlooking the river I could see the sun rising on the opposite side and realised with a startle that the flow of the Ganga was towards the north while she should actually be making her way south towards the Bay of Bengal. Realisation fell like a lightning bolt, as I understood the message she had secretly been giving to millions who took a dip in her year after year for thousands of years. She who had emanated from Shiva's locks in the Himalayas was showing the way back to the source – hurry back home she was saying. Practicing as I was the *urdhavaret* breath of the Kundalini Kriya Yoga I felt an uncontrollable surge in the spine at this realization of an open secret visible throughout the ages but realised by a few. This for me summed up the practice of Kriya Yoga as well.

❅

Nirodh not *Virodh*

An antidote to the vagaries of the truant mind, the practice of Kriya Yoga introduces not an opposing but an overriding command that calms archaic persistent patterns of thought. Enabling the mind to flow without conflict in tune with the circadian rhythms of the universe becoming an ever-expanding awareness. From personal experience I consider the Kriya breath a cure for all ills, delves as it does into the root cause of the disease, whether physical, mental, emotional and even intellectual facilitating release of its grip on the human psyche.

"To ease disease of random mind," says Gurunath in his poem Mind Transformation, "a remedy suitable we must find. A rhythmic breathing tension free, with Kriya Yoga the sovereign key." Then the same unruly mind, "Tamed and tuned to natures flow, mind melts into the opal glow. Which radiates from the soul within, where wisdoms mystic fire is king" Though drawn to the path of Kriya Yoga without conscious awareness either of the practice or the masters preceding Gurunath and complete oblivion when it came to Babaji, the moment I stepped on the path woken by the gesture of the master the familiar path revealed its Self. Settling back into the groove made from previous lives guided by the master in this one to deepen the groove further, made it impossible to spill out distracted. Kriya yoga is the tool fashioned by the master to chisel the disciple's transformation. The mind then follows the breath that is trained by the Kundalini *pranayam* and instead of leading the practitioner on a wayward chase starts to flow beautifully alongside, joyous and natural. Once again the paradox is not missed that the spontaneous mind in reality is the trained mind.

Being quite practical and not whimsical when it comes to the practice has helped me come to certain realizations that are fundamental to me. Thinking long and hard about the various visions, experiences and revelations that came seemingly effortlessly for me since stepping on this path I infer that this is evidence of the random mind being tuned. The same mind that can confuse and as Gurunath says take one into a bedlam of misery starts to bring clarity. Through subtle and overt messages it assists in the inductive leap towards a more harmonious living. It is as if once on this path the universe comes forth to help the *mumuksha*, the seeker of gnosis through bringing forth directions via illuminating visions.

Now whether these revelations come in the form of conditioned visions of gods as depicted for centuries or more natural spontaneous ways is dependent on the limitations of the mind of that particular seeker. Though I had visions of Shiva in the human form that's because over the ages I have been conditioned to behold him in that figure, with a moon on his forehead and a garland of snake. Shiva on mars will not be sporting a human figure, I'm sure! The external figure of these cosmic beings is dictated by how we want them to look the features, number of arms, heads, weapons, mode of transport are our poetic expressions corresponding to the image we want to invest them with. The *dvait* of form and *advait* of formless a state revealed as per the disciple's progress and inclinations.

However that may be, what matters is the end result of the experienced revelation. Establishing whether the experience brings one to live in harmony or conflict, in joy or in sorrow, contented or in discontent, in love or in hate, in clarity or in confusion, balanced or teetering will bring one closer to understanding the authenticity of the experience; if even after wonderful visions one is in misery then one is bound to question and discard the experience. I consider the experiencer is the best judge of that. The veracity of the vision can be measured by its influence to love humanity devoid of any judgement or denominations.

Finally when the disciple is well set on the path all visions fall away as the mind now rested in the stillness needs no props to tune or train it. Gurunath sums it up in the following words. "Then stiller than stillness itself, with bated breath, I do behold; My rising Self-Sun's nectar gold." Then pausing, he says," I dissolve in that mystery untold." As is usual with Gurunath every time he recites his poetry the *prana* that is carried in his voice transports the sensitive disciple to the state he describes and they too momentarily dissolve in that 'mystery untold', a taste of the state that will come someday.

※

The essential appeal

There are some core fundamentals of Kriya Yoga, that attract me personally and which as a teacher helps me to guide students into a practice that is so universal.

One, the simplicity of the initiation took my breath away at my first introduction to this practice by Gurunath. Coming from a *brahminical* background where much ado is made of secretly giving the gayatri at the overlong *upanayanam* ceremony, mind you only to the boys, I found the simple introduction by the master into such a powerful path refreshing. Kriya yoga does not discriminate; it's given freely to all who want to invest their time in pursuing this yogic path. This simplicity in fact flows into all the other aspects that follow.

Two, I see Kriya Yoga as an inner discipline where the yogi practitioner contained in the physical body temple realises themselves to be the immaculate spark of divinity. External forms of worship are redundant and Kriya Yoga does not demand any external ritual to be effective. Practicing the technique is most supreme and keeps the disciple truly attuned with the master.

Three, Kriya Yoga stands alone needing no other supportive practice to take the disciple to the highest states of enlightenment.

Four, the energy of Kriya Yoga is love, its practice supports ones becoming love and radiating love. Gurunath leads us into this state by connecting us with our inner fountainhead of love. The advanced seeker knows the quality of this love is not conditional, regional or limited and transcends human frailties.

Five, by dedicated sadhana, the disciples increase their gravity and move gracefully through life. As the disciple becomes more constant life under any circumstances becomes more full of ease for them. *Ishwar pranidhan* the surrender to the guru comes naturally to them. Mind you this surrender is not the mindless abject surrender of the piteous rather a surrender in full realisation.

Six, by steadfastness in practice and utter connection with the master the disciple becomes self-reliant and connects with the core of their inner knowingness as Gurunath calls it. The external physical master introduces the disciple to their inner essential master. This is an advanced stage that I know comes to all disciples eventually. As disciples we just need to keep the connection with the satguru as this process can go on for a while as layers upon layers of ignorance are peeled away, hence the peeling of an onion.

I am rather fond of repeating what I strongly believe, "I have no interest in what Krishna, Buddha, Jesus or Nanak said. I only know that my master has shot me like an arrow and there is no turning back." The living master then becomes the cornerstone on which the foundation of the evolution of the disciple rests.

I have no interest in what Krishna, Buddha, Jesus or Nanak said, I only know my Satguru has shot me like an arrow and there's no turning back. #ayukahat

9 ANCIENT YOGIC TECHNIQUES

9 ancient yogic techniques

Note: When a technique is given to you by a satguru it flowers into its potency. These meditations blessed by Gurunath will bring transformation as you practice. Observe the changes in yourself when you have practiced these exercises regularly. Gurunath especially released these techniques for this book in 2004.

Solar detoxification:

Even as you read this page, you can practice this meditation. This is a very effective method to clear the body of toxins – physical, emotional and mental. As you breathe in, visualise the golden light of the sun flowing into you, filling your hollow body with radiant light. Hold this light within you for a few moments and, as you breathe out, expel all disease, pain, emotional and mental trauma and stress, out of the body. Repeat this as often as you like till you feel cleansed and rejuvenated.

❦

Rainbow wash:

Sit with your back straight yet flexible. Take your attention six inches above your head. Visualise a stream of radiant light flowing towards the top of your head. As this light enters your head it turns violet in colour. The light flows down to the forehead, changing to indigo. It further moves down to the base of the throat and becomes electric blue. As it reaches the solar plexus it turns green. Further down to the navel it is yellow. The light flows down to the coccyx and is orange. At the base of your body it is red. Pause at every step till you feel completely saturated.

※

Surya/Chandra osmosis: (protective/healing shield)

Stand facing the sun, hands by the side, palms turned towards the sun. With eyes closed, experience your body absorbing the sunlight like a sponge. Once your body is saturated, the light spills over and out covering your whole body in a balloon of light. Carry this light around as you go about your daily chores. Repeat the Surya osmosis exercise on a full moon night, replacing the golden light of the sun with the silver light of the moon. This fills you with peace and healing energy.

※

Resonance healing:

Sit in a relaxed posture with your back straight yet flexible. Take a deep breath and chant the 'Om' loudly, letting the resonance of the word vibrate and fill your body. Then, continue with the humming sound of 'Hmmmmm' until all thought waves are calmed. You will notice a marked difference in your mental health and sleep patterns.

※

Yogic relaxation (A):

Lie down flat on your back on a blanket or mat. Take a few deep breaths and relax the whole body from the top of the head to the tips of the toes. With every outgoing breath, consciously release all physical tension from the heels, the calves, the thighs, the butt, the back, the shoulders, and the back of the head. Now, feel your body sinking a few inches into the ground, pulled in by the gravitational force of the earth. Visualise roots growing from the bottom of your body and going deep into the earth, anchoring you. They drain all the tension from your body, then detach themselves and fall away. Your body is released and comes back.

❋

Yogic relaxation (B):

Lie down flat on your back on a blanket or mat. Take a few deep breaths and relax the whole body from the top of the head to the tips of the toes. With every outgoing breath, consciously release all physical tension from the heels, the calves, the thighs, the butt, the back, the shoulders, and the back of the head. Now imagine yourself starting to rise and float a few inches above the ground. Without body consciousness, you are free of all tension and heaviness. Stay for a few moments with this sense of freedom. Come back slowly and feel the ground once again underneath.

❋

Moon meditation:

Sit comfortably facing the full moon, wearing loose clothes, preferably white in colour. Take a few deep breaths to relax the body and gaze gently at the moon. Visualise the pearl- coloured light of the moon flowing into and filling the pelvic area. The energy is cool and calm like the waters of a still lake. The cooling balm spreads in your whole body down to the toes and up to the top of your head, filling you with serenity. When you feel completely saturated, gently rub the essence of the moonlight on the whole body.

❄

Power to the self:

Sit comfortably on a mat. Make sure your stomach is empty (at least three hours since a meal). Keep your back straight but not stiff. Now, take a slow, fine breath through the nose, down to the navel, filling and extending your stomach. Exhale the breath explosively through the mouth, while at the same time pulling in the stomach sharply towards the spine. Repeat six to ten times. You will feel a warm glow spreading from the stomach; relax in this sensation for a few minutes. If you feel any discomfort during the exercise, reduce the intensity or stop and consult a Yoga teacher.

❄

Express yourself:

Sit comfortably on a chair or on the ground. Make sure you are in a calm and serene mood. Take a deep breath and then shout from your innermost core, explosively and continuously, 'Haaaaaaaaaaaa' until all your breath is expelled, taking away all unexpressed words. Then, as the breath flows in, visualise the throat area filling with a cool electric blue light. Repeat the exercise three times.

❄

WINGS TO FREEDOM ILLUSTRATION

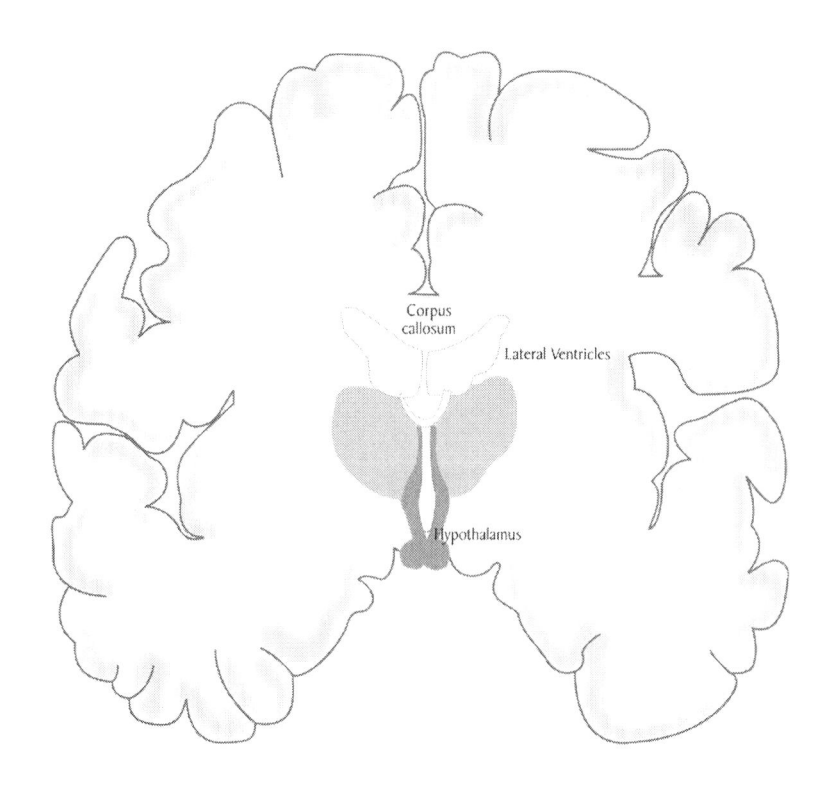

This diagram taken from Gurunaths book Wings to Freedom, illustrates his legacy revealing the secret of the Luminous Swan. This is his contribution to the treasury of yogic knowledge, where he has clearly revealed the reason why the soul is referred to as the Jeevahamsa, that the lateral ventricles in the human brain form the shape of the swan and are the residence of human consciousness. "When the yogi, through meditation and pranayama activates the Kundalini energy, these ventricles in the brain open," describes Gurunath. "Then, by further practise, the yogi moves into higher states of awareness to finally dwell in the 'cave of Brahma', which is located in the mid-brain called the third ventricle, with the thalamus glands as its walls, the hypothalamus as its floor, and the plexus of the third choroids ventricles as its roof."

The yogi then realises the soul in the shape of a swan.

GLOSSARY

Aam ras. A delicious thick mango juice
Aarti. Waving of lamps in temples
Adesh. Command by the guru to the disciple
Adinath. Title of Shiva
Advait. Non-Duality
Agraraham. A brahmin village built around a temple
Akhada. Habitat of the Nath order of yogis
Amaltas. The Cassia tree, bearing bright yellow flowers
Amma. Mother in Tamizh
Amrit sarovar. Pool of nectar; bestows immortality.
Anandamaya Kosha. The intuitional body, last of the five – the others being physical, etheric, emotional and intellect
Annas. Old Indian currency
Appa. Father in Tamizh
Ardhanareshwar. Shiva as half-man, half-woman
Asan. Yoga mat
Asanas. Postures prescribed in yoga
Ashram. Holy sanctuary, Hermitage
Avalokiteshwara. The Bodhisattva who embodies the compassion of all Buddha's
Ayurveda. A system of medicine that originated in ancient India
Ayurvedic. Pertaining to Ayurveda
Babaji Gorakshanath. Mahavatar Babaji who Gurunath has identified as Shiv Gorakshanath

Glossary

Bael. A hard-shelled fruit (Aegle Marmelos), favoured as an offering to Shiva

Baglamukhi. A tantric goddess meaning 'the powerful one'

Bajra. Pearl Millet

Bhagavad Gita. Literally the 'Song of God' – contains Krishna's discourse to Arjuna on the battlefield of Kurukshetra, in the epic Mahabharata

Bhairon. A tantric god who eliminates the effects of black magic and other negative influences and powers

Bhakta. Devotee

Bhakti Sutras. A collection of devotional renditions

Bhang. A substance derived from the cannabis herb

Bhavati, Bhiksham Dehi. A call by yogi mendicants at the door, literally means "Mother, give alms"

Bhikshus. Ascetics who call for alms

Bhil. A tribe in Central India

Bhoot. Ghost

Biryani. A spicy rice delicacy

Bodhi. Enlightened

Brahma. The creator, from the trilogy of the creator, preserver (Vishnu) and destroyer/redeemer (Shiva)

Brahaman. The highest universal principal; the ultimate reality

Brahmin. A class of people believed to have emerged from the head of Vishnu; keepers of knowledge by oral tradition. Later corrupted to caste system

Brahmarishis. Illustrious sages from ancient times

Brahminical. Pertaining to the rites of Brahmins

Buddha Purnima. The full moon in the month of Vaisakh in April-May. Buddha was born, enlightened, and attained nirvana on this day

Buddham sharanam gacchami. Take refuge at Buddha's feet

Bum Bholey. A chant eulogising the glory of Shiva

Carnatic. Pertaining to South India

Chai. Tea

Chaitanya Mahaprabhu. A Bengali vaishnav saint, devotee of Krishna

Chakra. Centres or vortexes of energy located along the spine super imposing upon the various biological plexuses

Chillum. Pipe used for smoking

Chimta. A traditional percussion instrument used to keep beat while chanting, also used to lift hot objects from the fire

Chitthappa. Father's brother; In India there's a separate terminology for every relation they are not clubbed under the general address of auntie and uncle

Chitthi. Means aunt wife of the above, but the author addressed her paternal grand- mother as such

Dakshina. An offering or fee for lessons imparted

Dal. Pulses

Dargah. Tomb of a Muslim saint

Darshan. To see or behold a 'vision of the divine' or the spiritual guru

Dasa Mahavidya. The ten aspects of the divine mother

Dasamdvar. 'The tenth door' connecting the individual soul to the divine

Dattatreya. Considered guru of all gurus who came to light the lamp of wisdom among the people

Devi. Goddess

Dharana. Concentration or single focus; the sixth stage of eight mentioned in Patanjali's Ashtanga Yoga

Dhoti. Piece of cloth worn on the lower body by Indian men

Dhyana. An aspect of meditation; the seventh stage of eight mentioned in Patanjali's Ashtanga Yoga or raja Yoga

Digambar. One of the two main sects of Jainism where the monks wear no clothes; literally sky-clad

Dupatta. Stole-like covering worn by women over the upper body

Glossary

Durga . Fierce warrior goddess regarded as the supreme power in the universe by some sects of Hinduism

Dvait. Duality

Gaalis. Very impolite swear words

Ganesh. Elephant-headed god of the Hindus, remover of all obstacles

Garba. A traditional dance of Gujarat, performed around a lamp

Gayatri. Popularly used to for a revered chant from the rig veda revealed to Rishi Vishvamitra; literally means a hymn or song in a particular vedic meter that when chanted brings speedy results

Ghee. Clarified butter

Gopi. Maidens who tend to the cows

Gorakhsha Gayatri. A secret chant to invoke Shiva; mystic mantra revealed in the ancient text Shiva Gorakhsha Rahasyam and taught by Gurunath to his disciples

Gufa. Cave

Guru. Spiritual teacher now distinguished from the satguru as master, but the author has used them interchangeably for Gurunath

Guru Purnima. Celebrated on the full moon day of the Hindu month of Ashad (July-August), to honour and offer respects to the guru

Gurudakshina. The fee for teaching often demanded by the Satguru is the guru's prerogative. In the olden days the guru could ask for any payment from the disciple; eg. Ekalavya and his thumb

Gurudwara. Shrine of Sikhs; literally means 'doorway to the guru'

Gurukul. A type of school in ancient India where the guru and his students resided together as equals, irrespective of their social standing

Gurumata. Wife of the guru

Gurunath Samadhi Yoga. A special meditation practice taught by Gurunath leading to Sahaj Samadhi

Guru-shishya parampara. The spiritual relationship that is centred on the transmission of teachings from a guru to a disciple

Hamsa. Literally means the 'swan'; Also used as synonym for the 'soul', see annexure Wings to Freedom Hamsa Dvij. The twice-born, once from the womb and the second time delivered from ignorance by the master

Hamsa Yoga. A special Hatha-Raj Yoga technique formulated by Yogiraj Siddhanath

Hamsacharya. An empowered teacher of the Hamsa Yoga Sangh

Hamsasanas. Yoga postures of Hamsa Yoga with breathing special to Hamsa Yoga.

Handi. A round shaped vessel used to cook

Hatha Yoga. A form of yoga dealing mainly with the three steps of yoga: asana, pranayama and pratyahar. Havan. Traditional brahminical purification ritual

Havan-kund. A receptacle to perform purification rituals using fire

Holi. A festival of colours

Indra. Lord of Gods; Zeus in Greek

Ishwar Pranidhan. Surrender to Guru and Divine

Jaggery. Dark brown sugar made from date palm or sugarcane

Jhunjhar. A warrior who continues to fight even after beheading.

Jivatma. Individual soul

Jivhamsa. Soul swan

Jowar rotis. Sorghum pancakes

Jwaladevi. An aspect of the goddess Sati, Shiva's wife Kali. Hindu goddess

Kama Sutra. A sanskrit text on erotic love compiled 300CE

Kamandal. A copper container with spout for water

Karma. Action or deed

Karmic. Dictated by Karma

Karthikeya. Son of Shiva and Parvati. His wives are Valli and Devasena. The peacock is his vehicle. He is also believed by some to be a manifestation of Mahavatar Babaji

Kayakalp. Body rejuvenation, reversing the aging process of the body

Kikar. Acacia nilotica, a genre of tree

Kirtan. Devotional rendering accompanied by music

Kolattam. A traditional stick and rope dance

Kolhapuri chappals. Leather slippers

Krishna. An incarnation of Vishnu

Krittika. Pleiades

Kriya Yoga. Practices of yoga to awaken Kundalini

Kumkum. Red powder applied to the forehead by worshippers, and also used to denote marital status in women

Kundalini. Primordial cosmic energy believed to be lying dormant in every individual, which, through the practice of yoga, can be accessed and hastens spiritual evolution

Kurta pyjama. A traditional Indian dress for men

Langar. A Sikh community meal distributed free to all at the gurudwara

Langur. A species of black-faced monkeys

Leela. Play of divine

Looh. Hot, dry summer wind

Maha. Very large; great

Maha Kumbhmela. The traditional bathing festival at the confluence of three rivers at Allahabad, India, that recurs every twelve years

Mahaprasad. An offering made first to the deity and then consumed by the devotees

Mahashiva. The eternal Shiva

Mahashivratri. The great night of Shiva

Mahavatar. The great incarnation

Mahavatar Babaji Kriya Yoga. Form of meditation taught by Yogiraj Siddhanath that transmutes the oxygen of breath into life energy, and blends it into the spiritual currents of the spine

Mahishasuramardini. Another name for Durga; slayer of the demon Mahishasur

Mala. A string of beads

Mantra. A sound or word endowed with special power

Mudra. Seal; system of sealing energy through hand postures

Mumuksha. Seeker of moksha

Murugan. Another name for Karthikeya, son of Shiva and Parvati

Naad Brahma. Transcendental sound of the universe

Nadi shodan. One of the most important breathing techniques in yoga, with far-reaching benefits

Nandi. Shiva's divine bull

Nath Sampradaya. An ancient lineage of spiritual masters

Navnath. The nine Naths of immortal splendour believed to be actively involved in the evolution of our universe

Nilgais. literally 'Blue Bull' – a species of antelope

Nirodh. Stop. Author's interpretation-antidote

Nirvana. enlightenment, liberation

Nirvanshatak. Set of six stanzas on the Supreme Self by Adi Shankaracharya

Nirvichar Avastha. A state of thoughtfree samadhi

Niyam. Observances, the second step Patanjali's Ashtanga Yoga

Om. All-pervading sound of the cosmic vibrations

Om Namah Shivaya. Mantra of Shiva

Omkara. The sound and vision of the sound of 'aum'

Palak paneer. A popular Indian dish of spinach and cottage cheese

Parah. Neighbourhood, Bengali word

Parampara. Lineage

Parikrama. Outer corridor of temple for perambulation

Parvati. Daughter of the Mountain, wife to Shiva

Pashmina. Shawl made from a type of wool that is obtained from a special breed of goats endemic to high altitudes of the Himalayas

Pind-Brahmand. Yogic theory of the blueprint of the universe in the human body.

Prana. Life force; vital energy

Pranayama. The breath control exercises of yoga to gain mastery over the Prana

Pranic. Pertaining to Prana

Pranpat. When the master breathes through the breath of the disciple in the spinal channel, clearing karma according to the disciple's karmic blueprint

Prasad. A portion of consecrated offerings infused with sacred energy returned for consumption by the devotees

Prakriti. Nature

Pratyahar. The fifth of the eight limbs of yoga

Puja. Worship

Pujo. Puja in Bengali

Purush. Universal Principle

Qawwalis. Devotional songs of the Sufis of the Indian sub-continent

Raas Leela. The cosmic dance of Krishna

Ragas. An array of melodic structure in music in India

Rangoli. Traditional drawing done with rice powder and natural colours on the front porch of the house

Rasayan. Alchemical Balm

Rishis. Ancient sages

Roomala. A piece of cloth offered in Sikh shrines

Rudraksh. reddish-brown seeds; sacred to yogis

Sadashiva. Title of Shiva

Sadhak. One who practices a spiritual discipline
Sadhana. A spiritual discipline
Sagura. One who has been initiated into a spiritual practice
Salwar kameez. A traditional dress in North India
Samadhi. Final step of the Ashtang Yoga of Patanjali
Samsara. World; endless cycle of birth-death-rebirth
Samshan sadhana. Practices conducted in the cremation grounds
Sanatana Dharma. The eternal religion
Sardarji. A respectful form of addressing Sikh men sporting a beard
Saris. Traditional dress worn by women of Indian origin
Sarovar. A pond
Sashtanga pranam. Literally to bow 'with all limbs'; prostrate
Satguru. True Guru, used more often now to distinguish from a teacher, though author has used both for her master.
Sati. The first wife of Shiva
Satsang. A gathering of like-minded people
Savitri. Wife of Brahma
Shakti. The female energy counterpart
Shaktipat. Transmission of the Kundalini energy by a spiritual master into the chakras of disciples, assisting them in their evolution
Shanti puja. Special prayers to appease the gods for peace
Shishya. Student, disciple
Shiva. Lord of destruction and transformation, the third in the Hindu trinity
Shivalinga. Represents the 'Universe' and is worshipped as an aspect of Shiva. According to Gurunath, "It has its centre everywhere and circumference nowhere"
Shivapat. When the master imparts his consciousness of natural enlightenment to the disciple
Shivbhakta. Devotee of Shiva
Shiv-Netra. lord Shiva's third eye
Shraddh. Prayer for ancestors performed by children

Shwetambar. A sect of Jainism where the monks are clad in white
Siddha. Perfected Being; a person of great spiritual attainment
Srishti. Creation
Surya Yoga. Solar meditation by Gurunath
Swayambhu: Self- manifested
Tabla. Indian musical Instrument, drum
Tantra. A form of yoga that draws from all sciences to achieve spiritual realisation through evolution of consciousness
Tantra Yoga. Refers to the spiritual disciplines that constitute the vast and complex Tantric tradition of India
Tantric. Person who indulges in the practice of tantra
Tapa. Austere penance
Tathastu. literally 'so be it'
Tithi. Lunar date in hindu calendar
Udaseen Sampradaya .A sect of yogis
Unmani avastha. State of natural enlightenment
Upanayanam. Rites of passage for brahmin boys
Upanishads. A collection of profound texts that has dominated Indian thought for thousands of years
Upasana. A practice to get close to a deity
Vairagya. Detachment to all things material; renunciation
Vaishnav. A person who worships Vishnu
Vedic. Pertaining to the Vedas
Vibhuti. Sacred ash from fire ceremonies
Virodh. Oppose
Vishnu. One of the Hindu Trinity; the Preserver
Vivar. A practice taught by Yogiraj Siddhanath that emulates the whirling movement of the galaxy
Yagna. A vedic sacrificial ritual
Yama. Restraints, the first stage of eight mentioned in Patanjali's Ashtanga Yoga
Yog. Yoga in Sanskrit

Yog paddhati. Contributions that help to 'illuminate' yogic perceptions
Yogi. One who is adept in the practice of yoga
Yogic. Pertaining to yoga
Yogini. Used to distinguish female adepts of yoga
Yugas. In Hindu philosophy the cycle of evolution of life is divided into four yugas: satya, treta, dwapar and kali

CONTACT

For more information on Yogiraj Siddhanath
www.siddhanath.org
www.youtube.com/hamsayogi

For more information on the author
www.ayu.yoga
jyotihamsa@gmail.com

Printed in Great
Britain
by Amazon